'This superb collection of essays, beautifully curated by Moss and Zeavin, moves beyond our clinical and institutional comfort zones to boldly place matters of pressing current concern – enduring racism and the resistance to real change, the emergence of fascist trends in politics, and the climate emergency – under a psychoanalytic lens.'

M. Fakhry Davids, *Supervising and Training Analyst, British Psychoanalytical Society/IPA, Author*, Internal Racism: A Psychoanalytic Approach to Race and Difference

'This deeply moving collection of contributions, edited by Moss and Zeavin, compels us all to re-think the received wisdom that has shaped our praxis. This new volume is a must-read for all analysts and therapists.'

Glen O. Gabbard, *MD, Author of* Love and Hate in the Analytic Setting

'Troubling and trenchant, these contributions will interest all those who are concerned with the political crisis we are living through, and with the ethics, application, and practice of the talking cure.'

Daniel Pick, *psychoanalyst, Fellow of the British Psychoanalytical Society, and Professor of History at Birkbeck College, University of London*

Hating, Abhorring and Wishing to Destroy

The kinds of hatreds that analysts have assumed make up part of the unspoken backdrop of Western civilization have now erupted into our daily foreground. This book, consisting of essays from eleven psychoanalysts, responds to that eruption.

The five essays of Part 1, "Hating in the first person plural," take on the pervasive impact of structured forms of hatred – racism, misogyny, homophobia, and transphobia. These malignant forces are put into action by large- and small-group identifications. Even the action of the apparent "lone wolf" inevitably enacts loyal membership in a surrounding community. The hating entity is always "we." In Part 2, "The racialized object/the racializing subject," the essays' focus narrows to an examination of racist expressions of "hating, abhorring, and wishing to destroy." A particular focus is the state of excitement attached to this form of hatred, to its sadistic origins, and to the endless array of objects offered to the racializing subject. In Part 3, "This land: whose is it, really?," its two essays focus on symbolic and physical violence targeting the natural world. We expand the traditional field of psychoanalytic inquiry to include the natural world, the symbolic meaning of its "trees," and the psychopolitical meanings of its land.

This book offers a psychoanalytically informed guide to understanding and working against hatreds in clinical work and in everyday life and will appeal to training and experienced psychoanalysts, as well as anyone with an interest in current political and cultural climates.

Donald Moss is on the faculty, New York Psychoanalytic Institute. He is the author of four books and over 60 articles, Chair of the APsaA Program Committee, and Member of the College of the *International Journal of Psychoanalysis*. Dr. Moss practices psychoanalysis and psychotherapy in New York.

Dr. Lynne Zeavin is a clinical psychologist and psychoanalyst in full-time practice in New York City. She is a training and supervising analyst at the New York Psychoanalytic Society & Institute. An associate editor of *JAPA*, she has written on a variety of topics exploring the status of the object in contemporary psychoanalytic theory.

The New Library of Psychoanalysis 'Beyond the Couch' Series
General Editor: Alessandra Lemma

The New Library of Psychoanalysis was launched in 1987 in association with the Institute of Psychoanalysis, London. It aims to promote a widespread appreciation of psychoanalysis by supporting interdisciplinary dialogues with those working in the social sciences, the arts, medicine, psychology, psychotherapy, philosophy and with the general book reading public.

The *Beyond the Couch* part of the series creates a forum dedicated to demonstrating this wider application of psychoanalytic ideas. These books, written primarily by psychoanalysts, specifically address the important contribution of psychoanalysis to contemporary intellectual, social, and scientific debate.

Current members of the Advisory Board include Giovanna Di Ceglie, Liz Allison, Anne Patterson, Josh Cohen, and Daniel Pick.

For a full list of all the titles in the New Library of Psychoanalysis main series and also the New Library of Psychoanalysis Teaching Series, please visit the Routledge website.

Titles in the 'Beyond the Couch' Series:

Reflections on the Aesthetic Experience: Psychoanalysis and the Uncanny
Gregorio Kohon

Psychoanalysis in the Age of Totalitarianism
Edited by Matt ffytche and Daniel Pick

Sublime Subjects: Aesthetic Experience and Intersubjectivity in Psychoanalysis
Giuseppe Civitarese

For more information about this series, please visit: www.routledge.com/New-Library-of-Psychoanalysis-Beyond-the-Couch-Series/book-series/NLPBTC

Hating, Abhorring and Wishing to Destroy

Psychoanalytic Essays on the Contemporary Moment

Edited by Donald Moss
and Lynne Zeavin

LONDON AND NEW YORK

First published 2022
by Routledge
2 Park Square, Milton Park, Abingdon, Oxon OX14 4RN

and by Routledge
605 Third Avenue, New York, NY 10158

Routledge is an imprint of the Taylor & Francis Group, an informa business

©2022 selection and editorial matter, Donald Moss and Lynne Zeavin; individual chapters, the contributors

The right of Donald Moss and Lynne Zeavin to be identified as the authors of the editorial material, and of the authors for their individual chapters, has been asserted in accordance with sections 77 and 78 of the Copyright, Designs and Patents Act 1988.

All rights reserved. No part of this book may be reprinted or reproduced or utilised in any form or by any electronic, mechanical, or other means, now known or hereafter invented, including photocopying and recording, or in any information storage or retrieval system, without permission in writing from the publishers.

Trademark notice: Product or corporate names may be trademarks or registered trademarks, and are used only for identification and explanation without intent to infringe.

British Library Cataloguing-in-Publication Data
A catalogue record for this book is available from the British Library

Library of Congress Cataloging-in-Publication Data
Names: Moss, Donald, 1944– editor. | Zeavin, Lynne, 1956– editor.
Title: Hating, abhorring and wishing to destroy : psychoanalytic essays on the contemporary moment / edited by Donald Moss and Lynne Zeavin.
Description: Abingdon, Oxon ; New York, NY : Routledge, 2022. | Series: New library of psychoanalysis beyond the couch | Includes bibliographical references and index.
Identifiers: LCCN 2021026367 (print) | LCCN 2021026368 (ebook) | ISBN 9781032102399 (hardback) | ISBN 9781032102375 (paperback) | ISBN 9781003214342 (ebook)
Subjects: LCSH: Hatred. | Violence. | Psychoanalysis and racism. | Civilization, Modern—21st century.
Classification: LCC BF575.H3 H36 2022 (print) | LCC BF575.H3 (ebook) | DDC 152.4–dc23
LC record available at https://lccn.loc.gov/2021026367
LC ebook record available at https://lccn.loc.gov/2021026368

ISBN: 978-1-032-10239-9 (hbk)
ISBN: 978-1-032-10237-5 (pbk)
ISBN: 978-1-003-21434-2 (ebk)

DOI: 10.4324/9781003214342

Typeset in Times New Roman
by Apex CoVantage, LLC

For our children Hannah, Ivan, and Isaiah – with gratitude for their commitments to better the world they have inherited

Contents

Acknowledgments   xi

Introduction   1
DONALD MOSS AND LYNNE ZEAVIN

PART 1
Hating in the first person plural   11

1   On hating in the first person plural: thinking psychoanalytically about racism, homophobia, and misogyny   13
DONALD MOSS

2   This is not about Trump: rage, resistance, and the persistence of racism   32
ANN PELLEGRINI

3   First world problems and gated communities of the mind: an ethics of place in psychoanalysis   51
FRANCISCO J. GONZÁLEZ

4   Insidious excitement and the hatred of reality   79
LYNNE ZEAVIN

5   A composite of King Kong and a suburban barber: revisiting Adorno's "Freudian theory and the pattern of fascist propaganda"   97
SAMIR GANDESHA

PART 2
The racialized object/the racializing subject — 117

6 On having Whiteness — 119
DONALD MOSS

7 "When reparation is felt to be impossible": persecutory guilt and breakdowns in thinking and dialogue about race — 135
JANE CAFLISCH

8 Murderous racism as normal psychosis — 158
ALAN BASS

9 Hunting the real: psychosis and race in the American hospital — 182
HANNAH WALLERSTEIN

10 A psychoanalytic contribution to understanding anti-Latino discourse and violence — 199
RICARDO C. AINSLIE

PART 3
This land: whose is it, really? — 215

11 Trees and other psychoanalytic matters — 217
LINDSAY L. CLARKSON

12 Shame, envy, impasse, and hope: the psychopolitics of violence in South Africa — 234
WAHBIE LONG

Index — 258

Acknowledgments

Many people have helped to bring this volume into being. First of all, we thank our contributors and their passionate commitment to the issues we are raising in this book. We wish to thank Sue Levy of the South African Psychoanalytic Association for inviting us to the marvelous SAPI conference in South Africa in 2019. That invitation was the impetus for Don Moss's paper *On Having Whiteness* and is when we first heard and met W. Long, whose paper is in this volume. We wish to express our gratitude to colleagues from the British Psychoanalytic Association, especially Michael Feldman, Priscilla Roth, Ignes Sodre, Daniel and Isobel Pick, and Irma Brenman Pick, whose teachings and friendship over the years have strengthened us as psychoanalysts, and we are appreciative of Alessandra Lemma who first read and encouraged this manuscript. We have benefited profoundly by many conversations concerning the environment with the other members of Green Gang, our dear friends and colleagues, Lindsay Clarkson and John Kress. Donald Moss has benefitted greatly from the opportunity to participate on the American Psychoanalytic Association's Holmes Commission on Racial Equality.

A special thanks indeed go to our daughter, Hannah, who lent her generous mind and spirit to several readings of the manuscript that included painstakingly and carefully copyediting it.

Permissions

Excerpts from *Beloved* by Toni Morrison used with permission of the Penguin Random House Publishers.

Caflisch, J. (2020). "When Reparation Is Felt to Be Impossible": Persecutory Guilt and Breakdowns in Thinking and Dialogue About Race. *Psychoanalytic Dialogues*, 30(5):578–594. doi:10.1080/10481885.2020.1797402, reprinted by permission of Taylor & Francis Ltd. Retrieved from: www.tandfonline.com.

González, F. J. (2020). First World Problems and Gated Communities of the Mind: An Ethics of Place in Psychoanalysis. *The Psychoanalytic Quarterly*, 89(4):741–770. doi:10.1080/00332828.2020.1805271, reprinted by permission of The Psychoanalytic Quarterly, Inc.

Wallerstein, H. (2020). Hunting the Real: Psychosis and Race in the American Hospital. *Psychoanalytic Perspectives*, 17(3):257–271. doi:10.1080/1551806X.2020.1801035, reprinted by permission of National Institute for the Psychotherapies. Retrieved from: www.nipinst.org.

Introduction

Donald Moss and Lynne Zeavin

> A belligerent state permits itself every such misdeed, every such act of violence, as would disgrace the individual. It makes use against the enemy not only of the accepted stratagems of war, but of deliberate lying and deception as well – and to a degree which seems to exceed the usage of former wars. The state exacts the utmost degree of obedience and sacrifice from its citizens, but at the same time it treats them like children by maintaining an excess of secrecy and a censorship upon news and expressions of opinion which leaves the spirits of those whose intellects it thus suppresses defenceless against every unfavorable turn of events and every sinister rumor. It absolves itself from the guarantees and treaties by which it was bound to other states, and makes unabashed confession of its own rapacity and lust for power, which the private individual has then to sanction in the name of patriotism.
> – Freud, *Thoughts for the Times on War and Death*

So what happens, then, when we psychoanalysts know, really know, that our long-standing clinical mantra, the one sponsoring the notion that the pursuit of love, work, and play unites us and our patients in a common vision, a common platform by which we can all guide ourselves, measure ourselves, satisfy ourselves – what happens when we come to know that this vision and this platform offer a grossly, even grotesquely, insufficient notion of what we might consider to constitute the basic requirements for living a full life? What happens when we know, really know, that tending to our private lives, our private gardens, no matter how successfully we might find ourselves loving, working, and playing in them – what happens when we know that such success, if treated as an end, marks us, not as successful, but instead as withdrawn, frightened, and uncertain? What happens when it marks us as the iconic citizens who, when, not too far into the

DOI: 10.4324/9781003214342-1

future, called to the dock, will assert, shamefacedly, "How could we have known?" or "What could we have done?" What happens when the dogged pursuit of work, love and play marks us not as the robust exceptions – the strong, the self-confident, the thoughtful, the pained – but instead marks us as the passive, the indifferent, the ones waiting for the moment to be over, the ones shoring up their walls, husbanding their intimates, saving their strengths? What happens when, in the name of pursuing the best of human possibilities, we in fact are replicating the behaviors of the enabling crowd, hugging the sidelines as the active collaborators get on with their grisly work?

We cannot continue as we have been. Our magnificent clinical experiment in keeping the doors closed, in barricading ourselves and our patients from our shared surround, has proven enormously successful We have founded a most remarkable discipline, a way of thinking, feeling, and speaking by which to sense, locate, and contact in ourselves and in others what has never before been sensed, located, and contacted. The constraining equilibria we can now disturb; the realms of possibility we can now open; the previously unimaginable impact we can now reliably have on another – these are the basic achievements of our ambitious 125-year experiment.

But the setup of this long-running experiment must now be modified. We need not open the doors, of course – there is nothing as fundamental as this that we must absolutely give up. But we do need to recognize that, all along, those closed doors of ours have been porous, have allowed in precisely what they were designed to keep out. That porosity has made it possible for us to develop, has in fact forced us to. Were the doors impermeable, we would still be where we were when we began, and we would, I think, have vanished, a memento of the moment, like the Charleston. Actual women infiltrated our offices, replacing the imaginary "feminine" with which we began. Actual gay and lesbian people infiltrated our offices, replacing the imaginary "homosexual" with which we began. We have been sluggish, but the real world has insisted. So, as we continue to work behind those porous doors, we can feel newer forces of infiltration – trans people, people of color, insisting that they too are here, that we cannot proceed as though they weren't, as though we could make of them whatever we wanted, that we wouldn't have to listen to what they actually say, and that instead we could know, in advance, what they would say, what they must say, given whom we knew they were. That moment, then, the one we thought we could control, is about to be over.

When we close our office doors, we want those doors to separate the materially bad object from the psychically bad one. In effect, we want to construct a special situation, the "psychoanalytic situation", in which badness is basically carried into the consulting room by patient and analyst, both in their idiosyncratic ways. The result – transference/countertransference – generates the analytic field, a "storm" of psychic realities that seems to erupt, materialize, in the session. It is this materialization of psychic realities that we can more or less expertly analyze – here and now, in the room. Our language designates our clinical aim. To turn psychic realities into material ones, here and now, in the room. We celebrate psychic reality and do our best to evade its material forms.

As we do, so does most of the human world – does its best to live behind closed doors, keeping disruptive material reality outside. Starting with Freud, we have long watched the rest of the world do this, and we have confidently known of the inevitable failure of this universal temptation to barricade doors, to keep the malign outside, to screen all passengers, to keep ourselves safe. This is the fundamental setup of most horror stories. The protagonists, alerted to the presence of danger, lock their doors, board their windows, thicken their walls, and meanwhile the viewers watch in alarm, knowing, as the protagonists do not, that the danger they are locking out is actually already in, that their project of keeping themselves safe is about to boomerang, that instead of locking the danger out, they are locking it in.

A reprise

Seeking the determinants of conscious experience, our original theory pointed inward toward the body and toward the body's exigent demands for satisfaction, for tension reduction. The "object" was theorized as a psychic representative, an idiosyncratically formulated "mnemic trace" of a perception association with satisfaction. "Wish" was defined as simply the urge to find that psychic representative – to form a perceptual identity: a seeking in the here and now for the perception of what I once found in the there and then. The most efficient form of finding that perceptual "object" would be to hallucinate it. "The bitter experience of life" was what Freud called the failure of that hallucination to provide the necessary satisfaction. Given that failure, wishing had to seek elsewhere for satisfaction. That elsewhere was the external world. This external world was mapped as the more or less resistant/accommodating field in which this second search ("secondary process" of wishing) had to occur. Mapped this way, the external world consisted of a vast field that either could or could not provide satisfaction (perceptual identity). The wishing subject was *driven* to find satisfaction. The source of that drive – the demand it made on the mind – was interior, a part of the body. Wishing, then, originated in the body and sought satisfaction in the external world. The external world was constructed as a place to look, a site of object seeking. At no point in this formative moment of our theory was the external world conceptualized as making demands of its own, primary demands, demands which themselves might possess force and power equivalent to those demands originating in our bodies, in our interiors.

This epistemological move yielded an enormously powerful theory, one capable of providing revolutionary depth and nuance to our capacities to understand and transform subjective experience, particularly subjective suffering. This same move, though, left psychoanalysis with an exposed flank, a fundamentally underdeveloped appreciation of the possibility that the external world generated its own demands, its own exigencies, its own primary disturbances.

Freud's idea of "the body" as a neutral biological entity – a source of erotic sources – warrants fundamental critique. The demands of "the body" are made not only by "the body" but by this particular body, placed particularly in relation to this mother, etc. – placed from the start, that is, in the pair's material world. As such, the "body" is subject from the start not only to demands emanating from its interior but also to demands and requirements emanating from the material world – demands that, together, have a primary determining power to regulate, insist, and define. We have long been accustomed to think that there is no such thing as a "baby" in itself. But now we must expand the reach of that "no such thing" to include "the mother" and "the mother–baby pair" – the reach of the phrase spreads outward – "the family," the "community." None of these is properly thought of as "in itself." Each entity rests within and is determined by a larger encompassing entity.

To oversimplify for a moment, Freud, in offering us a way of thinking of the external world as a reservoir of objects, tilted the discipline toward considering that external world as though it were one super-object: the set consisting of all possible external "objects." This epistemological move made enormous sense, given an initial aim of illuminating "psychic reality." The idea was to diminish the number of variables so as to focus on this one. Psychic reality assumed not only pride of place but sole place. Meanings apparently residing in the external world were interpreted as a product of drives and wishes – fantasies – originating in the internal one. (Beginning with Marx, varieties of historical materialism represented an inverse and complementary epistemological move. There, internal subjective meanings were interpreted as determined by external conditions.) Both epistemological strategies resulted in weakened and vulnerable theories and practices. In each, an epistemological move was mistakenly taken to be more than what it was – the part taken for the whole.

After Freud, psychoanalysis and psychoanalysts were left with an exposed flank – the external world continuously pressed in and the discipline was unsure what to do about it. We traditionally tried to fend it off, to treat exteriority's demands as the boomeranging result of processes originating in the interior. Really, we have too often said, that demand out there must have originated in here. Of course, we always may have been right. The problem we must face, though, is that we also may not have been right. We need to develop our capacities to actually think about events occurring at our exposed flank, rather than to be left doggedly trying to defend that flank by committing to a theory that, in principle, asserted that the demands of the exterior are best understood as the ghostly emanations of ones originating in the interior. In effect, our theory drove the discipline toward a committed belief in ghosts.

In this book, we hope to contribute to the unmistakable and widespread contemporary effort to examine, repair, and reconsider our discipline's exposed external flank. We want to fortify our capacities to theorize and work with all of the demands that impinge on all of us. None of these demands, whether their origins be inside or out, warrant a priori treatment as derivative and secondary. The drive, originating in the body, demands that we work – that we seek and find a satisfying object, one that promises to move us in the direction of calm and quiet. The processes – primary and secondary – by which we represent the demand and the object, the complexities through which we settle for substitutes, the strategies by which we both evade and court punishments – this complex nest of activity has long served as our fundamental clinical ground. In this book, we mean to expand that ground, to take on some of the determining forces originating in the external world, in the world of external "objects." Our book's "subject" – the living persons we encounter in our offices and homes and also in our streets – finds themselves living precisely where these two sets of determinants converge. The external world we mean to outline is not a secondary one, one functioning as merely a medium for object seeking, but is, just like the Freudian drive, a primary one. As we work outside ourselves to satisfy demands originating in our interiors, we also work inside ourselves to contend with demands originating in our exteriors.

Here is an exemplary moment, told to us by a colleague: A Black family has moved into her predominantly white neighborhood. Her five-year-old has befriended the five-year-old boy from that family. Her son invites his new friend to lunch. Our colleague feels herself resisting, feels that having the boy to lunch would be crossing some line, disrupting some foundational sense of order. Is this permissible? Should she take the risk? What risk, she wonders? What losses might she be courting? Nothing about it makes much sense. And yet she can feel the tension rise in her body. She is about to do something dangerous. Violating some regulations/seeking something that is wrong. Questions pour into her. What is a Black person? What is food? What appetites are in play? With whom can I eat? With whom can I find pleasures? What are the forces in play? Is this coming from me, is it coming from them, from somewhere else? Outside or in? Of course, she overcomes the resistance.

It seems clear to both of us that looking to her interior will likely unearth privately formed determinants – appetitive regulations – that have been stirred and aroused by the prospect of this psychically disruptive presence at her lunch table. It also seems clear that looking to the external world, to the force field generated by structural racism, she will also unearth abundant determinants – other appetitive regulations – that impact her in the form of primary demands. This mix of appetitive regulations – rooted both inside and out – yields a foundational sense of what constitutes the proper order of things, of how the world ought to be. Why, we wonder, would inviting a Black boy into her house for lunch be a violation of that order? In order to "analyze" her reluctance to host the boy at her lunch table, we psychoanalysts will have to consider every source of demand, appetite, and regulation, as separate, independent, converging in a kind of supercondensate: I should not be doing this/I should be doing this. I should preserve order/I should foment disorder.

In essence, we want to help expand the discipline's sense of where to look when we are looking for the primary sources of wishing, the primary sources of disturbance, the primary sources that drive us to look for satisfaction. We want to be able to look to the external world as a primary source without having to – *having to* – think of that turn toward the outside as primarily a turn away from the inside. The external world matters – full stop. We pay a dear price when our theory, either directly or indirectly, fails to recognize this. We humans find ourselves both in and determined by the external world no less than we find ourselves both in and determined by the internal one. We are placed in both places, doing our best to contend with demands emanating from inside and out. That sense of being placed "in" both of them – "in" our interiors as well as "in" our exteriors – informs each of the essays in this book.

The door closes. Analyst and patient are alone in a room. How alone are they? What kinds of presences accompany them? Of course, we know that each brings their traditionally conceived "objects" into the field. Each brings their desires. These objects and desires constitute the standard field of observation and work in clinical psychoanalysis. However, if we really ask what each wants from the other – which is, after all, the basic question being asked all the time in clinical work – we immediately have to face the immensities of history – each person's, of course – but also the histories surrounding each person, the histories that made it possible for this one to become a patient here and that one to become an analyst. There we are, conducting our analyses, and if you ask either of us if, while doing that, about, say, our white racial identities how might we really answer? We might offer a wan account and hope to move on. But what if you keep it up? What if you ask for more, ask how our racial identities affect our work, affect what we all see, hear and think? Push it just a bit, and we will likely soon run out of answers. Neither of us will really know. The theory has not provided us with an adequate way to think of that question. We will be pushed to a point where we will want you to stop asking.

We hope this book pushes the limits of that point – for the two of us, of course, but also for you, its readers, as well. We hope the book expands analysts' capacities to grasp for and think about the fullness of identities, racial and otherwise – their own and their patients'.

This book means to create a skein of questions – about our interior and exterior surrounds, about our private and social places, about race, about our relations to the natural world. Each question that arises will be partial. Gathered together, they form an epistemological thicket. This thicket marks both a necessary minimum and an irreducible excess. We are helpless to clearly find our way into it and equally helpless to honorably stay away from it.

The project of exclusion has been exhausted. The wind blows through the cracks, seeps under our doors, and, of course, hits us in our faces the moment we step outside. Here, then, is a cluster of psychoanalytic voices, contending with the contemporary wind. Each of these voices aims to work against a primary and elemental human impulse to exclude all sources of pain, an impulse that Freud so bluntly characterizes as *"hating, abhorring and wishing to destroy"* all that threatens our ongoing pursuit of pleasure and safety.

On Part 1: Hating in the first person plural

We want the reality we live in to function as a massive commons – capacious and safe enough to allow for the seeking and finding of what we think we want. Feeling sane, we feel other than alone. Common sense, common feeling, common mission, common belief – each undoes the threat of exile associated with absolute idiosyncrasy and singularity. To be utterly alone with an idea, a thought, an impulse – to be unable to give an account of yourself, unable to win the listener's nod of recognition and identification – is to fall into sharp contact with the threat of irreversible abandonment. Sanity's commons, then, will necessarily segment into zones of danger and safety, places to congregate and places to avoid. We bring an attitude of something like love and fellow feeling toward those with whom we congregate and something like hate and repulsion toward those from whom we flee. "I" am never alone, then, in sanity's Commons. I "love" with others; I "hate" with others. Problems arise, though, in sanity's Commons when "we" fellow congregants neurotically supplement the actual dangers – material threats to our bodies and material impediments to the realization of our wishes – we might all face. That neurotic supplement leads us to collectively imagine and construct gratuitous dangers and gratuitous hatreds. This excess results from the pooling of our common unconscious fantasies of danger. From that pool we can all extract frightening figures whom we can collectively locate and map into the external world. Suddenly, these figures common to our interior unconscious fantasies will seem to us to have become consciously perceptible, really there and really outside. What a relief that might be. Our imperceptible interiors might now seem safe. Our interiors secured, we might be able to relax a bit. All we have to do is to stay vigilant, to keep spotting the dangerous outsiders and then to manage and defeat these figures from the perceptible external world. The more we all do this, the more we all gather to fend off those pooled dangers we all can now so clearly see, the closer we all might start to feel toward each other. If only we can keep seeing them, those externalized dangerous figures, as we huddle together, close to each other, nodding – see, there's one, and there, there's another. United in keeping our common enemies at bay, we might be unburdened from some of the work of actually trying to see who each of us is, to see whether we, in fact, might find our way toward loving one another. Instead of the difficult work of recognizing idiosyncrasies, of bridging differences, of contending with unwanted limits, we can instead excitedly embrace our manufactured commonality; generating warm fellow feeling by way of our shared project of militant, even violent, defense and self-protection. Creating shared objects to hate might unite us, might turn us into an apparently impregnable unit, and therefore might protect us all from ever having to contend with the threat posed by our own idiosyncratic singularities, the threat of irreversible abandonment. And then again, it might not.

The chapters in this part take up the tensions arising from the difficulties of simultaneously living as a member of the Commons and as an idiosyncratic individual, bound to the particulars of what can easily feel like the most private, the most isolating demands generated by membership in our nuclear – separated – personal histories.

On Part 2: The racialized object/the racializing subject

Each of these five texts addresses some malignant features of "Whiteness" in contemporary American life. The texts share the premise that these features derive from a kind of foundational infiltrate inherent in the very category of "Race." Woven into its initial encounters with North America's indigenous peoples and its enthusiastic embrace of the African slave trade, "race" narratives offered Euro-Americans a bioreligious category that provided an ethical imprimatur to their overarching project of dominion. The category of "race" necessarily led to a vertical mapping of the people involved in the formation of the United States of America. Whiteness was positioned at the top of this map, nonwhite below. Some 500 years, approximately 20 generations – one necessarily carries the weight of all that time, all those generations. Born white, we are born into a history of

Whiteness. No matter how strongly we might wish to start afresh, that history informs us. It marks our deepest interiors – our bodies, the bodies of our mothers and of their mothers, the standings of those bodies, their places in the world, their points of arrival and of departure. Consciousness is a big help. With it, we can twist our heads around and at least get a glimpse of where we have come from and of the residue we are carrying.

On Part 3: This land: whose is it, really?

In widely divergent ways, Lindsay Clarkson and Wahbie Long remind us of the enormous damage wrought by separating ourselves from the world around us, the "trees" for Clarkson and "the land" for Long. Psychoanalytic work is grounded in an appreciation of the otherness of the other person and as such is also grounded in an awareness of the deforming consequences that result from our various ways of evading that appreciation. The impulse to eliminate otherness, in all its forms, marks one tactical extreme that this evasion can take. The impulse to become the other marks the contrary extreme. The work of maintaining oneself in relation to the other, living between the excesses of elimination and overidentification – this not only defines our clinical work, it also defines our work as people and our efforts at making such work seem worth it to those around us. The other with whom we are speaking is, of course, more than a psychic site, more than an individual body – the other with whom we are speaking is an integral part of all the otherness with which we are surrounded. I speak to you not only as a singular "I" speaking to you but also as a representative of otherness speaking to you – I speak to you as one of them, one of it, one of all who might be speaking and of all the world – speaking and not – whom you might encounter.

Part 1

Hating in the first person plural

Chapter 1

On hating in the first person plural

Thinking psychoanalytically about racism, homophobia, and misogyny

Donald Moss

There is scant sign of idiosyncrasy in the malignant hatreds of racism, homophobia, and misogyny. No matter that they may be rooted in our most private, urgent experiences of unmet desire, the objects that these hatreds both construct and target are standardized. With little variation, people of color are hated for their primitivity; gays and lesbians for their contagious transgressions, their "homosexual agenda"; women for their weakness of character and insatiable sexuality. The prescribed ideas, attitudes, and inclinations to be adopted toward these standardized objects of hatred also lack originality. For the hating subjects, these objects are self-evidently dangerous, and the appropriate sentiments and behaviors, no matter how violent, all share the stated aim of promoting safety and diminishing threat. Knowledge of the hated objects' noxious qualities and of the prescriptions and proscriptions related to their proper handling are felt to be derived from sources that both predate and supersede any particular experience. The primary function of any personal experience with the objects in question is neither the discovery nor the generation of new ideas and affects but rather the gathering of confirmatory evidence. With such evidence in hand, people can tap into what feels like the wisdom of the ancients. This wisdom is codified into systems of belief, structures of knowledge linked to a taxonomy, an organizing notion that the human world is, at bedrock, made up of hierarchically arranged groups.

Therefore, when we hate – racistly, homophobically, misogynistically – we are hating not as isolated individuals but as part of a group, not in the first person singular but in the first person plural. Within the sphere of these hatreds, "I" hate not as "I" alone, but as a white person, a straight person, a man. Our hatred is directed, as it were, taxonomically downward. Disidentification downward, identification upward; this dynamic may seem to offer

DOI: 10.4324/9781003214342-3

the only purchase against taxonomical descent. The zones occupied by the objects beneath us function for our hatreds as Freud's idyll of Yellowstone National Park functions for sexuality. They are bounded preserves, simultaneously offering a site of external indulgence while implicitly supporting local order. Whether we permit ourselves the indulgence of their explicit enactments, or try to constrain them to fantasy, we are in either case enlisting in a struggle for self-definition – asserting both a disidentification from the groups we target and an identificatory allegiance elsewhere. Felt as markers of a coveted identity in the taxonomy, these hatreds give partial expression of a yearned-for solidarity with like-minded others.

The basic assumption of fight/flight (Bion, 1959) that underlies these hatreds, as well as the psychological and physical violence linked to them, shackle our every public, private, and professional effort at fully realizing both the democratic and clinical ideals of truly free association. The horizontal/egalitarian operations of free association and the vertical/hierarchical operations of these malignant hatreds are mutually exclusive. As psychoanalysts and as citizens, we have openly committed ourselves to the ideal of democratically structured discourse – discourse shorn of the gratuitous influence of fixed, transference-based, taxonomical hierarchies. Any links to such hatreds, therefore, will be felt as putting the lie to that commitment and will spur us to try to liberate ourselves from their stunting influences.

In addition to doing the analytic work necessary for this kind of liberation, we might also be tempted to approach these hatreds from a personal/professional posture of disidentification. Such disidentification might be thought of as the reflexive response to the forceful influence of raw ethical principle. Such principle impinges upon us with the exigent character of a drive. At a minimum, its satisfaction would require a renunciation of all identifications and appetites that might lead to participation, no matter how indirectly, in the malignant sport sanctioned by these hatreds. Self-analysis, though, like clinical analysis, is grounded in identifications – the owning, usually against resistance, of the "not-me" aspects of our mental lives. Therefore, that ethically driven impulse to disidentify will directly oppose our impulse to perform analytic work.

The working analytic "dyad" here may actually be constituted by two people, or, in the case of self-reflection, simply two or more internally housed points of view. In either case, without the effect of identifications, the resulting discourse is limited. Regardless of whether the dyad includes a patient or not, if, at the crucial moment, the transgressive other is first felt and then perceived as "not me," the limits to analytic discourse are severe. Here, dangerous identificatory proximity provokes disruptive flight rather than disruptive recognition. Then, midflight, anxiety averted, contact lost, suddenly stranger is speaking to stranger, outsider to outsider. The opportunity for influence, from the inside, has been lost. Identifications are the only reliable counter to such estrangement. In principle, identifications create, at least transiently, a feeling that communication has no limit, that there exists an unimpeded, open line between the two parties. In the clinical setting, of course, this feeling of limitless communication appears and vanishes beguilingly. We are particularly alert to its comings and goings, trying to read indirectly the operations of wish and defense by reading, more directly, fluctuations in our sense of openness and identificatory contact. Contact, taken to its limit, is what for the moment I mean by identification – the sense that, no matter what is about to be said, access to the object will not be lost. Without the belief in such contact, one is confirmed in the idea that there are, indeed, sectors of mind that if spoken will result in abandonment. Without such contact, interpretation aimed at these sectors comes, as it were, from outside and is therefore reduced to the status of mere commentary. The analytic work, then, for both parties, becomes a matter of fulfilling obligations – the patient to present himself, and the analyst to witness. For patient and analyst, if the sentiments and fantasies associated with homophobia, misogyny, and racism remain walled off from identificatory contact, the clinical engagement with these systematized hatreds, if it occurs at all, will, in confirming the status quo, more likely produce rueful anecdote than disruptive change.

I will argue here, using personal, cultural, and clinical material, that if we are to have something psychoanalytic to say about racism, homophobia, and misogyny, the temptation to disidentify, though easily understood, must be resisted. Disidentified from these hatreds we will treat them, at base, moralistically, as both an outrage and an offense. When Flaubert wrote, "Madame Bovary, c'est moi," he succinctly outlined the methodological task for thinking psychoanalytically about racism, homophobia, and misogyny. It is only an intimate familiarity – finally unbearable and therefore transient – with these deadly hatreds that gives us any chance to diminish their influence.

In general, while doing clinical psychoanalysis, an analyst aims at a particular coupling of understanding with effect. We try to grasp the dynamics and determinants of the immediate moment while we are simultaneously imagining a possible one. The pursuit of this coupling of immediate understanding to imagined effect lies at the heart of psychoanalytic work. Such work is predicated on finding ways to sustain identifications with our patients – to reside, at least momentarily, in what seems like the patient's ongoing sense of a past, present, and future. Without such identifications, the feasibility of achieving this coupling of understanding with effect is limited. Insufficiently able to partake in our patient's immediate psychic present, we might become compensatorily caught up in an image of the patient's transformed future. Such a partial identification might, then, unwittingly limit us to a manipulative pursuit of effect, to making the patient "better." Or, conversely, were we unable to actually imagine our patient getting better, we might find ourselves in sterile pursuit of dynamics alone. Clinical work aims, via identification, to bring immediate idea and imagined effect into vital union. Such work can be particularly difficult when we are confronting systematized hatreds like racism, homophobia, and misogyny. We can easily feel deprived of secure points of identification, and find ourselves instead driven back and forth between fleeting states of alienation, excitement, and moral condemnation. None of these states seems to give us much of a purchase for psychoanalytic work, and yet, for sustained periods, they may be all we can find. I have used the following personal memory as an orienting aid – a technical assistant – when I have found myself in the midst of this kind of clinical difficulty.

When I was five and six years old, in the late 1940s, I often went alone to the movies. What I remember most from those matinees are the newsreels: the war footage in general, the footage of the Nazi concentration camps, and the Nuremberg trials in particular. We were shown the accused in uniforms and judges in robes. We were shown large numbers of bodies and large numbers of barely living survivors. Each newsreel had an instructive voice-over: someone telling us some of what had happened and how many it had happened to. The purpose of the footage was moral instruction. We were to see what had been done to people like us by people like them. Innocents had been slaughtered. Evil had no limits. We were to remember these lessons forever. As Jews and Americans, we were to vow to defend both ourselves and other innocent people. The lessons I learned were, in fact, unforgettable.

Although the moral instruction of this forceful, somber footage definitely took, while watching the footage, while using my eyes to see, stare, gaze – *connect* – to it, something else was also taking place, something entirely independent of the voice-over's message of reflection and remembrance. While the voice-over's lessons directed my focus to what should be done after seeing what we were seeing, the focus of this other activity was the present tense – what could be done now. Here, rather than work to do, there were appetites to feed. These marginal appetites, unintended and unbidden, seemed in direct opposition to the voice-over's intended ethical lessons. Along with my ethically reassuring sense of horror, I found myself in a state of raw and hungry fascination.

I was amazed by all the bodies, their vast number, so many of them dead, and by the incomprehensible apparatus of cameras, movies, and photos that had brought them here for me to see. And indeed, they seemed placed on the screen for me, and for me alone, to see. Not only, as the voice-over assumed, to learn from them, but also to do with them whatever my eyes, and I, might want to do. At the margin, all of my once fellow participants in ethical life turned not only irrelevant but imperceptible; they actually seemed to dissolve, fall out of focus, and no longer exert the pressure of their presence. At the margin, I had neither need nor wish for any of those whose companionship at the center provided both the reason and the reward for the successful completion of my ethical lessons. Here the matinee audience, my friends, family, all the stand-up Americans, the good ones, the fighters, had no place. Here, in service to appetite, I felt unlimited license – alone with my eyes and with the rest of my body, in contact with no one but the figures on the screen. Without any such contact, my body and I felt also without any obligations, beyond the reach of the voice-over's ethical grasp.

But, because the centers of consciousness do abut and therefore influence the margins, we were not beyond the reach of ethics per se. Even at the otherwise unobliged margins, an accounting felt necessary, an ethical accounting, a way of orienting myself in relation to an idea of operative justice, the bedrock machinery through which the world's order was maintained. At both the center and the margin, the situation to be accounted for was identical: my being here, and they there. At the center, though, the ruling idea was that what we were seeing must never be allowed to recur. At the margin, the idea was that what I was doing with what I was seeing could be repeated at will.

The problem to be addressed was likeness: I was a Jew; the victims on the screen were Jews. This likeness was not diluted by the logistics of geography and immigration. And likeness meant identification. I was one of them: reduced, naked, and dead. But I was also using them. They were my objects, in both the vulgar and the original psychoanalytic senses of the term: "the thing in regard to which or through which the drive is able to achieve its aim." This relation had to be accounted for. Whereas the voice-over's ethical injunctions were grounded on the premise and the demands that linked identity to likeness, the ethical account here, on the margin, would be grounded on the premise and the privileges that linked identity to difference.

Such ethics linked me to the killers. There was no limit to what we could do to people both unlike and beneath us. Like the ethics of identification that had me joined to the victims, this link too was intolerable. It could not be so. I was not one of them. I was a Jew. I had no third option, no stable means by which to represent the simultaneous presence of such identificatory incompatibilities. Self-reflection seemed useless. I wondered what kind of justice was operating, that gave all of us exactly what we deserved; wondered if I were better, cleaner, smarter, bigger, whiter, more American, cooler; whether I knew more, whether it was the Yiddish that ruined them, the clothes, the shapes of their faces. Adorno (1951/1978) catches well the same psychic operation, the same urgent attachment to an exculpatory fantasy of a world ruled by the impersonal operations of ruthless justice, when he writes: "In early childhood I saw the first snow-shovelers in thin shabby clothes. Asking about them, I was told they were men without work who were given this job so that they could earn their bread. Then they get what they deserve, having to shovel snow, I cried out in rage, bursting uncontrollably into tears" (p. 190).

The idea of an impersonally ruthless justice machine was not an interpretation of experience but rather an escape from it. So was the idea that my eyes alone, not I, were responsible for what was taking place – the idea of my body as a rogue entity to which I was only coincidentally bound. The problem with both of these extraexperiential solutions was the ongoing experience of pleasure. No matter how forcefully I might disavow my implication in both my ethics and my body, I could not, finally, dissociate myself from the pleasures I was taking. Those pleasures were mine. My arousal and fascination – my pleasures – left me dumbstruck. I dreaded the newsreels, but wanted to see more. I hoped to cure myself of my fascination with them. Maybe if I looked again, differently, I thought, I could wall off the exciting margin, could train and tame my gaze, and end my implication in what I was seeing. Hoping to achieve both more pleasure and the kind of mental hygiene that would render such pleasure impossible, I kept looking. I was aiming for the properly ethical gaze: the one intended for me, for all of us in the theater, the one that would have us all entirely disidentified from the killers and entirely identified with the victims and with the judges who act in their names.

Retrospectively, this experience with the newsreels seems to have been my first conscious encounter with the power of unconscious fantasy: its inaccessibility, its capacity to thrive at the margins, its ferocity, tenacity, its capacity to attach itself, transfer itself, onto any element of conscious experience, its authoritative obliteration of innocence. Fifty years later, the news and the newsreels continue: different bodies, different killers. I still watch them; still hope to use them self-curatively. But the cure eludes me; I remain implicated – neither my identifications with the victims, nor my disidentifications from the perpetrators, are ever quite what they are meant to be.

This kind of implication, in both the attitudes and appetites of the perpetrators, has been for me a requirement in my feeling I might have something psychoanalytic to say about the determinants of contemporary malignant social phenomena: Nazism for me then; homophobia, racism, and misogyny for all of us today. It is akin to the identificatory implications necessary in clinical practice. There, effective interpretation seems to depend on sensing patients' wishes and appetites as recognizable versions of my own. Clinical theory offers robust means by which to locate these linking similes, these often obscure points of contact between analyst and patient. Without such contact, the analyst speaks, in principle, as a stranger speaks and is heard in principle, as a stranger is heard. Absent identificatory contact, we might be able to fulfill our formal obligations as commentators, and patients theirs as informants, but for neither will there be much real hope, or threat, of influence.

Because it is grounded in such points of contact, I consider the theory and practice of psychoanalysis as in principle incompatible with what might be called the theories and practices of homophobia, racism, and misogyny. That is not to say that psychoanalysis cannot support homophobic, racist, or misogynist practices. Numerous flash points dotting its history demonstrate both that it can and that it has. The incompatibility between psychoanalysis and these structured hatreds refers not to content but instead to epistemology and method. The cardinal difference is that for homophobia, racism, and misogyny, the other as object is by definition transparent, and knowledge about it is available through revelation. For psychoanalysis, though, the other as object is by definition opaque, and knowledge about it is available only through inference and experience.

Internal to the structure of psychoanalytic thought is the accumulated clinical experience of patients saying no to both the manner and the particulars of interpretation. In clinical theory this no, this elementary exercise in refusal, has a privileged status. Intended as both self-defining and limit setting, establishing boundaries and therefore the possibility of definitions, it is the founding developmental and political unit of discourse. It points to perennially contested borders, between self and object, inside and outside, private and public. It marks points of conflict and opposition that both dot and constitute those borders. Its patterns of usage reliably map the complementary relations linking the forces of desire to the forces of regulation, power, and subjectivity. Since neither party in analysis accepts the other for very long "at face value," much of what actually takes place can be thought of as an exchange of noes. The very possibility of effective clinical work, then, will hinge on each party's handling of this volatile exchange. In my experience with the concentration camp footage, such an exchange has not yet been completed. Its terms are still contested. My employing the example here, turning outward, going public, is yet another effort, perhaps, to move the sluggish "analysis" to a termination phase.

In both the theory and the practice of homophobia, racism, and misogyny, the object's no is transparent and dismissable on its face. Each of these discriminatory structures directly reads the object's body and its sexual practices. They are legible to the clear, learned, eye. Such readings yield – or, more precisely, affirm – the presence of fixed, natural hierarchies. These hierarchies, once secure, are now threatened. Their security is to be restored. The project is not constructive but reconstructive. As such, guided not by an idea but by a perception, the reader can process these objects with a sense of unshakable certainty. Contemporary experience of the object can only redundantly confirm that sense of certainty. It can never disconfirm it. To the methodologically refined, negative findings are always illusory; the object's no always means yes. Knowledge of the object comes not through piecemeal construction but through revelation.

Access to the hated object through revelation rather than through thought is reflective of both ego and superego deformations. Tentative apprehension and cautious moral assessment vanish, replaced by a potentially lethal combination of direct perception and merciless judgment, the kind of immediacy familiar to us all, say, in a common experience of disgust. The reaction is immediate: the object appears; judgment and perception converge. One simply knows what the object is and what ought to be done with it. The possibility of danger for the provoking object increases exponentially when affects such as disgust lose a quality of subjective idiosyncrasy and instead seem an element of one's unquestionable identity. When they are loosed from the first person singular and located in the first person plural, such affects seem to be features of one's fundamental, and crucial, attachment to like-minded others.

Bion's classic text, *Experiences in Groups* (1959), is directly relevant to a consideration of the plural voice's deforming effects on the possibility for individuals to think on their own. Bion's book can be read as an extended study of the usually covert effects of direct, unmediated modes of knowing on individuals' capacities for thought, for the ability to "learn through experience." Bion is particularly interested in the ways that membership in groups, though essential, necessarily exposes us to forces that oppose individual thought and experience. The opposition comes, says Bion, through the influence of shifting sets of alternate "basic assumptions." These basic assumptions, such as "fight/flight," establish an underlying tone, a mood and posture, that permeates the group's every activity. The group treats the elements of these assumptions as beyond the reach of individuals' questions. Participation in the assumptions, no matter how indirect, coincides with membership in the group. These basic assumptions are, then, akin to what I mean here by "revelatory knowledge." They offer a kind of information that precedes and exceeds the kind offered by experience. They promise direct access to reality and therefore seem to make secondary process superfluous. Bion focuses on the irreconcilable tensions between thought and revelation, between apprehending the object by way of "work" and apprehending it by way of basic assumptions. Thought's piecemeal and tentative constructions are, for Bion, the product of an appreciation of experience and are housed in "the mentality of the individuals." Revelation's certainties, by contrast, are the products of basic assumptions and are housed in what he calls "group mentality." Group mentality is a concept that approximates the notion of "first person plural voice" that I am using here. At the heart of this group mentality is "the feeling that the welfare of the individual does not matter so long as the group continues, and there will be a feeling that any method of dealing with neurosis that is neither fighting . . . nor running away . . . is either non-existent or directly opposed to the good of the group" (p. 64). That is, the group, the "first person plural" collective, is constituted by its homogeneous commitment to fighting and/or running away and to its absolute opposition to thought, to what Bion calls work. In this sense, the first person plural voice directly opposes any individual's efforts to assess, via experience, the object's particular qualities.

When, as a feature of one's sense of identity, hating the object seems intrinsic to perceiving it correctly, we can assume that the ego-deforming force of Bion's group mentality is exerting a corrupting influence also on superego function. This corrupting influence corresponds to the one exerted on the ego. Writing about what she calls the "pathological superego," O'Shaughnessy (1999) catches its effects well:

> The pathological superego . . . is dissociated from ego functions like attention, enquiry, remembering, understanding. . . . [It] is not trying to know; it is denuding and condemning. . . . It is full of hate and prejudice, skeptical of all renaissance; its aim is to destroy links within the self and between the self and its objects.
>
> (p. 868)

I would only add to this clinically derived, precise, description that the pathological superego described here can, when structured within the first person plural voice, indeed destroy links with objects, while also serving as a deep elemental link between other objects.

O'Shaugnessy is writing within and about phenomena observed in the clinical setup, where analyst and patient each think and speak as both person and working/theorized entity – "psychoanalyst"/"patient." There, site and theory construct each other and both, together, construct the participants. By "construct" I mean that the clinical situation transforms what would most likely be an inert interaction into a productive one. It does this by considering all that contributes to that baseline inertia, to intrapsychic and interactive stasis – i.e., defense – as its energizing central problem. But, outside the clinical situation, when I am writing or speaking about homophobia, racism, and misogyny, neither my function nor the audience's demand has been theorized. Necessarily identified with and proxy for the object of my interpretations and unprotected by site/theory specificity, the analyst's desires are necessarily exposed while the audience's rights to disidentificatory silence are privileged and protected. Then, without controls, where psychoanalytic effect is neither measurable nor even necessarily relevant, we can confidently say that psychoanalysis is reaching beyond its own clinically grounded theoretical grasp. Here, then, both parties can rely only on sincerity – their own and others'. Sincerity is premised on self-transparency, on the claim that here, now, I am what I appear to be. In the clinical setup the claims of sincerity carry almost no intrinsic force. But in the public sphere, when talking of homophobia, racism, and misogyny, we are for the most part deprived of the structuring impact of the object's demand. Entre nous, then, sincerity seems all we have to lean on.

The opening paragraph of the "Strike" section of Hubert Selby's (1957) *Last Exit to Brooklyn* provides an extraclinical representation of the emergence of both misogyny and homophobia as structured hatreds, providing disidentificatory relief from an otherwise unbearable and unstructured mixture of desire and identification.

Harry, a working-class man, is watching as his naked son plays with a diaper. Harry looks at and touches his son's penis, wondering what it might feel like to a baby boy. He is pleased to imagine how he and the boy might be alike. Unexpectedly, Harry's wife walks in and sees that Harry has his hand on the baby's penis. Harry backs off and watches as his wife diapers the baby and kisses his stomach, her mouth brushing against the baby's penis. He has the thought that she might put it in her mouth. With that, his stomach knots, and he feels nauseated.

Harry's lush and idiosyncratic homoerotic daydream is instantaneously transformed into a stock, prototypically misogynist tale of woman's insatiable heterosexual appetite: "she" was going to put it in "her" mouth. The sequence is clear and exemplary. It begins with Harry's sight of his son's penis: Harry "stared . . . touched . . . wondered." At first, the daydream occurs safely. In Harry's consciousness, both he and his objects, the son and the son's penis, are experienced as opaque. This opacity is, for the moment, bearable. Though conscious that he can never really know, Harry is nonetheless curious as to sexual similarities and differences. Both the sense of safety and the sense of the object's opacity end abruptly, though, with the appearance of the wife. Curiosity and arousal are replaced by certainty and dread. Opacity is replaced by transparency. To Harry, the wife is a transparent object, an interdicting third party; the implication is that, of course, It is she, and not he, who both interdicts and transgresses. Harry's interior has been expelled; he is now reacting to external perceptions. He is no longer an aroused, sexually curious man, tentatively identifying with his object. Now he is sexually shut down and alarmed – vigilant, alert to, and disidentified from the sexual excesses of his suddenly transparent objects: the wife's seeming readiness to put the baby's penis in her mouth, the son's to have it put there.

What put Harry into danger was the transformation of his sexual aim from a private to a public sphere. The wife as third party, as witness, will for Harry demand an accounting that he cannot adequately provide. Neither the language nor the imagery available to him can simultaneously represent what he has just been doing and represent competent masculinity. This inadequacy stirs him into symptom formation, whose twofold aim is the restoration of safety and the restitution of a sense of competent masculinity. What has signaled danger is the image of the wife. Harry then reconfigures the externally located signal and expels the internally located aim. "It looked as if she were going to put it in her mouth." Interdicted Harry, once he is safely nauseous rather than dangerously sexual, becomes the one who, turning the tables, would now interdict the wife's unregulated sexual appetite. He is now the third party, the witness; the public's representative, a seer. He occupies a middle rung in an ancient sexual taxonomy. The rung is occupied by competent heterosexual men. As one of them now, he sees and is sickened by what any competent man would see: the insatiable woman/the wanting boy. The internal world again safe and the voraciousness of the external one revealed, Harry can flee – toward what he wants to be, an outraged and therefore competent man, and away from what he is not: an insatiable woman or a wanting boy. Selby catches this complex effort at flight well when he describes how, minutes later, their child asleep, Harry and his wife take to their own bed.

His wife's desire for him leads to a situation in which he feels there is nothing he can control. This scene echoes the earlier one with his son. That is, in both situations he could not find an adequate way to account for feeling out of control. It is not the absence of control, per se, that drives Harry into misogynist/homophobic flight. Rather, it is the absence of any theory, any means of representation, by which controlling nothing can be reconciled with competent masculinity. What he sees opaquely he cannot put to use, so therefore he must see transparently, must *see through* everything. He does not read his wife's desire for him; he *reads through* it. That desire reveals her as a "fuckin' bitch." Once provided with that revelation, Harry is also provided with a solution, a way of controlling something: he finds momentary relief in imagining his wife and baby leaving, allowing him a desireless tranquility.

This kind of sequence, this reversion to the epistemology of transparency, is evident also in a recent documentary, *License to Kill*. We are shown excerpts of interviews with men who have killed other men who they thought were homosexual. Each man refers to an experience of "rage" prior to the killing. Without exception, the rage is accounted for as the killer's reaction to the victim's presumption that the killer might be open to homosexual activity. The rage reaction is characterized by a sense of certainty about three interdigitated items: (1) that the victim presumes the killer to be homosexually available; (2) that the presumption is wrong; (3) that the victim therefore warrants elimination.

One man is particularly articulate. He tells of his long hatred of "whatever is inside me" that drives him to seek out homosexual contact. Most notable here is the phrase, "whatever is inside me." No matter how painful the effects of this "whatever" that drives him, the man has been able to endure, for a long period, his own sense of its opacity. In addition to this source of pain, he spoke of the egregious insult associated with often being rejected in these encounters. He found it especially terrible to be rejected at what he "hated having to do in the first place." His solution was that the problem would vanish only if he could "rid the world of homosexual men."

We might think of the experience of murderous rage here as an experience of revelation – the sudden, harmonious unification of affect, idea, impulse, and perception. Lacking direct clinical access, we can still sketch out a plausible formal structure of the sequence in question. In the mind of the killer, along with the single idea, say, of the victim sexually wanting *him*, had come other ideas, other fantasies, dangerous ones, inexorably associated with the first idea and experienced mentally in the form of conclusion or consequence: "Being wanted by another man means castration, means punishment, means abandonment, etc." Wanting and anxiety had coalesced into a single, untenable, though transparent mental presence. Then, suddenly, the killer *knows* the score. The untenable becomes both legible and bearable. He now *knows* all the pertinent dynamics, the configuration of forces, and, most malignantly, exactly what to do. Deed will solve the problem. In this movement away from untenable mental content and toward revelatory illumination, a movement Freud (1905) aptly conceptualized as topographical regression, the killer's conflicting ideas have become a single idea; conflict has been replaced by clarity, thought by perception. And perception, yoked to impulse, turns into deed. The origin of the trouble has been spotted and can therefore be eliminated. Now, via these transformations, there is the promise of satisfaction. This sequence of transformations represents the resolution of a problem. Topographical regression is an act of radical simplification. The opaque intrapsychic complex has turned both external and transparent; as such, it can be fled or destroyed.

A brief contrasting example might be clarifying. An analytic patient recently said to me, regarding his ambitions to become an artist and a husband, "Wanting or trying to do something, anything, just brings on the damning voice. 'Who are you,' it says to me, 'to want that?'"

For this patient, even though the source of this voice's prohibitive authority is inaccessible and thus opaque to both of us – now, in the analysis, and for the many years in which he has been aware of its influence, he nonetheless knows that source to be in *his* interior. That knowledge structures his treatment. The voice often changes its apparent location. It can often seem to come from me. "You will be jealous if I get this project, and I can't afford that if I want to get better," he said, for example, as he pursued a coveted commission. But his sense of the voice's shift in location never achieves the force of revelation. No matter how difficult our work on this problem gets, we both share a confidence that what constricts him is at bottom the effect of some form of memory and is therefore within our therapeutic reach. Each of us readily refers to the source of that memory through phrases like "whatever it was," and thus we jointly acknowledge the memory's opacity. Our confidence in analytic access to "whatever it was," however, would vanish – would indeed turn incoherent – were "whatever it was" to turn into a transparent perception.

In principle, the self-certainty of perception leaves no room for psychoanalytic interpretation. Perception locates the problem sensorily and thus, implicitly or explicitly, transforms the private singularity of "whatever it was" to the potentially unanimous voice of "there it is."

We can hear the perceptual certainty, the potentially unanimous "there it is" that joins nature, culture, and reality itself – in, for example, the epithet "faggot." The "we" lodging the epithet are the cognescenti, the ones who, in giving a name to what they see, are staking their claim to their taxonomical place in relation to it. The epithet refers to a hierarchy and locates its users in superior relation to the homosexuals beneath them. Its violent overtones also make clear that if the taxonomy is threatened, appropriate measures must be taken: exile, elimination, disappearance. This commonplace epithet comes into especially brutal relief in testimony from the trial that produced Pvt. Calvin Glover's conviction for premeditated murder in the recent baseball bat killing of a gay colleague. One witness reported that his drill sergeant unapologetically bellowed a homophobic cadence in leading the platoon on a five-mile run: "Faggot, faggot down the street/ Shoot him, shoot 'til he retreats" (*New York Times*, December 12, 1999, p. A33). The cadence here delineates a culture for whom the transparency of its objects is a grounding assumption; the first person plural voice unites all the marchers in perceptual certainty and ethical charge.

A clinical example of the operation of what might be called the "hermeneutics of transparency" might be useful. In the exchange to be presented, the patient, a woman in her late forties, was in the sixth year of her analysis. She was raised in a household whose dominant mood of misogyny was, if not more intense, then certainly less disguised, than in most. Throughout her childhood, her father spoke casually and frequently about women as entirely sexual vehicles, as, variously, sluts, crones, whores, dried up, and voracious; he was explicit, both at home and in public, about his fantasies of raping them, beating them, driving them into servitude, even killing them; of controlling them; of the necessity that, for them to be worthwhile, they be dominated, cared for, and beautiful. He wanted to protect his own beautiful daughter from ever having to fall into a life among commoners. As teenagers, while the mother stayed home, he took both the patient and her sister out on "dates," where at a local bar he would show them off and compliment them on their beauty. The patient's mother, an overtly passive, depressed, compliant woman, complained openly to the patient about the irrecoverable cost to her figure of having children, frequently took to bed for days at a time, and, no matter the problem, always provided the patient the same advice: "Cheer up, dear, smile; make other people happy and you will be happy." The patient's analysis has been, as she has frequently put it, a sustained effort to separate from her parents, to "get my feet on the ground," to "clear my head of crazy ideas." What follows is intended to illustrate the defensive use of a transparent and demeaned object in the maintenance of the patient's misogynist conviction:

PATIENT: I told John [her husband] I was going to shave my bikini spot. He said he was glad. Something disgusting about all that hair. He's right, I know. He's so squeamish about women. So am I. Disgusting, that hair, covering something over. Like something icky is about to pop out. And my Dad referring to a world filled with women squirting out babies. It's so hard to take my own side against all of that. I'm afraid you're really seeing me. Unvarnished. I'm trying to make up with my family. My father used to tell how he started to soil himself when he was three years old. He said it was because a brother was born. But now my mother tells me it's not so. What really happened was his mother dressed him up as a little girl after he wet himself. My father just forgets, I guess.

ANALYST: You're hoping to get me to think of him as the despised girl and deflect my attention from you and your sense of yourself as despised, disgusting.

PATIENT: Physically, I'm measurably good enough. Here, though, with you just staring inside of me, I can't say I'm basically okay. There is nothing lasting about the physical, though. I did wax drips on my legs after remembering what my father said about babies squirting out. Clean myself, somehow. I didn't want to.

ANALYST: You imagined the waxing would join you to me in hating you for being a woman.

PATIENT: That is where the safety lay. You once said if kids aren't loved, they're just repellent creatures. Love is the only thing that makes another person not ugly. I don't want to have to dye my hair, have facelifts and all that. There are always things to find fault with.

ANALYST: The more fault you find in yourself, the stronger you feel.

PATIENT: That's the *reality* of it. I'm not trying to hide my feelings. I can bear what's true. It's stronger to simply accept the indictment. More dignified. Beat them to the punch. It's better than trying to defend something on faith. If you're a woman, they can always list things to hold against you. There's nothing concrete to fight back with. But last night, for just a few minutes, I had a sneaky feeling of okayness. Like I have something, something to offer. I was alone with it. No one but me could really know.

From this rich material, my focus here is primarily on the patient's efforts to steady her self-esteem by maintaining identificatory contact with an admired grandiose object. That object's exalted stature, like her own diminished one, is transparent to her alarmed psychic gaze. Object loss is the threat, though beginning to be modulated, perhaps, as marked by her association to "a sneaky feeling of okayness" while alone. She can barely bring herself to think of what she is saying, of what John is saying, of what her parents have always been saying. Thinking would, at the least, be an act of taking her own side and, as she says, "It's so hard to take my side against all of that." Thinking – treating her own impulses (i.e., to wax her legs) and her objects as interpretable, opaque items – is a labor that exposes her to excessive separation and the threat of irreparable abandonment. Thought is jettisoned, and all turns transparent, at least for the moment, when she declares, "That's the reality of it." Thought is predicated on separateness, on the possibility of difference. This contrasts with perception, which presumes sameness. We do not merely think an item is "red," say, but we know it, and are certain that everyone like us will know it, with equal certainty, as "red." Misogyny in this case, with its "hermeneutics of transparency," provides the patient an unassailable sense of connection: "That's the reality of it." That sense of connection is not at all disturbed by her awareness that she is the explicit target of the "reality" she is affirming. "That's the reality of it" actively transforms the private and fluid dynamics of thought, fantasy, and history into the static and public dynamics of straightforward perceptual certainty. By way of this sense of certainty, the singular voice fades out, replaced by the plural. She is then united with a powerful cluster of objects, from which she derives what she feels is her only secure source of vitality.

Freud (1927) well describes a predicament similar to that of my patient:

> No doubt one is a wretched plebeian, harassed by debts and military service; but, to make up for it, one is a Roman citizen, one has one's share in the task of ruling other nations and dictating their laws. This identification of the suppressed classes with the class who rules and exploits them is, however, only part of a larger whole. For, on the other hand, the suppressed classes can be emotionally attached to their masters; in spite of their hostility to them they may see in them their ideals; unless such relations of a fundamentally satisfying kind subsisted, it would be impossible to understand how a number of civilizations have survived so long in spite of the justifiable hostility of large human masses.
>
> (p. 13)

It is precisely this combination of "identification" and "emotional attachment" that finds such elegant expression in the transformation of the first person singular voice into the first person plural.

For me, for Harry, and for the patient in my last example, structured hatreds promised relief from otherwise unbearable constellations of identification and wishing. My impulse to identify with the Jews on the screen, Harry's to identify with his son, the patient's to identify with herself – to, as she put it, "take her own side" – proved too dangerous. Retaliatory threat was too imminent, too real. For all of us, this retaliatory threat imposed itself not as idea but as perception. The object stirring each of us was opaque, while the object of retaliation, when it appeared, seemed a fact, a presence. None of us had the capacity to think through the apparent concreteness of our predicament. Each of us then tried to escape. In the hoped-for escape, private horizontal yearning would be obliterated, to be replaced by affiliated vertical hating. Instead of privately wanting our original objects, we would instead publicly renounce them. "I want" would turn into "we hate." Our original aims and objects could be reconfigured and displaced, focused now on the pursuit of fellowship and union – Harry's with competent men, mine with impermeable killers, the patient's with the grandiosity of sadistic men. First renounce the opaque object, then render it transparent and identify with its tormentors – this is the scheme by which the overwhelmed singular voice here tries to transfigure fragile yearning into mighty hatred. The maintenance of that sense of might depends on disidentifying from what we once loved. Psychoanalytic engagement with it entails identifying with what we now hate.

References

Adorno, T. (1951/1978). *Minima Moralia*, trans. E. F. N. Jephcott. New York: Verso.
Bion, W. (1959). *Experiences in Groups*. New York: Basic Books.
Freud, S. (1905). Three Essays on the Theory of Sexuality. *Standard Edition*, 7:130–243.
Freud, S. (1927). The Future of an Illusion. *Standard Edition*, 21:5–56.
O'Shaughnessy, E. (1999). Relating to the Superego. *International Journal of Psychoanalysis*, 80:861–870.
Selby, H. (1957). *Last Exit to Brooklyn*. New York: Grove Press.

Chapter 2

This is not about Trump

Rage, resistance, and the persistence of racism[*]

Ann Pellegrini

I wrote and completed the first version of this essay the weekend before the 2020 presidential election in the United States. That election took place against the backdrop of a deadly pandemic, whose death toll in the United States was compounded by the extraordinary incompetence and even dereliction of the Trump administration – and of a president indifferent to anything that did not promote his own interests. When I finished that first draft, there had been just over 223,000 deaths attributed to COVD-19 in the United States. Seven weeks later, as I type these words and complete the final version, that number has surpassed 300,000. When you read this essay, that number will have been surpassed by the tens of thousands. When you read this essay, Donald Trump will no longer be president of the United States. But the forces of racism and reaction that brought him to power and that he stoked during his four years in office have a much longer history and will outlast him. I will have a lot to say about Trump in what follows, but, in the end, this essay is not about him or his personal racism. Trump is a symptom, not a cause.

Some moments from the long year that was 2020: On February 5, the Senate impeachment trial of President Donald J. Trump ended with his acquittal. That same day, there were eleven confirmed cases of COVID-19 in the United States.[1] But from on presidential high, Americans were told not to worry; all was well and under control. Not only that, miracles were coming our way: "One day – it's like a miracle – it will disappear." President Trump spoke those words during a February 27 meeting with African American leaders.[2] At that same meeting, he also asserted that "nobody has done more for black people than I have." He has repeated versions of this claim throughout the four years of his presidency, and it is closely related to another of his refrains, namely that he is "the least racist person that anybody's going to meet"[3] "in this room"[4] or "anywhere in the world."[5]

DOI: 10.4324/9781003214342-4

There were no miracles for Ahmaud Arbery. On February 23 – the same day the presidential thumb tweeted that everything was "very much under control" – Arbery, a twenty-five-year-old Black man, was chased, shot, and killed by three white men while jogging in his South Georgia neighborhood of Satilla Shores. There were no miracles for Breonna Taylor (killed on March 13) or for George Floyd (killed on May 25). And there were no miracles for the 295,000 and counting who had by then died of COVID-19 in the United States, each one of them more than a statistic to the family and friends who called them by name and loved them. By the time you are reading this essay, tens of thousands more will have died from COVID-19 in the United States. And this number – 302,314 as I type these words on December 15, 2020[6] – is most certainly an undercount. Multiple studies of "excess deaths" indicate that deaths related to the pandemic are much higher than the officially reported figures. There have been "nearly 100,000 additional fatalities that are indirectly related to COVID but would not have occurred if not for the virus."[7]

These "excess deaths" are disproportionately affecting people of color. From January 26 to October 3, 2020 (the period examined in a study released by the Centers for Disease Control and Prevention [CDC] on October 20, 2020): "deaths were 11.9% higher [for white people] when compared to average numbers during 2015–2019. However, some racial and ethnic subgroups experienced disproportionately higher percentage increases in deaths." The report lists the following further breakdown of excess deaths by "racial and ethnic subgroups":

> [T]he average percentage increase over this period was largest for Hispanic persons (53.6%). Deaths were 28.9% above average for AI/AN [American Indian and Alaska Native] persons, 32.9% above average for Black persons, 34.6% above average for those of other or unknown race or ethnicity [which, continuing with the language of the report, included non-Hispanic Native Hawaiian or other Pacific Islander, non-Hispanic multiracial, and unknown], and 36.6% above average for Asian persons.[8]

"Excess deaths" is a jarring term, abstracting individuals and individual lives, each one rich in detail and difference, into the anonymizing and massifying calculation of "life" in general. This is what Michel Foucault called the "biopolitics of the population,"[9] one-half of a "great bipolar technology" that characterizes modern forms of governance. The other half, he says – and these two pieces work together – concerns the "disciplines" of the individual and individual body.

Biopolitics addresses itself to "man-as-species,"[10] its basic unit is the population, and it concerns itself with the calculated management of life, developing expert sciences, practices, and bureaucracies (e.g., federal and state departments of health and human services, the CDC) to track and administer "problems of birth rate, longevity, public health, housing, and migration."[11] Identifying "excess deaths" is part of this technology for managing and administering the life of the population, the national body, which can be further subdivided into racialized groups, as we have just seen in the language of the CDC study, with its reference to quasi-naturalized "racial and ethnic subgroups." The CDC defines "excess deaths" "as the difference between the observed numbers of deaths in specific time periods and expected numbers of deaths in the same time periods."[12] This difference between the observed and the expected fatalities is important information, and the further breakdown of "excess death" rates by racialized groups *could* be used to ask critical questions about why some groups have experienced higher death rates and, then, to develop strategies to address these differences in outcome. Such strategies would emerge not out of the good graces of some beneficent state[13] but through cultivating practices attentive to the conditions of the living and dying of those members of the population historically left outside the calculation of lives who matter to and for the nation. In this regard, Black Lives Matter could be seen as conducting a kind of "biopolitics from below"[14] by forcing to public attention the enduring links between health disparities and racism, thereby revealing racism as a comorbidity.

Racism is not just an incidental feature of modern biopolitics; racism has been indispensable to power as it is exercised in the modern state. How so? Racism, Foucault argues, introduces "a break into the domain of life under power's control: a break between what must live and what must die."[15] So, if it is difficult to conceive of modern forms of governing *outside* the terrain of biopolitics – outside, that is, the management and administration of life – it is not less arduous to imagine a nonracist state. Frantz Fanon, Sylvia Wynter, and others have brilliantly shown how the very category of the human whom the modern state presumes to protect and make live is in fact a specific "ethnoclass genre of the human" (in Wynter's phrasing) that is "overrepresent[ed] as if it were isomorphic with the human, its well being, and notion of freedom."[16] Wynter's crucial emendation of Foucault, then, is that the species of life comprehended by modern biopolitics was always limited to a narrow and racialized conception of the human. Insofar, then, that racism has been a constitutive feature of modern governance, the management of life can easily become the management and bureaucratic administration of *racism*. Importantly, such racism is more often delivered not in the register of hate but as a form of neutral bureaucratic administration. We thus need an epistemological and ethical reorientation in the ways events and bodies are counted and measured. Otherwise, some bodies – some people – will continue not to count; they are excess lives even before they are excess deaths.

In the wake of these staggering losses, *rage*, *resistance*, and *racism* are very much with us and, if anything, beating with more urgency. What can we do with our anger, and who are the "we" who should/would be doing something about it? In what follows, I want to explore what we might think of as the "uses of anger."[17] In this phrase, I am invoking the title of Audre Lorde's essay to inquire into the contemporary politics of anger in the United States. How do we distinguish between moral and political anger that protests social injustice and the kind of defensive anger that, in fact, perpetuates social dominance and inequality? We need to be able to answer this question because those who participate in or gravitate towards right-wing populism and white nationalism also understand themselves to be acting in the service of "just" causes. For them, movement towards more equitable treatment of previously minoritized groups may feel like a loss, like they are being asked to give something up or, rather, like something is being forcibly taken away. If right-wing populism and white nationalism speak a language of hate, this language records a deeper love: for family, tradition, nation. Love and hate synthesize in ways that fortify group belonging (us) and actively require a powerful enemy (them).[18] Social progress comes to feel like an attack on "us," "our" families, and on "traditional" American values. But the thing is, an increase in equality and freedom for some may indeed lead to a loss for some others. Therefore, so much depends on which side of the ledger sheet you've been placed on. For those who have enjoyed the historic and ongoing privileges that accrue to Whiteness, maleness, heterosexuality, and/or Christianity, extending legal protections and expanding public space for racial, sexual, gender, and religious others *will*, in fact, entail loss – a loss of social dominance and a loss of the material, symbolic, and psychic benefits that come with it. It is not easy to reckon with such loss, to mourn the social world you thought you knew, and, most importantly, it is not easy to relinquish willingly your exalted place in it. Grief can easily curdle into grievance.

White grievance – and a social order dedicated to comforting it – are not new, of course. Legal and social institutions in the United States have long been organized to protect and comfort white grievance. There are so many examples to choose from here, but one that comes to mind is the legal principle of "separate but equal," which was endorsed in *Plessy v Ferguson* (1896). In an 8–1 decision, the Supreme Court held that racially segregated train cars were constitutionally permissible. The state, the Court opined, "is at liberty to act with reference to the established usages, customs, and traditions of the people, and with a view to the promotion of their comfort and the preservation of the public peace and good order." In his famous dissent, Justice Harlan wrote, "There is no caste here. Our Constitution is color-blind." Note that the comfort being promoted in *Plessy* is the comfort of the white majority. But note also that the Court seems unaware of that. 8–1. The Court is unaware of, if not disinterested in, the fact that the comfort that is being protected is not the comfort of Black people but of a white majority – who constitute an exclusionary We the People. This is what subtends the Court's belief that the separation of Black and white in a public accommodation amounts to "public peace and good order." Although separate but equal was officially overturned in *Brown v Board of Education*, in 1954, we are not done today, in 2020, with the cultural logics that look to preserve and protect the feelings of a white majority. We are not done, that is, with understanding public peace and good order as the set of conditions that will ensure what counts as peace and order for white citizens – even when, or perhaps especially when, their days as a *numerical* majority are numbered.

Consequently, when I turn, as I will do momentarily, to discussing President Trump's September 2020 executive order undermining attempts to address systemic inequality, I do so *not* because what Trump says and what his administration has done are exceptional instances of racism that we should all note as such, but because Trump so openly exposes a sensibility that runs through so many aspects of American life, actively shaping institutions of governance, up to and including the Supreme Court. There has been much media commentary, by self-proclaimed conservative "never Trumpers" as well as by moderates and liberals, about "how President Trump has pushed the boundaries of norms in office." This was in fact the title of an August 2020 NPR interview with the *New Yorker*'s Susan Glasser.[19] Over the course of Trump's presidency, the *Washington Post*'s Amy Siskind published "The List." It is a week-by-week accounting, which she culled from 34,000 entries, of Trump's steady assault on norms of democratic life. She started the list days after the 2016 election to "chronicle," as she says, "the ways Donald Trump has changed our country."[20] The weekly list ends in week 208 on November 7, the day the major news networks called the election for Joe Biden, while Trump tweeted in all caps ("I WON THIS ELECTION, BY A LOT!"), golfed, continued his flurry of lawsuits, and Trump's personal attorney Rudy Guiliani held a press conference at the wrong Four Seasons. I want to underline the importance of Siskind's tracking the erosion of core features of the democratic process, especially if such mindfulness can serve as wake-up call to slow down the slide into authoritarianism. Indeed, the Republican party's willingness to go along with Trump's fraudulent claims that the election was stolen indicate that we cannot remain alert enough. But, with respect to race/racism and also sex/sexism, I want to suggest that something more complex is at work here: more specifically, I want to argue against the wish to see Trump and the Trump presidency as some malignant bump on the otherwise "unstoppable" American project of extending freedom and equality to all. This wish is a white liberal version of Make America Great Again.

Not only that, this version of greatness – American equality as an unstoppable force in the world – is not new and was endorsed by Trump himself in a speech on September 17, 2020 announcing a "1776 Commission" to teach "patriotic education." Here are his words: "America's founding set in motion the unstoppable chain of events that abolished slavery, secured civil rights, defeated communism and fascism, and built the most fair, equal, and prosperous nation in human history."[21] This belief in the inevitability of racial progress and freedom's expansion provides the heroic frame of an "Executive Order on Combatting Race and Sex Stereotyping."[22]

President Trump signed this executive order (EO) on September 22. This EO builds on and extends a memorandum issued two weeks earlier (September 4), by the Office of Management and Budget (OMB), that had effectively banned diversity training at all federal agencies.[23] The EO is part of a cluster of coordinated recent attacks on "Critical

Race Theory," an intellectual movement that arose in the U.S. legal academy in the 1970s and 1980s to explain the persistence of racism despite important civil rights victories (from *Brown v Board*, in 1954, to the Civil Rights Act of 1964, to the Fair Housing Act of 1968).[24] Critical Race Theory attempts to understand "structural racism," the various ways racism is built into the everyday life of everybody and into such social institutions (and state bureaucracies) as law and education.[25] Importantly, the concept of structural racism better explains ongoing racial inequalities than does a focus on the racist acts or racist motives of a few (or even a lot of) racist individuals. This is not just a story about "bad" "racist" white people; "good" white people are implicated in structural racism too. The disproportionate impact of COVID-19 on people of color is an example of structural racism at work, and its deadly effects cannot be traced to the deliberate, intentional actions or omissions of a racist individual or group of individuals, who alone are to blame. The force of racism pours through the social, contouring individual and group possibilities.

So we must do without angels *or* devils, good *or* evil – splittings that psychoanalysis, in any case, teaches us to distrust. Drawing on a somewhat different lexicon, religious studies scholar Donovan Schaefer writes, "If theodicy is interested in why bad things happen to good people, affect theory is interested in why good people do bad things."[26] I'd add a twist to his formulation: affect theory (and psychoanalysis offers powerful ways to think about affect) is interested in how good people do bad things and yet think of themselves as basically good people. This is not, or is not always or necessarily, a matter of hypocrisy. Let's return to Trump's refrain: "I'm the least racist person you'll find anywhere in the world."[27] The question is *not* whether or not Trump believes his own claim. Rather, claims such as these – which would seem to be easily controverted by the long and public record of Trump's racist actions prior to entering the White House let alone while President – evidence larger dynamics of "racial dissociation" (Eng and Han's term).[28] Racial dissociation means that many white people can genuinely believe of themselves that they are not racist and harbor no racist views even as they say (or retweet) racist things, do things that have racist effects, or benefit from a racism baked into state policies and into the structures of everyday life (for example, who can safely jog around their own neighborhood, who cannot).

The "Executive Order on Combatting Race and Sex Stereotyping" has three stated rationales, which it lists in its opening sentence: first, "to promote economy and efficiency in Federal contracting"; second, "to promote unity in the Federal workforce"; and third, "to combat offensive and anti-American race and sex stereotyping and scapegoating." A few things to note right away: the first, "to promote economy and efficiency in Federal contracting," sets the tone of the EO by situating it within the economic and bureaucratic logic of neoliberalism: promoting efficiency. Bureaucratic organizations, as I have just suggested, are also conductors of *structural* racism. Even well-intentioned individuals can and routinely do devise and carry out policies that have racially discriminatory effects without doing so "on purpose." This is also why being "woke" is not enough to end racial inequality.

As legal scholar Charles Lawrence – a pioneering figure in Critical Race Theory who introduced questions of unconscious bias into studies of U.S. law's assumptions and applications – argues, we need to move away from the "false dichotomy between the 'evil' acts of avowed racial bigots and the 'innocent' acts of good people."[29] This false dichotomy unfortunately underlies the way the modern Supreme Court has come to interpret the injury of racism. Starting with its 1976 decision in *Washington v. Davis*, the Court has required that "plaintiffs seeking constitutional protection from racially discriminatory practices and conditions" prove that these practices and conditions were racially motivated.[30] That is, the plaintiff asserting injury must prove that the legislators who crafted the law were motivated by explicitly racist motives. As Lawrence explains, it is not simply that this is a "heavy and often impossible burden" – what would be the smoking gun to prove racial bias – but "the injury of racial inequality exists irrespective of the motives of the defendants in a particular case."[31] The concept of structural racism – the way the practices and habits of thought of white supremacy live on in our institutions and in so many of us, even in us "good white people" – allows us to see how white supremacy informs the law and produces disparate impacts. Crucially, it may well do so without someone or some ones *deliberately* acting with racial bias and intending racial injury. Combatting racial inequality thus requires a shift in orientation from ferreting out the bad motives of bad racist people to tracking and ameliorating the injurious effects of supposedly neutral social policy.

But let's go back to the EO and its three stated rationales: "to promote economy and efficiency in Federal contracting, to promote unity in the Federal workforce, and to combat offensive and anti-American race and sex stereotyping and scapegoating." It is the third and final stated element – "to combat offensive and anti-American race and sex stereotyping and scapegoating" – that gives this EO its proper name: the "Executive Order on Combatting Race and Sex Stereotyping." This turn of phrase is what makes this Executive Order deceptively appealing. After all, who is going to speak up *for* "Race and Sex Stereotyping"? But note, too, this important recalibration from combating race and sex stereotyping (in the EO's title) to combating "*offensive and anti-American* race and sex stereotyping and scapegoating" (emphasis added) in the body of the EO. As we will come to see, what makes a particular claim about race or sex "offensive" is that it runs counter to the nation's founding story.

This founding story appears in Section 1 of the EO. It marches us through a triumphant history of We the People as always already committed to principles of equality for all people – a kind of originalist All Lives Matter:

> From the battlefield of Gettysburg to the bus boycott in Montgomery and the Selma-to-Montgomery marches, heroic Americans have valiantly risked their lives to ensure that their children would grow up in a Nation living out its creed, expressed in the Declaration of Independence: "We hold these truths to be self-evident, that all men are created equal." It was this belief in the inherent equality of every individual that inspired the Founding generation to risk their lives, their fortunes, and their sacred honor to establish a new Nation, unique among the countries of the world. President Abraham Lincoln understood that this belief is "the electric cord" that "links the hearts of patriotic and liberty-loving" people, no matter their race or country of origin. It is the belief that inspired the heroic black soldiers of the 54th Massachusetts Infantry Regiment to defend that same Union at great cost in the Civil War. And it is what inspired Dr. Martin Luther King, Jr., to dream that his children would one day "not be judged by the color of their skin but by the content of their character."

This is a strange origin tale, which starts at the Civil War of the mid-nineteenth century, leaps to the civil rights movement of the mid-twentieth, and then identifies in both a fulfillment of the Founders' dream that "all men are created equal." Fascinatingly, the "heroic Americans" mentioned in this passage are all either black ("heroic black soldiers of the 54th Massachusetts Infantry Regiment," civil rights activists of Montgomery and Selma, Martin Luther King Jr.) or in some way allies in struggles for black equality (Lincoln and those who gave their lives on the Battlefield of Gettysburg).

Unnamed in this text are the forces that required such acts of heroism, the obstacles that heroic black Americans and their allies had to overcome: white supremacy. By starting at the Civil War, the EO leaves out the whole history of slavery. We get a flash of 1776, but left out of here is 1619, the year that the first kidnapped, enslaved Africans were brought as property to what would become the United States. Then, by leapfrogging to the Montgomery Bus Boycott of 1955–1956, the EO's story of America rushes past both the extralegal as well as the legal, state-sanctioned violences of Jim Crow. By this rhetorical sleight of hand, anyone who is American is baptized after the fact of our original sin (slavery), ostensibly uninvolved and unimplicated in the conditions that established the nation. Bathed in the blood of those who fought and died at Gettysburg and of those who marched and were bloodied from Selma to Montgomery, "we" Americans are all heroes now. What's more, "we" are bleached of the stains of the past.

Section 1 of the EO contains two references to Dr. King's dream of a color-blind future. Turns out the future is now. Having leeched out the enslavement of African people from American history and having contorted this history into an *anti*-racist teleology, the EO insinuates that color blindness is the end game of anti-racism. Taking us down a rabbit hole of false equivalences, the EO scrambles not only history but also our thinking: down is up and up is down. This is how we end up with the following, perplexing proposition: it is, we are told, *opposition to* racism and sexism – not racism and sexism themselves – that offend American values, thus necessitating this executive order. The EO lists certain "divisive concepts" that are to be banned from any federally funded diversity training to ensure that this opposition will not be allowed to offend American ideals. These "divisive concepts" turn out to be any ideas intimating that racism and sexism are structural, historically enduring, and in excess of any individual's motives or acts. Here is where that recalibration I mentioned previously – from combating race and sex stereotyping to combating "*offensive and anti-American* race and sex stereotyping and scapegoating" (emphasis added) – kicks into high gear. The EO refers ominously to a "destructive ideology . . . grounded in misrepresentations of our country's history and its role in the world." Though never named in the executive order, we know from the larger context of the EO's issuance that it is taking aim at Critical Race Theory and at Black Lives Matter, as well. Although the EO explicitly names "sex stereotyping" as an area of concern, in fact the *historical* conditions cited to explain the reason for the EO only pertain to race; no references are made to sex/sexism in the heroic foundation story that leads off the EO. This may lead one to speculate that concerns over sex stereotyping are just tacked on for added heft or, perhaps, to take the heat off racism.

In one particularly astonishing passage, critical analysis and teaching about the ways whiteness is built into American law and social institutions are equated to "discredited notions of the nineteenth century's apologists for slavery who, like President Lincoln's rival Stephen A. Douglas, maintained that our government 'was made on the white basis' 'by white men, for the benefit of white men.'" In other words, an *analysis* of how white supremacy is structured into U.S. laws, institutions, and everyday life is equated with white supremacy. Put still more bluntly, the institution of slavery was somehow Critical Race Theory before the name. The EO cannily collapses the difference between using racial categories as a way to analyze and combat discrimination and the use of racial categories to *ground* discrimination: to name race is itself the preamble to racism. A color-blind approach, the EO's logic suggests, is more equitable to people of color, who will not have to shoulder the weight of their difference, because their difference *from* whiteness will no longer be called to the attention . . . of white people. In the end, the doctrine of color blindness comforts white people, because it shields them – shield us – from having to consider other races and our own racialization. Within the rhetoric of the EO, this conflation, in which calling attention to race and racism equals racism, is motored by taming Dr. King's words and activism and insisting we have arrived at the color-blind future he only dreamed of.

The Roberts Court has elevated color blindness into a determinative legal principle in cases concerning racial injury. In *Parents Involved in Community Schools v. Seattle School District No. 1*, a 2007 decision concerning school desegregation policies in Seattle and Kentucky – policies that were put in place to remedy ongoing racial inequalities in educational resources – a split Court struck down the desegregation plans as themselves discriminatory. Chief Justice Roberts, writing for the 5–4 majority, held, "The way to stop discrimination on the basis of race is to stop discriminating on the basis of race."[32] Gallingly, Roberts claims the mantle of *Brown v Board of Education* in doing so, saying that the principles established by that case as to the invidiousness of racial distinctions also apply in this instance. As a result, Justice Roberts' "color-blind Constitution" cannot distinguish between laws and policies that use racial categories in order to *remedy* discrimination (as was the case in the school desegregation policies examined in this 2007 case) and those that use race to discriminate (as in *Brown*, where the Court was asked to examine policies *enforcing* racial segregation).[33] All this in the name of fulfilling Dr. King's dream of a color-blind America.

What if we take seriously this word "dream"? Thinking/speculating with José Esteban Muñoz's conception of queerness and queer utopia as an always receding point on the horizon that we squint to see but never finally arrive at,[34] what if Dr. King's dream of a time when his children "will be judged not by their color of the skin but by the content of their character"[35] is also in a future perfect, a will have been that never arrives? The struggle "towards" is the point. We may never get "there." What's more, the "there" at which activists for social justice aim may have to keep shifting because the forces that oppose social justice adjust to conserve power.

In *The History of Sexuality*, Michel Foucault famously asserts that "power is everywhere," but so too is resistance: "Where there is power, there is resistance, and yet, or rather consequently, this resistance is never in a position of exteriority in relation to power."[36] That this is so tells us nothing about the motives of any given instance of resistance or its likelihood of success. In fact, Foucault suggests, any success is only ever temporary because resistance generates fresh resistances in its wake. Power "regroups." But, then again, so does resistance. Foucault offers a picture of relations of power flexibly responding to fractures in it, recuperating breaks and challenges. Struggle continues; victories are not once for all. Derrick Bell, another key figure in the development of Critical Race Theory, gives flesh to this dynamic in a 1992 essay on "Racial Realism," where he points out that "racial patterns adapt" to legislative and judicial victories in ways "that maintain White dominance."[37]

As sociologist Victor Ray astutely points out,[38] the EO conflates Critical Race Theory with diversity training focused on exposing implicit or unconscious bias in individuals. These are very different approaches to understanding and solving racial inequality. Critical Race Theory, remember, draws attention to structural racism, which cannot be explained/ explained away by reference to the racist acts of individuals. We can see this strange "hodge podge" (as Ray calls it) at work when the EO blasts the idea that "an individual, by virtue of his or her race or sex, bears responsibility for actions committed in the past by other members of the same race or sex." This is one of the "divisive concepts" the EO bans in federally funded diversity training. Also barred as "divisive" is teaching that "any individual should feel discomfort, guilt, anguish, or any other form of psychological distress on account of his or her race or sex." This "divisive concept" confuses an individual's or group's emotional distress at learning about racism or sexism with racism or sexism, such that the real injustices the state needs to address (and hence the need for *this* EO to combat it) are the violences of *teaching* people about racist or sexist violence.

This confused caricature of Critical Race Theory, diversity training, and studies of implicit bias would be unrecognizable to practitioners of all three. But they are not the addressees of this EO. The outrageous mishmash is calculated to promote outrage at social justice projects by reassuring white people of good will that they are . . . people of good will, who can now stop thinking about race. It's a kind of get-- f–jail-free card. The EO speaks to and from white grievance, and this grievance is positioned as the reasonable response to the excesses of social justice scolds. It is these scolds who turn out to be the real racists. Moreover, if they can't be stopped, at least they will be stopped from speaking and teaching on the taxpayers' dime.

In the last section of the EO – "Sec. 10 General Provisions" – we learn that "Nothing in this order shall be construed to prohibit discussing, as part of a larger course of academic instruction, the divisive concepts listed in . . . this order in *an objective manner and without endorsement*" (emphasis added). But we are given no guidance as to what constitutes "objective manner and without endorsement" or about who decides. The "Executive Order on Combatting Race and Sex Stereotyping" had immediate impact, as worries about running afoul of it led some colleges and universities – almost all of whom, public or private, receive federal monies – to either cancel altogether or put on pause planned diversity training.

In a few instances, public lectures on topics connected to white privilege were even canceled.

This transpired at a time when it is all the more important for universities and colleges to offer spaces for tangling with the enduring legacies of white supremacy. Such engagement will not feel comfortable, certainly not for white people and likely not for people of color either. But why should we expect the hard work of addressing racial inequality to be easy or feel comfortable? In this regard, the language of "safe spaces" promoted by many campus diversity initiatives may mislead if it seems to promise conversations and encounters in which no one's feelings ever get hurt. There may even be anger – the anger at racial injustice and an often defensive anger at being asked to think about one's implication in it. How do we slow – and, here, I am speaking of we white people – the reflexive anger that defends against accountability? Or the no less *un*helpful recourse to white guilt, which becomes its own way of doing nothing?

Audre Lorde's extraordinary and still necessary 1981 essay on "The Uses of Anger" can help orient us, or, perhaps more exactly, it can give us something to hold onto amidst the often vertiginous experience of accountability. In that essay, Lorde distinguishes between guilt (and she is writing specifically about white feminist guilt) and responsibility, describing the former as "a device to protect ignorance and the continuation of things the way they are, the ultimate protection for changelessness."[39] This is guilt as a deflection of the other's experience and one's implication in it. She goes on to dare women of color to upset a feminist fantasy of unity without difference or differences of opinion, urging women of color to name and speak their anger aloud and challenging white feminists to hear it without getting defensive:

> The angers between women will not kill us if we can articulate them with precision, if we listen to the content of what is said with at least as much intensity as we defend ourselves against the manner of saying. When we turn from anger we turn from insight, saying we will accept only the designs already known, deadly and safely familiar.[40]

Instead of turning from anger, we need "to stand still, to listen to its rhythms, to learn within it."[41] Lorde suggestively connects anger and grief: "Anger is a grief of distortions between peers, and its object is change."[42] The difference between grief and grievance is also the difference between accountability and disavowal. Both may involve anger, but only one tends toward justice and repair. This is slow work, necessary work, and it may never get us where we hope to be. Perhaps justice and repair share something of the temporality of queer utopia described by Muñoz: we point towards the horizon, we never arrive, our hearts are even broken in the trying, but even our failures are a kind of change.

Reparation starts with the grief – not the *grievance* – of recognizing that injury has been done. Grievance short-circuits accountability and rockets right into resentment and rage. Mourning the injury done to an other – and mourning one's connection to this injury (however historically attenuated) and to this other – may give rise to anger. This kind of anger, rooted in an accountability for injury done to another, may even become the stuff of social solidarity, of movements for social change. But this "grief of distortions" (the distortions of structural racism, the distortions of historical amnesia, the distortions of not wanting to know) can only work towards change if those of us who have done injury or who are the beneficiaries of structured inequalities can develop the capacity to stay with the anger of others, to bear the pain of their anger and our own accountability.

I want to close with a few thoughts about white defensiveness. We are in the midst of an important national conversation about antiblack racism. To be sure, this conversation is not new, even if there is some sort of special amnesia affecting white people – let's call it white privilege – that can make the reality of white supremacy seem like new news each time white people are asked to think about it. Many white people are in fact grappling hard with concepts like structural racism and may profess agreement with it. But still a kind of defensiveness creeps in; they see how "the system" perpetuates racist violence but do not see their own material implication, let alone their own psychic *investments*, in it. So their defensive response to the challenge of white racism is "*maybe* the system, but not me."[43] The "Executive Order on Combating Race and Sex Stereotyping" says *definitely* not the system.

But consider how affirming "yes, me, yes I am racist" may be its own kind of nothing burger. First, members of white nationalist groups are the last ones to say of themselves, "I'm racist." Instead they understand themselves to be defending themselves and their own. Ordinarily, "racist" is something we say of other people. About the only people affirming their racism are a species of woke white people. And the longer version of "I am racist" is something like: how could I *not* be racist, I live in a racist society. Then, what? A shrug of intellectual self-congratulation and back to everyday life. Or maybe, "I am white, I am racist" become the defensive turning in on oneself: "I am a wretch, a worm, let me tell you all the ways." Here the self-indictment can become a species of white narcissism: "Enough about your inequality, let's talk about my guilty conscience." Again, a big plate of nothing burgers.

I just wrote moments ago of the urgent necessity of working to stay with the anger of others, to bear the pain of their anger and our own accountability. But another and perhaps still scarier project is required. White people need to study our own investments in racism – not just what we get out of racism in a material sense (i.e., the resources that flow to us on account of our race). We also need to investigate how racism may get us off – what it provokes and excites in us. Here I am thinking alongside Sharon Holland's discussion of the "erotic life of racism"[44] and with psychoanalyst Avgi Saketopoulou's recent work on the excitement and energy that surcharge racial difference.[45]

Education and training aimed at revealing implicit or unconscious bias are uncomfortable, but they at least promise that if once we can make all the racist (and sexist) stereotypes we harbor conscious, we can defeat racism. I earlier pointed out that this focus on eliminating individual racism misses the ongoing force of structural racism. But there is another problem with focusing on unconscious racism. Strictly speaking, there is no such thing as "unconscious racism." The unconscious has no content. Its churning, unformulated energies and forces press for representation – through embodied acts, through speech, through artistic expression, and even through political protest. Racism is one of the cultural forms available to capture and channel the wild aggressive energies of the unconscious. Part of what makes this such a good fit is that the anger, heat, and driving passion of racism are an energetic "match" for the energetic force of unconscious life. But these energies do not belong to racism. Black Lives Matter thrills with its fierce intellectual force and its energetic, defiant, enraged, and also joyous taking *of* the streets. Perhaps collective movement for social justice also offers an outlet, a channel for the wild energies that stir us from within. This is the rage for justice, and its time is now, now, now.

Notes

* I am grateful to Don Moss and Lynne Zeavin for the exciting invitation to participate in this volume; to audiences at the University of Georgia and

Northwestern University's Feinberg School of Medicine, who offered feedback on earlier versions of this essay in October and November 2020; and to Avgi Saketopoulou, who pushed me past the finish line with her fine-tuned comments on this essay.

1. Kathryn Watson, A Timeline of What Trump Has Said on Coronavirus. *CBS News*, April 3, 2020. Online. Retrieved from: www.cbsnews.com/news/timeline-president-donald-trump-changing-statements-on-coronavirus/.
2. Remarks by President Trump in Meeting with African American Leaders, February 27, 2020; issued on February 28. Retrieved from: www.whitehouse.gov/briefings-statements/remarks-president-trump-meeting-african-american-leaders/.
3. Trump said, "I am, as I say often, the least racist person that anybody's going to meet," in a January 2018 BBC interview with Piers Morgan. Retrieved from: www.bbc.com/news/av/uk-42830165.
4. Trump said, "I am the least racist person in this room" at the Presidential debate with Joe Biden, on October 22, 2020. See Caitlin O'Kane, Trump Says He's the "Least Racist Person in the Room": Biden Says He's "One of the Most Racist Presidents." *CBS News*, October 23, 2020. Retrieved from: www.cbsnews.com/news/trump-biden-racism-debate/.
5. Trump told reporters, "I'm the least racist person you'll find anywhere in the world," on the South Lawn of the White House, on July 30, 2019. Qtd. In Jonathan Capehart, Trump Says He's "the Least Racist Person in the World": That's Rich. *Washington Post*, July 30, 2020. Online. Retrieved from: www.washingtonpost.com/opinions/2019/07/30/trump-says-hes-least-racist-person-world-thats-rich/.
6. Coronavirus in the U.S.: Latest Map and Case Count, updated December 15, 2020, 2:06 P.M. E.T. *New York Times*. Retrieved from: www.nytimes.com/interactive/2020/us/coronavirus-us-cases.html.
7. Roni Caryn Rabin, The Pandemic's Real Toll? 300,000 Deaths, and It's Not Just from the Coronavirus. *New York Times*, October 20, 2020. Retrieved from: www.nytimes.com/2020/10/20/health/coronavirus-excess-deaths.html?searchResultPosition=1.
8. Lauren M. Rossen et al., Excess Deaths Associated with COVID-19, by Age and Race and Ethnicity – United States, January 26–October 3, 2020. *MMWR (Morbidity Mortality Weekly Report)*, October 20, 2020. Retrieved from: www.cdc.gov/mmwr/volumes/69/wr/mm6942e2.htm?s_cid=mm6942e2_w.
9. Michel Foucault, *The History of Sexuality, Volume I: An Introduction* (New York: Vintage Books, 1980), 139.
10. Michel Foucault, *"Society Must Be Defended": Lectures at the Collège de France, 1975–1976* (New York: Picador, 2003), 242.
11. Foucault 1980, 140. For related points, see Foucault 2003, 243–246.
12. Rossen et al.
13. Felipe Demetri, Biopolitics and Coronavirus, or Don't Forget Foucault. *Naked Punch*, March 21, 2020. Online. Retrieved from: www.nakedpunch.

com/articles/306?fbclid=IwAR2t01tud4nuprA2cyHR6acFBc6B2EDdbyBLVZBL_boUZMm9opbf2MnpPzA.
14 *Panagiotis Sotiris, Against Agamben: Is a Democratic Biopolitics Possible? Critical Legal Thinking*, March 14, 2020. Retrieved from: https://criticallegalthinking.com/2020/03/14/against-agamben-is-a-democratic-biopolitics-possible/.
15 Foucault 2003, 254.
16 Sylvia Wynter, Unsettling the Coloniality of Being/Power/Truth/Freedom: Towards the Human, After Man, Its Overrepresentation – an Argument. *CR: The New Centennial Review*, 3(3) (Fall 2003):329. See also Frantz Fanon, *Black Skin, White Masks* (New York: Grove Weidenfeld, 1967).
17 Audre Lorde, The Uses of Anger: Women Responding to Racism. In *Sister Outsider: Essays and Speeches* (Freedom, CA: Crossing Press, 1984), 124–133.
18 Jeff Sharlet, A Heart Is Not a Nation: Confronting the Age of Hate in America. *Bookforum*, December, January, February 2021. Online. Retrieved from: www.bookforum.com/print/2704/confronting-the-age-of-hate-in-america-24245?fbclid=IwAR2RApZcY-eFWzvgmdLI4fbk3jGd5uvhr6k_a509BtsSUTw3bnXxmcliM34.
19 Retrieved from: www.npr.org/2020/08/20/904383253/how-president-trump-pushes-the-boundaries-of-norms-in-office.
20 Retrieved from: www.washingtonpost.com/graphics/2020/outlook/siskind-list-trump-norms/.
21 See Remarks by President Trump at the White House Conference on American History, September 17, 2020. Retrieved from: www.whitehouse.gov/briefings-statements/remarks-president-trump-white-house-conference-american-history/.
22 Retrieved from: www.whitehouse.gov/presidential-actions/executive-order-combating-race-sex-stereotyping/.
23 From the OMB memo: "The President has directed me to ensure that Federal agencies cease and desist from using taxpayer dollars to fund these divisive, un-American propaganda training sessions."
24 See Victor Ray, Trump Calls Critical Race Theory "un-American." Let's Review. *Washington Post*, October 2, 2020. Online. Retrieved from: www.washingtonpost.com/nation/2020/10/02/critical-race-theory-101/.
25 Critical Race Theory has also come under attack by the Council of Seminary Presidents of the Southern Baptist Convention (SBC), which released a document simultaneously "condemning racism in any form," while also declaring "that affirmation of Critical Race Theory, Intersectionality, and any version of Critical Theory is incompatible with the Baptist Faith & Message." The document nowhere says why Critical Race Theory is "incompatible with the Baptist Faith & Message." It needs to inasmuch as it presumes a theological understanding of worldly power as being derived from the right relation to Jesus. Critical Race Theory's focus on structures of power that perpetuate racism and its relative de-emphasis on individual actions is indeed incompatible with both the SBC's conception of Divine Power,

upper-case P, and its focus on the individual-to-be-saved. From this theological perspective, racism is a personal sin, not a structural problem. For the SBC statement, see George Schroeder, Seminary Presidents Reaffirm BFM, Declare CRT Incompatible. *Baptist Press*, November 20, 2020. Online. Retrieved from: www.baptistpress.com/resource-library/news/seminary-presidents-reaffirm-bfm-declare-crt-incompatible/?fbclid=IwAR1v7ipki9p2Mv9o0gz63r4kObz-0I1HiNCIIAgHqIAUF0R-kyfyS9hCbvU.
26 Donovan Schaefer, *Religious Affects: Animality, Evolution, and Power* (Durham, NC: Duke University Press, 2015), 145.
27 Trump told reporters, "I'm the least racist person you'll find anywhere in the world," on the South Lawn of the White House, on July 30, 2019. Qtd. In Capehart.
28 David L. Eng and Shinhee Han, *Racial Melancholia, Racial Dissociation* (Durham, NC: Duke University Press, 2019), 174.
29 Charles R. Lawrence III, Unconscious Racism Revisited: Reflections on the Impact and Origins of "The Id, the Ego, and Equal Protection". *Connecticut Law Review*, 40(2008):931–978, 947.
30 Lawrence, 944.
31 Lawrence, 944.
32 Qtd. in Lawrence, 955.
33 Lawrence, 955.
34 José Esteban Muñoz, *Cruising Utopia: The Then and There of Queer Futurity* (New York: New York University Press, 2009).
35 It is also worth stressing that a world in which individuals are not judged on the basis of their skin color is not or need not be a world in which racial belonging does not or cannot affirmatively matter.
36 Foucault 1980, 95.
37 Derrick Bell, Racial Realism. *Connecticut Law Review*, 24(Winter 1992):363. Qtd. in Ray.
38 Ray.
39 Lorde, 130.
40 Lorde, 131.
41 Lorde, 130.
42 Lorde, 129.
43 Patricia Clough in conversation with Judith Butler, What's Systemic About Racism? *Couched*, October 14, 2020. Podcast.
44 Sharon Patricia Holland, *The Erotic Life of Racism* (Durham, NC: Duke University Press, 2012).
45 Avgi Saketopoulou, Risking Sexuality Beyond Consent: Overwhelm and Traumatisms That Incite. *Psychoanalytic Quarterly*, 89(4) (2020):771–811.

Chapter 3

First world problems and gated communities of the mind

An ethics of place in psychoanalysis

Francisco J. González

Respirator masks are once again commonplace. Most of us already have one.

Two years in a row, the fires raged. For a time, the San Francisco Bay Area claimed the unhappy distinction of having the worst air quality in the world. If in the first year stores quickly sold out of the coveted N95 government-approved masks, by the second year people had learned to stockpile them. By the time the virus hit, it was the medical providers who couldn't find them. San Francisco was a ghost town, streets deserted, a scene from a cheap zombie movie. A few people milled about wearing flimsy surgical masks or scarves, anything that might prevent the transpiration of harmful particles, or maybe simply as a guard against a greater onslaught: the loss of hope against the infiltration of despair about the end of the world.

When I started writing this, news of recent fires – the Kincade, the Tick, the Getty – were stirring the kinds of symptoms that could only be called post-traumatic, an ironic word now, as if the trauma were already behind us. The beginnings of a sickening new routine in the Bay Area – anticipating the fire season, fearing the winds, anxiously watching the smoke roll in as we pulled out the masks – now seem almost quaint in the face of the new global assault. The frequency and magnitude of the fires were frightening, but at least we had a living memory – collectively, if not always individually – that even fires could be survived.

Now it's different. As of this writing, the confirmed cases of COVID-19 caused by the novel coronavirus have passed 10 million worldwide, the United States claiming about a fourth of worldwide deaths; and the numbers keep rising.[1] For now, the San Francisco Bay Area is still relatively sheltered, not yet assailed by the dreadful surge that nearly inundated metropolitan New York, where the really harrowing stories were coming from. Still, to the scenes of horror the fires seared into us – pictures of burned-out car husks, dazed animals wandering in smoky fields, the faces of stunned residents, tear-streaked and dirty, watching their lives burn to ash – we are now forced to add other agonies we had yet to imagine: refrigerator cars for corpses, people dying isolated from those who love them, exhausted health care workers in space suits.

Pandemic literally means *all people*, and the consulting room, of course, could not be immune. The afflictions of shared social trauma touch not just every*one* but the dense network of connections that connect those everyones: acquaintances and fellow strangers, as well as intimates, the invisible reticulation of interdependencies. It is as if the very matrix of our in-between is sullied, the psychic air contaminated and dangerous, the collective environmental mother herself terribly stricken.

If last year the buildings outside my window in downtown San Francisco were barely visible, shrouded in the dull brown smog of the fires, the sun an eerie orange disk filtered through the haze, this year the eerie scene couldn't be more different: the sun blazing in the clearest sky, the streets utterly deserted, everything in sharp relief. Last year, the smoke itself was a literal residue, no abstract symbol, but real lives turned to cinder, aerosolized trauma. This year, what we breathe into our lungs is imperceptible, undetectable: not the residue of an external conflagration that has already happened, but the indifferent harbinger of dreadful potential, of a life-threatening internal conflagration to come. The invisible monster – a hundredth of the diameter of a human hair – the SARS-CoV-2 virus, like others in its class, exists in a nether world between life form and inert chemical matter, a true species of the undead of horror films, utilizing human bodies as the matrix of their mindless replication.

But as with the smoke from the fires, we are once again plunged into a fog of blurred edges, where the line between internal and external becomes ominously indistinct and surfaces shimmer with hallucinatory danger. As with the fires, those of us with the means to do so take refuge, "sheltering in place" in roomy houses, retreating to second homes away from the fray. But the enclaves of home and consulting room offer no ultimate security; neither fire nor virus ultimately acknowledge the distinctions of class and privilege. I recall one patient during the fires who felt irritated, the butt of a cruel joke: *we didn't move here to have air quality that is worse than Mumbai or Shanghai* . . . . For months, Wuhan remained a place firmly elsewhere. But the soap bubble fantasy then burst: whether smog or sickness, privilege could no longer protect *us* here from the miasmas that daily beset *them* there.

What would seem to be so completely unrelated to the conduct of psychoanalysis in a private practice office in twenty-first-century California – Mumbai and the Cold War language of political economy – finds its way, through association and displacement, into the discourse of my patients with some regularity. It's not at all uncommon that a patient, after a long complaint about loneliness or the pains of relationship brushes it all away by sighing: *oh well, first world problems.*

A common ironic meme meant to dismiss the trivial irritations of life in the rich capitalist West (like the heartbreak of an espresso drink made with the wrong milk product), the phrase is psychic sleight of hand, cloaking concern in the guise of (false) humility. At the most obvious level, it seeks to foreclose. The patient fails to elaborate the loneliness, refuses association, doesn't speak the transferential accusation of a lack of receptivity in, say, the analyst. We are familiar with these kinds of defensive dismissals.

But a meme – like a gene – is a mode of transmission, of replication and dissemination, but with a grounding in the *social* unconscious of *collectivities*. And so this "first world" meme invokes problems in the collective sphere which are increasingly becoming a focus of attention for psychoanalytic practice. And in this guise, the evocation of "first world problems" has surfaced in a denser, more poignant way in my practice as of late than the defensive minimization of personal emotional experience. A first world problem implicates other worlds and their problems, performing a dismissal at a collective level too. At its core the phrase houses, then, a double disavowal: let's not think about *me* (and, implicitly, the collectives to which I belong) by not thinking about *them* (the collectives I explicitly disavow).

Uncannily, the term can be traced to an article published in 1979 by Geoffrey Payne, a housing and urban development consultant, entitled "Housing: Third World Solutions to First World Problems." Addressing a frustration any even upper-middle-class home buyer in the metropolitan Bay Area would instantly recognize today ("the bottom rung of the housing ladder moving upwards consistently faster than income levels" [p. 100]), Payne suggests anarchic innovations from the third world: perhaps unauthorized building and squatting could ease the housing strain. The irony couldn't be more complete: a line from an article seeking solutions *from* the third world to a very real problem of housing inequity *in* the first world, flips into an erasure of problems by the disavowal of inequities.

But psychoanalysis teaches us something about the processes of disavowal: namely, the biting return of reality. And if San Francisco will not go to Mumbai or Wuhan, then Mumbai or Wuhan will come to San Francisco. The smoke of climate change is hard to keep out, and the changing climate is far more penetrating than only atmosphere, as catastrophic as that promises to be. Late last year, the crowds rioting in Santiago, Chile, echoed the crowds rioting in Beirut and Hong Kong and Paris as country after country struggled with growing inequity; early this year, the abandoned plazas of St. Peter's mirror the vacancy of Times Square, empty avenues near the Eiffel Tower, the desolation of common streets the world over, as country after country locked down against the horrifying pandemic. In a shrinking world that gets ever faster and more "liquid" (Bauman, 2000), groups with radical differences are thrown ever more tightly against each other. There can be no denying now that Hubei is intimately conjoined to Seattle, Milan, Teheran, São Paolo. The air quality in Mumbai cannot be dissociated from that of the Bay Area. If the UN Refugee Agency estimates that almost 71 million people were forcibly displaced worldwide by the end of 2018, then some of them, no doubt, live close by. In short, the teeming cities and comfortable suburbs of first world America can no longer be seen as impermeable to the crises shaking the other worlds coinhabiting the planet. And with the closing of the gap – with this intimate global touch – the fear of infestation, of a threatening contamination by the other, often becomes the impetus for a pressing imperative of safety: close the door, round the wagons, please just keep all of it – and all of them – out.

Focusing on a throwaway phrase from the hipster lexicon against the dark background of great fires and a historic pandemic rings of bathos. But by doing so, I hope to highlight concepts and modes of working that give shape and coherence to emergent trends in psychoanalysis today, a psychoanalysis that progressively recognizes it can ill afford to be a gated community, even in the name of protecting internal reality from the taint of the social. My goal is to work in part through illustration and clinical vignette and, in part conceptually, to interweave psychoanalytic and critical theory in order to figure a horizon of thought that is increasingly being developed clinically and theoretically but that cries out for more development. It is, in fact, the horizon of a response to a cry in the world, which psychoanalysis – as an art of listening to what remains shrouded but insistent – cannot help but hear. And as it is at the heart of our ethic that true listening is mutative, psychoanalysis cannot help but be changing. This change has broadly to do with the recognition that the social field is an essential constituent of psychoanalysis, both within its unfolding as clinical praxis, and as a foundational element of its theoretical evolution. More specifically, and critically, work in a social field concerns *positioning* – what I might call an ethics of *place* – for patients and ourselves as practitioners, but also for the collective we are as a discipline. As the importance of positioning is crucial to my project, I will continue, then, by attempting to locate *myself* psychosocially through a psychoanalytic story.

Fat cats and invisible people

David is a well-off businessman, almost 70, whom I have been seeing for just over a decade in weekly psychotherapy. An immigrant from Latin America, he pronounces his name in English rather than the Spanish (*David*), which is just one way he signals ambivalence about his pre-immigrant past. He grew up in a lower-middle-class household and came to the United States as a young adult, when he struggled economically before slowly working his way up to his now highly successful position. He himself was homeless for a time and depended on the kindness of friends to get by, for which he is deeply grateful. In the series of sessions I have in mind from a few years ago, he is very concerned about being overweight. He is clear that he knows how to lose weight and has in fact done so before but cannot seem to find the motivation to embark on this project now, as much as he feels the pressure to do so for his health and comfort. He is associating to this problem. Even as I too have the words in mind, he says with a chuckle that he is thinking of himself as a *fat cat*, which opens a dialogue on his economic position. A session or two later, he enters the consulting room quite animated; there was much in the news about the Occupy movement at the time and the slogan "We are the 99%." He had just read an article on current wealth statistics. *It turns out I am in the 1%!!* – he says, apparently dumbfounded. I myself am taken aback with disbelief that he could have thought anything otherwise and tell him so; he is an educated and well-traveled man, it seems curious to me that this would not have occurred to him before. He has a quick response: *I don't really look down, I look up. Believe it or not, in my circles there are many people who have a lot more money than I do. I am really towards the bottom of the pack. In the parking garage, my Mercedes is the least expensive car.* The parking garage is in a high-end hotel not far from my office in downtown San Francisco. On the way into my office, I have seen people with needles in their arm, shooting up; I routinely hear what I presume to be a psychotic homeless person, shouting incoherently for an hour at a time just under my window. *Didn't you walk here from the garage?* – I ask – *did you happen to see the people on the street?* He had not, he says, seeming a bit confused. During the conversation, I search for and decisively dismiss any possible feelings of envy I might harbor concerning his wealth, while vaguely settling into a warm and pillowy moral superiority. The following session, he picks up without missing a beat. On leaving my office the previous session, he had conducted a little test as he walked back to his car. With each person he passed on the street, he asked himself, *Do I think this person has more money than I do?* And with each one, the answer was the same: *No, definitely not.* It had suddenly become possible to see invisible people.

Tellingly, it is only now, through the writing of this chapter that placed me in dialogue with colleagues and an imagined readership, that is, in dialogue with a collective social object that – for the first time, astoundingly to me – I turn to see the door within myself that I have shut on my patient, Davíd.

The first time I returned to Cuba – the country my parents and I left when I was a small child – I invited the extended family in Santiago to eat at a *paladar*. *Paladares* were the in-home restaurants newly sanctioned by Castro as he struggled to improve the disastrous economy of the so-called *período especial*, the "special period" following the collapse of the Soviet Union. Of the 15 of us present, only I ordered the local lobster, everyone else thrilled to taste chicken again, which they hadn't seen in years. I don't remember what the bill came to; it might have been $50 – little for me, but about one-and-a-half months of my cousin's salary, a doctor with a decade of experience. When I went to pay, the waitress told me it was taken care of, apparently by my uncle – aging, unemployed, and the patriarch of the family. I became irritated with him – I had been planning this dinner from the beginning of the trip, this was to be my treat, a gift. As we walked home, one of the frequent power outages now suddenly hit, and in the hot darkness that accompanied us as we picked our way among the potholes in the empty streets, my anger melted into shame. I realized how cheated I felt, how fiercely I had wanted to be the benevolent one. And now, rather than luxuriating in the anticipated generosity of my first world largesse, I was left with the humiliating emptiness of narcissism laid bare, knowing the next morning I would board a plane and fly back to my comfortable life, leaving this third world of my family behind. Davíd was clearly not the only one with first world problems.

Social nausea

I use this clinical story to highlight an intricate transference/countertransference mesh involving class, ethnicity, political upheaval, immigration, biculturality, and language. It is a story that could be read in conventional individualist terms, along the lines of Oedipal dynamics, envy, and survivor guilt, for example, but such readings would ignore important structural elements, an erasure that would constitute a kind of violence.

For now, let me look in a different direction and say that the true recognition of privilege and the acknowledgment of the social inequities that undergird it almost inevitably lead to disruption (Swartz, 2019). For psychoanalysis as a discipline, this disruption is often confined to the psychic; we recognize it in the oft conceded charge against our discipline of its elitism, of its white fragility, and guilt. But increasingly the disruption is structural, as we question what constitutes the canon of psychoanalytic literature and grapple with changes to the teaching curriculum, as we reconsider the session frequency that defines an acceptable training case, and as we struggle with painful issues of diversification in our institutes. Our journals and conferences are crowded with the complexity of these issues. But precisely because a true encounter with otherness is disquieting and disruptive, the conservative forces of psychic equilibrium will seek to restore homeostasis, reinstalling old paradigms, to quell the disruption and prevent change. We know this from our clinical practice, but it no less true for the institutional resistances within the discipline of psychoanalysis than it is for the resistances of the individual analysand.

In Jenny Erpenbeck's (2017) acclaimed novel *Go, Went, Gone*, a retired philology professor from former East Germany finds his life deeply subverted when an initial curiosity about a group of African asylum seekers becomes deep engagement. In a review of that novel, literary critic James Wood (2017) gets to the troubling heart of our resistance to change when he reflects on his disturbing experience of reading the novel and his retreat from this disturbance. Wood writes:

> I am like some "flat" character in a comic novel, who sits every night at the dinner table and repetitively, despicably, intones, without issue or effect, "This is the central moral question of our time." And, of course, such cleansing self-reproach is merely part of liberalism's dance of survival. It's not just that we are morally impotent; the continuation of our comfortable lives rests on the continuation – on the success – of that impotence. We see suffering only intermittently, and our days make safe spaces for these interruptions.

It is precisely the safety of these spaces that is the matter at hand; for this safety can be the way that these interruptions are domesticated, minimized, and brushed aside. Through the influence of philosophically inflected cultural criticism, a growing body of analytic literature has begun to take up this problematic, and indeed some quarters of institutional psychoanalysis have been adept at naming the social disturbances that daily besiege us, but we too often settle back, reinscribing the old paradigm: individualistic and introspective, wary of the structural changes that deeper social engagement compels. It took nearly one hundred years of theorizing for the Establishment (the term here is Bion's) to begin to problematize the workings of power as a properly psychoanalytic category, and this mostly through the lens of feminism and gender; we have much further to go in unpacking the operations of racism, economic disparities, migration, climate change, political upheaval, globalization, technological acceleration, and a host of other forces, which might rightly be called shared social traumas. These domains have typically been relegated as *external* to psychoanalysis proper, but this sense of propriety is itself already shot through with the workings of the unconscious, an unconscious that operates at a different level than that of the individual, namely, the social unconscious. These new changes in psychoanalysis are due, in no small measure, to the recovery and accentuation of a lineage of thinking that has always been with us but has often been relegated to the margins.[2]

As an example, I will focus now on some ideas from the work of Janine Puget, the Argentinian analyst who has long been writing on the necessity of psychoanalytic work in the domain of the social. Puget (1988, 1991, 1992) has insisted that there are two distinct psychoanalytic domains with heterologous logics: the domain of the personal, Oedipal, conventional psychoanalytic project and the domain of external reality, uncertainty, and groups, of the social psychoanalytic project. As part of this work, Puget (2018a) has written on those who are made invisible – specifically, the homeless, the unemployed, and the "desaparecidos" of the Argentinian dirty wars. We could easily add Judith Butler's (2004) register of precarious life, those who pass unmourned because they are considered socially unmournable; or the status of nonbeing relegated to black subjects, in the line of Frantz Fanon (1987/1952), Saidya Hartman (1997), and Achille Mbembe (2017). Puget (2018a) places such subjects under the rubric of disposability, operating in a state she calls a naturalized "dis-existence." Cloaked in invisibility, they become recognizable only when they amass into a group, in a moment of protest, like the refugees in Erpenbeck's novel. More often than not, we relegate them to a third world or pass them in the street as ghostly entities, if not quite seen, yet still with the power to haunt.

For if there are holes in the social fabric through which people effectively disappear, they do not exactly vanish without a trace. These "invisibles" trouble my consulting room with great regularity, as we saw in the example of Davíd. In one now seemingly distant week, when people still left their houses and all talk did not involve references to the coronavirus, several patients from tony parts of the city told a similar story: leaving home in the morning, they step over the sleeping body of a homeless person at their doorstep, and are left with a kind of social nausea, trailing malaise, awkwardness, guilt, fear, disgust. *I don't want to bring up my child in these conditions* – says a single mother. *I want to help but I don't want to enable them* – says a venture capitalist. And the common refrain: *they should do something*. Often, the greater the frustrated disgust of the patient in question, the more precarious the economic position the patient occupies. Despite our attempts to insulate ourselves, to edit the scenario out of the psychic picture, an encounter with these "invisibles" leaves a mark, an affective vestige. The homeless person does more than confront us with someone who can, all too often, be reduced to a depository for projected abjections which return to threaten us from the realm of the uncanny. The homeless subject also challenges us with the radical and disquieting alterity of a form of human living that seems alien, confronting us with the stranger within. Such an encounter puts us face to face with the precarity we all inhabit – though unquestionably in radically unequal ways – within the incomprehensible complexity of the social order. Few of us working in the urban centers of this privatized first world do not feel it: I need to command the fee that pays the mortgage, and the nameless person sleeping on the stoop can obviously not pay that fee.

One patient, a successful artist from a war-torn country, works a reception job, barely eking it out – despite critical acclaim. At the community clinic where I work, asylum holders and seekers live in shared rooms and SROs, where tensions run high and an argument can end in eviction and thus the streets. But such precariousness does not affect only my poorer patients. A South American immigrant from a well-off family, Ivy League schooled, came to the land of start-up opportunities but can't quite get it to gel, and everything threatens to unravel: house, family, marriage. An American-born woman, Ivy League schooled, is holding on with a tech job consultancy but looks into immigrating to Mexico, where she knows from past experience she can afford Montessori schools, health care, and a nanny. More than one patient cannot stop working, despite significant wealth: one literally works himself ill, overwrought but unable to slow down, he develops strange somatic disturbances despite extensive negative medical workups; another, mortgage-free and with many millions in the bank, frets he does not yet have enough money.

Each of these patients comes sporting the complicated childhoods that conventional psychoanalysis is well equipped to address: psychic intrusions large and small, insufficient holding, inadequate containment. But it is difficult to sit for a day of analytic sessions and not hear the relentless press of a world gone mad, the steady shrill pitch of unreconcilable political discord, the nauseous unease of a collective holding environment turned toxic, the fear of contagion, illness, and death. The accelerated speed of social and technological change; globalized political ferment; the bombardment of information, of misinformation, of case numbers; the constant pinging of the next message, the next tweet – a relentless and exhaustive uncertainty that goes well beyond the nameless dread and existential uncertainty of one's own individual death or even the death of those one loves, to something more diffuse, more all-encompassing, like the collapse of whole systems of material sustenance, the death of an intelligible social order, the annihilation of the planet.

Our ability to create livable forms and adequate structures of containment are overwhelmed by what analyst Rachael Peltz (2005) calls our "manic society" and sociologist Zygmunt Bauman (2000) calls "liquid modernity." We are born into a social order we did not create but to which we are inextricably bound, stepping over its bodies. Overwhelmed by its complexity, we remain relatively powerless to change it, even as organized collectives, much less as individuals. The anxieties exposed here concern our unstable belonging. And the interruptions of daily comfort that opened this deluge of anxieties can only create "subliminal ailments and defensive formations [malestares subliminales y formaciones defensivas]" (Puget, 2018a, 27)[3] as we attempt to ward off the chaos.

The excess of the social

Social subjectivity, in Puget's terms, regards that arena of living in which a social reality that exceeds us, one that is well beyond our control, produces its effects on the mind and on relationships, producing "new marks for which we have no previous inscription [nuevas marcas para las cuales no tenemos inscripción previa]." I quote from her paper "Coartada social [Social alibi]":

> These marks are incorporated as intrusive, representing the alienness of the world as much as the alterity of others, and making a place for them produces a kind of displacement from known positions. It breaks with inherited models and forces a difficult coexistence between what is known and what is alien/foreign. A typical defense [against this difficult coexistence] attempts to articulate the present and the past as if they corresponded to similar logics when they tend to be heterogeneous logics.
>
> It also includes the necessity of processing belonging to a world in which events take place that populate the life of the subject, without depending on his having generated them. It includes the culture to which he belongs, which must needs clash with his inherited culture.

> Estas marcas se incorporan como intrusas, representan tanto lo ajeno del mundo como la alteridad de los otros, y hacerles un lugar produce una suerte de descoloque de posiciones certeras. Rompe con modelos heredados y obliga a una difícil convivencia entro lo conocido y lo que es ajeno. Una defensa habitual lleva a intentar articular el presente y el pasado como si correspondieran a lógicas similares cuando suelen ser lógicas heterólogas.
>
> Incluye también la necesidad de procesar el pertenecer a un mundo en el que suceden eventos que pueblan la vida de un sujeto, sin que

dependa de él haberlos generado. Incluye la cultural a la cual pertenece, que habrá de chocar con la cultura heredada.

(2008, 324)

The brave new world in which we live cannot be domesticated through the logic of yesterday. That is, current social events and traumas (the California fires, the churning political turmoil, the symptoms of white supremacy, the coronavirus pandemic) cannot be simplistically reduced to intrapsychic (or even intersubjective) terms using the psychoanalytic logics and hermeneutics of the previous century. But neither can the disjunct in our theorizing be reduced to a lag resulting from the acceleration and liquidity of contemporary life. The shrinking and quickening of globalization generate heat and energy, to be sure, but what this compression more clearly reveals are the fissures that were always there in our thinking. In truth, psychoanalysis has always struggled with the brave newness of the world, and from the beginning. The psychoanalysis of the individual was always in an unstable tension with the heterogeneous logic of the group and the social (Kaës, 1995/1993).

Like Lynne Layton's (2006) critique of conventional psychoanalysis for its attacks on the social link, Puget (2008), reading Steiner's famous 1985 paper against the grain, asserts that it is we who have "turned a blind eye" on the social realities of our time. As in the Oedipal myth, such repudiation comes at a great cost. It is not an exaggeration to say that the vibrancy and relevance of psychoanalysis as a useful discipline for the next century hangs in the balance. We have undoubtedly come some way since Winnicott famously noticed that bombs were dropping outside, during the controversial discussions, only to have Klein chide him for forgetting that psychoanalysis concerns itself with the internal world. Most contemporary analysts at least acknowledge the daily bombardments of twenty-first-century living. Nor is it to say that narratives concerning social events might not fruitfully be reinterpreted as characters to "dream the session" of the patient's intrapsychic world as one might do following post-Bionian field theory. It is more to assert that, following Freud on the function of dreaming, strictly hewing to the oneiric function could also serve as a kind of wish fulfillment to help keep patient and analyst asleep to a social reality which threatens the psychic stability, creativity, and vibrancy of both parties and their web of relations, and that this "external" force has as much impact on the psyche and requires as much metabolization as do the forces of an endogenous drive. And if, rather than dream making, a usable accommodation to reality is to be our guide for healthy psychic functioning, there are urgent matters before us, literally matters of life and death, to which as individuals and collectives we continually turn a blind eye. The contemporary catch phrase used to signify newfound understanding of the pervasiveness and reach of structural racism – being "woke" – has been an easy target for the caricature of politically correct culture, but it is hardly a metaphor easily dismissed. No one (on either the political left or right) is likely to deny the anger, divisiveness, dismay, and anxiety – indeed, the jarring rudeness – of waking from the fantasied promises of the mid-twentieth-century American dream, the apogee of institutional psychoanalysis.[4]

What, then, is an analyst to do?

Puget (2008) recounts a clinical vignette that opens a door. A patient recounts his disdain at seeing homeless people gathering up trash and cardboard for money: it's a shame, he says, they should get a job. Puget finds herself uncomfortable, her ethical stance at odds with her patient. In another case, a patient recounts smuggling something across the border, gloating about getting away with it. Puget is initially silent while feeling complicit with a socially accepted culture of corruption. Recurrence to interpretations about childhood seems an easy way out, but this feels disingenuous. In both these instances, Puget recognizes that the patient's positions, derive from a political and ideological stance, as do her own; in both cases she opts for speaking out, in effect disclosing something of her own ethical position. The patient becomes angry, but a rich analytic process ensues. In a similar vein, Eyal Rozmarin (2009) has written about countering a fellow Israeli patient's insistence on serving in the army, with his own ideologically dissimilar position, again with complications for the analytic process. Rather than interpretation, what is sometimes needed is *opinion*, Puget (2008) says, since this demonstrates the alterity of two subjects.

Now, bringing opinion to the toolbox of technique (and suggesting that it is on par with interpretation) implies a rather different relationship of the analyst to what psychoanalysis is about and how it works. This difference, however, should not be constituted or understood as a call for politics in analysis. Considered psychoanalytically, opinion as technique is neither an act of political suasion nor bullying, but a form of intervention whose goal is making apparent ideological differences undergirding the analytic encounter. Opinion emanates from social positioning; it begins to make visible facets of the larger structure in which the two subjects are embedded. That is, it touches on the kind of technique that will become more necessary as we develop tools for making the *social* unconscious more conscious.

An opinion, as opposed to other more conventional forms of intervention (interpretation, elaboration, etc.), reveals the positioning of the analyst, the analyst's ideological investments. Not only the alterity of the other, but how that alterity is located in a sociopolitical field. Analytic use can be made of this if it helps to illuminate the psychic reality of the social unconscious, which exists in a plane well beyond individuals. There are, of course, limits to how much alterity any given analytic dyad can bear and still remain clinically useful to the patient, a matter which implicates our thinking on the social. Franz Fanon famously worked with both resistance fighters and their torturers at the Blida hospital in Algeria (Macey, 2012) and, to do so, did not reveal his political affiliations. An interesting thought experiment[5] is to consider not only whether one could work as an analyst with someone of wildly divergent political views (a progressive analyst with a Trump supporter patient, say), but whether one can imagine being the analysand of an analyst holding such views (the Trump supporter now as the analyst). It is not uncommon that a queer person wants a queer analyst or a person of color, an analyst of color. These preferences cannot be reduced to matters of individual subjectivity or something like "ego fragility"; they reflect an intuition by the patient about the social dimensions of the unconscious, and its impact on the formation of the analyst. A gay patient with a kind, understanding analyst who is also hell-bent on dissolving the "pathology" of homosexuality – certainly not an uncommon scene even 50 years ago – represents an annihilating alterity for the patient.

Doors, membranes, walls, threshold, skin

Classically considered, the frame is an essential mechanism that turns attention toward the "inner" world and that in Jose Bleger's (1967) terms constitutes the "non-process" of the analytic setting. For Marion Milner (1987), who is credited with the introduction of the psychoanalytic concept, frames simply and profoundly "show that what is inside has to be perceived, interpreted in a different way from what is outside" (p. 81).

Institutionalization has tended to reify the term, prosaically reducing it to such things as the length of the session and the fee. But recent interest has turned not only to the quality of attention in the analyst's mind that makes the frame portable but more trenchantly to how the conventional frame comes packing a great deal that is socially unconscious (Tylim & Harris, 2018). Indeed, in the face of the social – especially at the level of social trauma but not only at this level – the question of framing becomes particularly complex, as both members of the analytic pair are *embedded* in complex realities beyond their making or control (Boulanger, 2013). This can appear to overwhelm or explode the frame, though more accurately what it does is decenter it, revealing its latent history and ideological underpinning (see especially Hartman, Gampel, and Puget – all in Tylim & Harris, 2018).

This decentering allows us to consider the frame less statically: less a noun and more a gerund, as *framing*. Framing still offers the nonprocess elements or ground *against which* something can be analyzed but considers this frame contingently, itself necessarily constructed, historically and institutionally bound, and so subject to the social unconscious. In this sense, it is a less of a door and more like a construction manual for doorways – a threshold phenomenon, like a border or skin.

Indeed, borders have always been an extremely generative site of development for psychoanalysis. Psychoanalysis is about coming and going: the patient transits through the world and returns, transits through the session and leaves. This weaving in and out makes psychoanalysis permeable. The cell wall, the skin, the doorway – all are sites of enormous activity. Interaction and exchange with the world is a necessary condition of vitality; metabolism, like breathing, requires transport across these thresholds. Too porous, and liquid processes leak out, diminishing the organism; not permeable enough, and the organism suffocates.

Wisława Szymborska (2000), in her poem "Psalm," marvels at "the leaky boundaries of man-made states," those frontier borders crisscrossed "with impunity" by insects, birds, and clouds, despite the vigilance of the border patrol. She concludes, "Only what is human can truly be foreign." Psychoanalysis has always been deeply engaged with this foreignness and the border crossings that constitute it. Indeed, elsewhere (González, 2016) I have argued that immigration is one of our discipline's animating tropes: from Freud's erogenous zones, through the great psychoanalytic diaspora following World War II, to contemporary theory, psychoanalysis is a study of boundaries, errancy, and otherness.

It is precisely against this fluidity that the frame is compelled. Both egos and groups establish and maintain – and at times police – a boundary demarcating inside from out. Psychoanalytic orthodoxy has tended to frame the social out of the purview of strict clinical work, but a psychoanalysis that attends more carefully to questions of social subjectivity – to the problems of collectivity, the effects of social reality, and the violence and strangeness of the world in which we must live – cannot be a psychoanalysis of closed doors.

Delimitation of the social unconscious: demarcation and place

So, the psychoanalytic encounter with the world and its social order, a matrix of unfathomable complexity, is an encounter with alterity, with the otherness of the other and with the otherness this opens within ourselves. Think of the encounter with homelessness already mentioned, of the refugee crisis in Europe, red and blue political divisions in this country, the coronavirus pandemic, and racialized difference anywhere. These encounters with otherness force us to a border, the frontier between a domain of familiarity and putative sovereignty and a foreign territory whose workings are beyond our ken or control.

I want to move our thinking now towards a *topological* consideration of this border. What do I mean by this? Topology derives from *topos* (Greek for a "site" or "place," akin to the Latin, *locus*). We are familiar with it in the rhetorical notion of a *topic*, a place where an argument or theme is developed, or in the idea of the *topography* of natural borders – a river or mountain range, say – that provides geographic distinction between countries. Consider, then, the *topology* of the border, as a place or site of the construction of borders in multiple registers of existence: whether as a topic in theoretical discourse or a patient's speech; the border of repression or dissociation, fencing off the internal otherness of our own unconscious; the construction of the me/not-me distinction; the sense of belonging to or exclusion from groups constituted through identity markers such as gender or race; or the geopolitical and discursive frontiers of nation-states. This is the *topos* of the border, in multiple registers. Thinking *topologically* about borders is a way of considering the continuities and transformations of these interrelated but different locations: the way that shutting the office door is like crossing the border into a land of dreams – or like entrapment in a reeducation camp.

Like any psychoanalytic work, work in and with the social requires some sort of delimitation of a vastly complex field. To distinguish this delimitation from the framing of conventional analysis and its work on the personal, I will use different terms. This is an artificial convention and used here only for heuristic purposes. Space constraints prevent me from an extensive elaboration, but I do not mean to say that the question of the social concerns psychoanalysis only in certain unusual or traumatic circumstances, though these make a great deal visible that otherwise goes unnoticed. I argue instead that subjectivity itself only arises at the intersections of the two domains of *personal* and *social* unconscious, each with its respective psychoanalytic logic.[6]

Rather than "frame" or "framing," then, I will use the term *demarcation*, by which I mean the temporary or contingent location of a portion of the social field, with all that corresponds to it unconsciously. Closing a door (real or metaphoric) creates a domain, it demarcates a terrain or territory. Framing – as we conventionally understand it – happens in a demarcated place. Demarcation of a social territory, field, or zone allows analytic work on social subjectivity to take place, a term I distinguish from the more typical emphasis on psychoanalytic space (González, 2016, 2018, 2019). A correlate of this thinking stresses that psychoanalytic processes – those relations that are open to analytic transformation, interpretation, interference, interruption, punctuation, elaboration, and so forth – are always materially anchored, an anchorage that itself is an important site of analytic interrogation.

I emphasize that demarcation is material, and in more than one way. Conventionally this material demarcation defines the place of the office, with its closed door, armchairs and couch, and two bodies. The realm of potential *space*, of dreaming, of free association that leads to an elaboration of the unconscious in the personal psyche is not possible without this material demarcation of *place*. Place is the subfloor of framing. While we have extensive allusions to it, we have yet to sufficiently elaborate how consequential the material dimension of our work is: the location of the office (neighborhood, building), the arrangement of waiting rooms and modes of crossing of the threshold to the consulting room, its furnishings as "thinking surface" (Leavitt, 2013), the lying down or sitting up, the movements of analyst and patient. The ritualization of the psychoanalytic encounter, to the point of cliché, has rendered this materialization relatively invisible; it has made it seem as if the psychoanalytic encounter did not take place in the physical world. As with so many aspects of conventional psychoanalysis, the material subflooring of framing is made more consciously visible by the encounter with a specifically social psychoanalysis. Consider the contingency of my office being located in downtown San Francisco, for example, where there are many homeless people, as part of materiality that generated the fat cat sequence. Such material contingencies are part of the heterologous logic of the social register of the unconscious and should not simply be collapsed to psychic determinism and its representations.

The current COVID-19 crisis underscores the significance of materiality to psychoanalysis. In the nearly universal move to so-called "remote" therapies via phone and video platforms, analysts the world over have been forced to alter their relationship to the material setting. It is not that analysis at a distance is dematerialized or lacks a frame or setting (telecommunications do not, of course, make us all suddenly spirit). Instead, these platforms reconfigure the relation of bodies to each other, the points of contact in voice and sight, the loss of a place *shared*. We are familiar enough with the profound psychic effects of a simple material repositioning, namely from chair to couch: we know that reorienting the relation of the perceptual apparatus of analyst and patient to one another can become a portal to the workings of psyche. Freud theorized about the effects of this (not the least of which was the safeguard it afforded of his own social privacy). Psychoanalysis might thus be seen as a discipline that investigates the relation of psyche to materiality: not just between mind and body, but in the living linkages between bodies and the variabilities of place, architectures of all sorts, the population of diverse topologies.[7]

There are, of course, many other material configurations where analytic process can and does take place. The most familiar of these are the same kind of office, now inhabited by three bodies, in the form of a couple and an analyst. Or perhaps in a larger room now with more chairs and an assembly of bodies, whether a multigenerational family or a group of relative strangers, as in family or group analysis. And this can be extended further, to large groups or to organizations and institutions, such as in organizational consulting or in community psychoanalysis. With the Mexican individual and group analyst Juan Tubert-Oklander (2014), I suggest there is a continuity from individual to group to social analysis and, further, that these modalities are in fact interdependent and coconstituent. Once we recognize other material platforms for fostering analytic process (from couples' therapies to community psychoanalysis), it becomes clear that framing is a contingent, artificial, and temporary demarcation of the social field that establishes usable terrain where psychoanalytic process can *take place*.

What demarcation does is isolate a field and its players, and in addition to the analysis that it enables within its walls, it also allows the appearance of what Daniel Butler (2019) has called the "phantomatic aspects of the setting." Butler's work is specific to black subjectivity, but it is, I think, applicable in a wider way. He extends the work of Bleger, bringing theorists of blackness (such as Fanon and Marriott) to bear on Bleger's more individualist theorizing. As we have seen, Bleger speaks of the setting as the "non-process": this is the dimension, Bleger (2012/1967) says, that sediments the "phantom world" of the patient, that is the psychotic part of the personality, that "most primitive and undifferentiated organization" (p. 230, as quoted in Butler). Like a number of other contemporary analytic writers (Bass, 2018; Gampel, 2018; Hartman, 2018; Puget, 2018b), Butler challenges the view that the frame is able to insulate the clinical pair from history and its structural racism. It is the very supposition that the clinic can be a pristine space isolated from ideology that in fact enacts the recapitulation of structural inequity, for the institution of the clinical frame itself is also historically placed and must needs carry its own "primitive and undifferentiated" world, which, as Brickman (2003) so clearly shows specifically for psychoanalytic theory, is here a historically racist one. What kind of setting is created by a psychoanalysis haunted by this invisible whiteness? Only one that inadvertently annihilates the fullness of black subjectivity. What, then, can be done to help to put things "in their proper place"? (Fanon, 1987/1952; González, 2019).

What the psychoanalytic clinic can do – and here I am thinking again of its multiple manifestations not only as a dyadic enterprise but in other more expansive configurations – is to be a place where this veiled history can come into apparent view and become amenable to imaginative transformations in those who are subject to it. As such it acts as a topological site, where transferences and traces from the domains of both the social and the personal unconscious iterate.

Let me share a brief vignette about this kind of work, from outside the dyadic setting.

For about six years, I have been part of a group of community mental health practitioners, activists, and psychoanalysts called Reflective Spaces Material Places. The group meets about five times a year. The open meetings – typically a mix of twenty-five to forty regulars and newcomers – are organized by a core group that meets regularly. The past two years have been strongly inflected by racialized dynamics, with an explicit focus on the workings of whiteness, racism, and colonialism. While this is not psychoanalysis in a conventional mode, I identify and am interpellated as an analyst in and by this group, among other identities and positions I hold. To some extent, then, and along with others, I represent psychoanalysis in this group. Loosely speaking, I work analytically in the group, and the group in turn is working analytically upon me. I do not mean by this a formal position as the "group analyst" but rather a vertex of listening beyond the apparent, a consideration of the operations of history (part of the social unconscious) and how they become enacted in the group, and a collective attempt to work through that historical repetition to new kinds of relationships in the group. Doing so requires occupying a very different position from the one I occupy in the conventional psychoanalytic setup. To the extent that I help contribute to a containing function in the group, it is not by operating in the typical way that I do in the consulting room. Without doubt, enormous transferential forces from a variety of domains map onto the field demarcated by this group and its setting, including its material home in an established and strongly culturally identified Latino mental health organization. A great deal of work along the lines of metabolization, containment, structuring, and to some extent interpretation happens within and through the organizing group which facilitates the meetings, more than through any one individual. We have experienced serious ruptures as well as important gains in this process.

I will mention one particular experience here. During a series of heated discussions in which a number of people of color were speaking more forcefully and directly than they had in the past, challenging a current of hegemonic whiteness in the organization, I found myself in the hot seat. I believe I represented a number of vertices for the group: as a founding leader, as a white man, and as an established psychoanalyst. Other aspects of my identity – as an immigrant, bicultural/bilingual Latino, and vocal queer man – were less prominent in this sequence. At one point, I made comments about *feeling afraid for the sustainability of the group given the intensity of affects and suggested that what we were doing might be precisely what real change actually looks like, but that I thought this kind of change takes a good deal of time.* These comments were met with anger by some people of color who I believe saw me as using my position of privilege to place my fears above others, of being condescending in lecturing patience from a position of relative comfort and power, and of generally trying to shut down dissent. I was quite rattled by the experience; it took me several days after the event to finally settle down. Initially I felt quite misunderstood and hurt regarding marginal aspects of my identity I wished to have recognized and held in solidarity (especially my ethnic provenance and status as immigrant). I felt like an object of transference and wanted to justify a psychoanalytic move on my part, centered on an interpretation of "their" projection with a concomitant reaffirmation of my goodness. It took a little longer to get to the self-analysis: I was tremendously displaced from my typically more sheltered position behind the couch; this sense of exposure felt humiliating and made it difficult to hear the truth in what was being said to me. I came to realize that I was, in fact, relatively unconscious about the position I was occupying in this social field. This was not an intellectual insight (I could have easily described this positioning before), but a lived experience of "seeing" for the first time the freedom I had to speak in a certain way granted by virtue of the place from which I was speaking. The visceral emotional shake-up I experienced was public and painful; it implicated deeply held unconscious identifications with privileged groups. I do not believe I took a masochistic position of self-denigration, nor was I wracked with a paralyzing white guilt; rather I feel I learned something about the unconscious way I inhabited my social position, a position that became more completely visible to me precisely because I was shaken out of it. Being decentered from whiteness and from cherished identifications provoked the anxious malaise that arises from troubling the supposed sovereignty of the ego at its foundational joint with the collective matrix that grounds it. It meant a reconfiguration of my relation to myself and to others that was disturbing, growth promoting, and impactful, allowing me to work and respond in the group in new ways. It was an encounter with the social unconscious, which would not have been possible without the demarcation of the social field the group made usable for me.

As with dyadic analysis, transferences and enactments from the register of the social unconscious – that is, historical transmission of inequities, unavowed group pacts, ideologically freighted categories of thought (Brickman, 2003, unpacked "primitivity," for example) – will inevitably take place. And as with dyadic analysis, these will have to be acknowledged, suffered, mourned, worked through, though now at the levels of both the group as well as the individual.

Ethical iterations

Demarcation, then, is the kind of framing that looks toward the social unconscious, one that seeks to explore the effects of social reality, to catalyze the appearance of the phantomatic setting, and to analyze the hidden ideologies in which we are embedded. It does not dispense with the work we have conventionally been trained to do regarding the personal unconscious and its manifestations in intersubjective life. Rather, it seeks to expand the possibilities for rich engagement in and with a troubled and troubling world. It has become, in my estimation, a necessary part of contemporary analytic practice, which for me includes many nondyadic forms of being an analyst.

I am fond of a metaphor regarding knowledge, which I believe I read once in Jorge Luis Borges: as the sphere of knowledge grows, so too does its contact with the unknown, only now exponentially. We might extend this to say that as the group under analytic consideration grows (from dyad to community), so too does its contact with the social, which must include its suprahuman complexity, its vast realms of unpredictable and unstable possibility. Such contact not only subjects the individual egos in the field to significant centrifugal forces, but exposes them to the enormous violence, pain, and suffering of the social sphere. To be fully open to the world would mean to be unbearably open to its suffering, a suffering we are only rarely able to usefully manage.

Fundamentally, this is an ethical question, one of our relation to the suffering of both individual and collective others.

Levinas (1969/1961, 1998/1974) has appeared a great deal in psychoanalytic writing lately. Levinasian ethics puts a transcendent primacy on the other, obliging us to a radical responsibility for this other, thus inaugurating critical inquiry into ourselves. The serious engagement with questions of the social, of collective aspects of individual subjectivity, of the group cannot but open a vein of critical self-inquiry for the discipline. Is this not one of the roots of the discontents our discipline currently faces? To investigate what it means for practice when we attempt to be open to collectives not usually served by psychoanalysis? To question the institutionalization of a frame that can shut the door on particular groups of people, while making invisible that very closure? The infamous elitism of psychoanalysis is not a demographic chance happening: it is predicated on this unconscious and structural closing off, which has become reified in the normative clinical practice that defines what psychoanalysis is supposed to be. This results in a widely accepted view that psychoanalysis is a privatized, office-based, closed-door encounter between two people. This material subflooring of conventional clinical practice naturalizes the idea of keeping the social "without" in order to make room for the personal psyche "within," as if the social were extraneous to psyche.

Complicating Levinasian ethics for psychoanalysis, Rozmarin (2007) claims we cannot be fully for the other in psychoanalysis: our hearing of the other is not simply a transcendent exercise. As he writes, the essence of psychoanalytic ethics is to hear the other "in his materiality and presence in this world" (p. 359) – that is, in his particularity. To be open to the social and its deleterious effects – what Fanon (1987/1952) called sociogeny – is truly to court the "plague" (as Freud, on his journey to the United States, famously characterized psychoanalysis, a phrase which now, in the shadow of the coronavirus, takes on, *nachträglich*, an eerie resignification). For there is no easy way out of the ethical problem that reiterates in every material field: in demarcating a portion of the field by closing doors, we shut out important elements of fruitful possibility, often violently but also necessarily, for such closures are constitutive, making available to analysis and possible understanding the very processes we aim to pursue.

Examples from the Community Psychoanalysis Track at my institute readily come to mind.[8] In projects at an agency working with highly traumatized refugees, the complexities of establishing workable limits were a pervasive dynamic. How much availability should a therapist allow a client in catastrophic need, when what hangs in the balance is deportation? What are the boundaries between the process group and agency as a whole, between the group and the analytic institute? The institutionalized fee-for-service frame was hardly relevant here, and the establishment of workable limits had to be grounded in other ways. When need is virtually infinite, the preservation of providers as human resources for ailing communities becomes its own priority. Transferences from an often inept, discriminatory, volatile, confusing, and underfunded system infiltrated the organization, affecting its providers, appearing as projective identifications in the candidates working with them. Demarcation of usable analytic fields was necessary, but closing doors was also deeply fraught ethically and only possible by some measure of dissociation.

This has become accentuated under the current conditions of practice during the global pandemic. In a recent episode of the IPA podcast *On and Off the Couch*, Marilia Aisenstein (2020) spoke of a "community of soft denial." We all keep a certain kind of sanity, like the "fat cat" patient, by not looking down.

But psychoanalysis has something to offer precisely here. Our practice is to question, to question continually, to note the significances and the problematics of doors, to promote the difficult task of articulating values, to try to become responsible for the choices we make.

What we can attempt to do is to make more conscious our ethical struggle – to question and problematize the framings that keep the other out, recognizing the necessity of demarcation, and using these delimitations of the social field as a way to make the social unconscious visible. This allows us to take up a relation to the social and towards history that might be analogous to Klein's depressive position, though now in collective terms. At the level of the singular subject, that means recognizing our individual limitation in the face of the collectives that supersede us, while not renouncing our agency and responsibility to act on what troubles us as neighbors and as citizens in the world. At the level of the group and institution that is psychoanalysis, recognizing that our forms of practice and our theories must carry the marks of a social unconscious that seeks to obscure the workings of power.

A psychoanalytic theory and method for the twenty-first century must be one that rigorously takes up the double provenance of the unconscious – as *both* social and personal. Problematizing the social ills of our patients, we problematize our own as psychoanalysts. That means working within our institutes and with other groups and collectives in order to broaden the cultivation and reach of the psychoanalytic process. It means questioning our institutional foreclosures. Working as a psychoanalyst does not have to mean working with one patient, on a couch, for fifty minutes four or five times per week. I do not mean to water down our thinking: quite the opposite. We will have a great deal of theoretical and clinical work to do, if we are to follow the rigorous tradition that is our inheritance.

But honestly, I don't see how we can keep from doing the psychoanalytic work of the social and still remain a viable practice. It is an inevitable catastrophic change.

You might recall the dream Freud recounts and that Lacan made much of. A father keeping watch over the body of his dead son, falls asleep, during which time a candle falls over, setting the son's bed on fire. From the vantage point of the social analysis I am describing here, let us figure this son as the future of psychoanalysis, ailing unto death at times, and beset now by what Baldwin would call "the fire next time." In Freud's (1900) recounting of the dream, the father sleeps on, and in his dream the son appears, imploring, *Father, can't you see I'm burning?* (p. 509).

We can ill afford to ignore the smoke that even now infiltrates through the closed doors of our consulting rooms and the imagined refuge of our offices.

Notes

1 It is a marker of the speed of the pandemic: in the first iteration of this chapter, the worldwide caseload was approaching 1 million.
2 A description of this lineage is well beyond the scope of this chapter, but a quick sketch of it might include not only the late works of Freud on culture and the group, but such figures as Burrow, Ferenzci, Reich, Horney, Sullivan, Pichon-Revière and South American psychoanalysis more widely, along with post-Lacanian thinking on the social, and the American Relational School. An indispensable part of theorizing the social link in psychoanalysis is the rich tradition of group analysis on the social (Bion, Dalal [1998], Foulkes, Hopper [2003], Kaës [2007], Tubert-Oklander [2014], among others). For introductions to this social lineage, see, for example, Aron and Starr (2013), Danto (2005), Herzog (2017), Jacoby (1983), Salberg and Grand (2017), and Zeretsky (2015).
3 Translations from Puget's Spanish are my own.
4 This was written before the uprisings sparked by the murder of George Floyd. It is even less deniable now.
5 I thank Jay Greenberg for this.
6 See González (in press), for a more detailed elaboration of the idea of subjectivity at the intersection of these two domains (personal and social) of the unconscious. For a grounding introduction to the domain of the social unconscious, see Hopper (2003), who is often credited with coining the term.

7 Analysis at a distance should make visible to us the virtuality underlying all analytic encounters. Well beyond the scope of this chapter, Deleuze's (1991) concept of virtuality is linked to the emergent, to what can "become." Events are pregnant with possibility. Rather than the common expression, "it is what it is," psychoanalysis is predicated on the premise that "it is more than it seems to be."

8 The Community Psychoanalysis Track at the Psychoanalytic Institute of Northern California (PINC), founded in May 2019, allows candidates to count a project – conducted at a partnering community mental health agency and under psychoanalytic group supervision – as a formal psychoanalytic case toward progression.

References

Aisenstein, M. (2020). *On and Off the Couch*. Podcast Series: Episode 43. A Report from Paris with Marilia Aisenstein, March 31. Retrieved from: www.ipaoffthecouch.org.

Aron, L. & Starr, K. E. (2013). *A Psychotherapy for the People: Towards a Progressive Psychoanlaysis*. New York: Routledge.

Bass, A. (2018). When the Frame Doesn't Fit the Picture. In I. Tylim & A. Harris (eds.), *Reconsidering the Moveable Frame*. New York: Routledge, 111–138.

Bauman, Z. (2000). *Liquid Modernity*. Cambridge: Polity Press.

Bleger, J. (1967). Psycho-Analysis of the Psycho-Analytic Frame. *International Journal of Psychoanalysis*, 48:511–519.

Bleger, J. (2012/1967). *Symbiosis and Ambiguity: A Psychoanalytic Study*, trans. J. Churcher. London: Routledge. Originally published as Symbiosis y mbigüedad: Estudio psicoanalítico. Buenos Aires: Paidós.

Boulanger, G. (2013). Fearful Symmetry: Shared Trauma in New Orleans After Hurricane Katrina. *Psychoanalytic Dialogues*, 23(1):31–44.

Brickman, C. (2003). *Aboriginal Populations in the Mind: Race and Primitivity in Psychoanalysis*. New York: Columbia University Press.

Butler, D. G. (2019). Racialized Bodies and the Violence of the Setting. *Studies in Gender and Sexuality*, 20(3):146–158.

Butler, J. (2004). *Precarious Life: The Powers of Mourning and Violence*. New York: Verso.

Dalal, F. (1998). *Taking the Group Seriously: Towards a Post-Foulkesian Group Analytic Theory*. Philadelphia: Jessica Kingsley Publishers.

Danto, E. A. (2005). *Freud's Free Clinics: Psychoanalysis and Social Justice, 1918–1938*. New York: Columbia University Press.

Deleuze, G. (1991). *Bergsonism*. New York: Zone Books.

Erpenbeck, J. (2017). *Go, Went, Gone*, trans. Susan Bernofsky. New York: New Directions.

Fanon, F. (1987/1952). *Black Skin, White Masks*, trans. C. L. Markmann. London: Pluto Press.

Freud, S. (1900). The Interpretation of Dreams. *Standard Edition*, 9.
Gampel, Y. (2018). The Frame as a Border in a Variety of Settings. In I. Tylim & A. Harris (eds.), *Reconsidering the Moveable Frame*. New York: Routledge, 164–183.
González, F. J. (2016). Only What Is Human Can Truly Be Foreign. In *Immigration in Psychoanalysis*. New York: Routledge, 15–38.
González, F. J. (2018). Re-Placing Objects. *Studies in Gender and Sexuality*, 19(1):41–47.
González, F. J. (2019). Necessary Disruptions: A Discussion of Daniel Butler's "Racialized Bodies and the Violence of the Setting". *Studies in Gender and Sexuality*, 20(3):159–164.
González, F. J. (in press). Trump Cards and Klein Bottles: On the Collective of the Individual. *Psychoanalytic Dialogues*.
Hartman, Saidya. (1997). *Scenes of Subjection: Terror, Slavery, and Self-Making in Nineteenth Century America*. New York: Oxford University Press.
Hartman, Stephen. (2018). When We Frame. In I. Tylim & A. Harris (eds.), *Reconsidering the Moveable Frame*. New York: Routledge, 141–163.
Herzog, D. (2017). *Cold War Freud: Psychoanalysis in the Age of Catastrophes*. Cambridge: Cambridge University Press.
Hopper, E. (2003). *The Social Unconscious: Speaking the Unspeakable*. New York: Jessica Kingsley Publishers.
Jacoby, R. (1983). *The Repression of Psychoanalysis: Otto Fenichel and the Political Freudians*. Chicago: University of Chicago Press.
Kaës, R. (1995/1993). *El grupo y el sujeto del grupo: Elementos para una teoría psicoanalítica del grupo*. Buenos Aires: Amorrortu Editores.
Kaës, R. (2007). *Linking, Alliances, and Shared Space: Groups and the Psychoanalyst*. London: The International Psychoanalytical Association.
Layton, L. (2006). Attacks on Linking: The Unconscious Pull to Dissociate Individuals from Their Social Context. In L. Layton, N. C. Hollander & S. Gutwill (eds.), *Psychoanalysis, Class and Politics: Encounters in the Clinical Setting*. New York: Routledge, 107–117.
Leavitt, J. (2013). Superficie, spazio e artefatto: La presenza materiale della memoria. *Rivista Psicoanalitica*, 59:549–571.
Levinas, E. (1969/1961). *Totality and Infinity: An Essay on Exteriority*, trans. A. Lingis. Pittsburgh, PA: Duquesne University Press. Originally published as Totalité et Infini: Essai sur l'extériorité. Le Livre de Poche.
Levinas, E. (1998/1974). *Otherwise than Being, or Beyond Essence*, trans. A. Lingis. Pittsburgh, PA: Duquesne University Press. Originally published as Autrement qu'être ou au-delà de l'essence. Martinus Nijhoff.
Macey, D. (2012). *Frantz Fanon: A Biography*, second edition. Brooklyn, NY: Verso.
Mbembe, A. (2013/2017). *Critique of Black Reason*, trans. L. Dubois. Durham: Duke University Press.
Milner, M. (1952/1987). The Framed Gap (1952). In *The Suppressed Madness of Sane Men*. New York: Tavistock Publications, 79–82.

Payne, G. K. (1979). Lessons from the Third World. *Built Environment*, 5(2):99–110.

Peltz, R. (2005). The Manic Society. *Psychoanalytic Dialogues*, 15(3):347–366.

Puget, J. (1988). Social Violence and Psychoanalysis in Argentina: The Unthinkable and the Unthought. *Free Associations*, 1(13):84–140.

Puget, J. (1991). The Social Context: Searching for a Hypothesis. *Free Associations*, 2(1):21–33.

Puget, J. (1992). Belonging and Ethics. *Psychoanalytic Inquiry*, 12(4):551–569.

Puget, J. (2008). Coartada social y psicoanálisis [Social Alibi and Psychoanalysis]. *Psicoanálisis*, 30(2–3):321–332.

Puget, J. (2018a). Habitar espacios en el hoy o en un para siempre [Inhabiting Spaces in the Now or in a Forever]. *Psicoanálisis*, 39(1–2):19–39.

Puget, J. (2018b). Revisiting the concept of frame. In I. Tylim & A. Harris (eds.), *Reconsidering the Moveable Frame*. New York: Routledge, 184–204.

Rozmarin, E. (2007). An Other in Psychoanalysis: Emmanuel Levinas's Critique of Knowledge and Analytic Sense. *Contemporary Psychoanalysis*, 43(3):327360.

Rozmarin, E. (2009). I Am Yourself: Subjectivity and the Collective. *Psychoanalytic Dialogues*, 19(5):604–616.

Salberg, J. & Grand, S. (eds.). (2017). *The Wounds of History: Repair and Resilience in the Trans-Generational Transmission of Trauma*. New York: Routledge.

Steiner, J. (1985). Turning a Blind Eye: The Cover Up for Oedipus. *The International Journal of Psychoanalysis*, 12:161–172.

Swartz, S. (2019). *Ruthless Winnicott: The Role of Ruthlessness in Psychoanalysis and Political Protest*. New York: Routledge.

Szymborska, W. (2000). Psalm. *The Iowa Review*, 30(2):24. doi:10.17077/0021-065X.5231.

Tubert-Oklander, J. (2014). *The One and the Many: Relational Analysis and Group Analysis*. London: Karnac.

Tylim, I. & Harris, A. (eds.). (2018). *Reconsidering the Moveable Frame*. New York: Routledge.

Wood, J. (2017). A Novelist's Powerful Response to the Refugee Crisis. *The New Yorker*, September 18.

Zeretsky, E. (2015). *Political Freud: A History*. New York: Columbia University Press.

Chapter 4

Insidious excitement and the hatred of reality

Lynne Zeavin

1

The following caught my attention one morning.

> Dr. Thomas R. Frieden, who ran the Centers for Disease Control and Prevention for eight years under President Obama, was arrested in Brooklyn on Friday morning on a sex abuse charge after an incident in October 2017, the police said.
>
> A 55-year-old woman came forward to the police in July and said that Dr. Frieden, described by the authorities as an acquaintance, grabbed her buttocks against her will nine months earlier, on Oct. 20, at his residence on Montague Street in Brooklyn Heights, the police said.
>
> (*New York Times*, August 24, 2018)

Grabbed her buttocks? He was arrested for grabbing her buttocks? Grabbing someone's buttocks is an arrestable offense? I realize I feel dismissive. Yes, it's crass of Dr. Frieden for sure, but going to jail for it? Isn't it excessive, maybe even wimpy on the part of the accuser? This is my own unchecked, unexamined response, one I will return to later in this chapter.

Unbidden, I recall being on the street in New York and my own shock and resounding humiliation when a man going by on his bicycle grabbed my own butt(ocks) and rode off. In hiding just behind that image is the recollection of my father, and me, at many different stages. As a little girl, the pinch, the pull and pat, and as a very young woman, in my teens, the all-out grab. When I would protest, he would disparage, disregard, much as I did about the woman in this article. He would claim ownership: "I am your father. I was the one who bathed and diapered you."

DOI: 10.4324/9781003214342-6

(Funny, or not, to think of all the times the conversation went in the reverse, where in trying to appeal to him I would say, "But I am your daughter").

Perhaps it's this kind of acculturation, a kind of underpinning that now skews my perspective in the face of some of the more mild and ambiguous #metoo accusations and the often potent reactions. I often feel bewildered in response to younger women, my daughter among them, who seem entirely clearheaded about what is and what should not be tolerated in patriarchy, in a culture where men feel it is their privilege and right to take possession of women in both crude and more subtle, quotidian ways. In a family where this behavior is normalized, where no one intervenes to question it, much less stop it, it becomes ever more difficult to get hold of the meanings that spiral through one's mind and body from both inside and out. That family culture is permeated by the culture at large, always, or anew, particularly now, I think, when we have had a president whose very victory came on the heels of his pronouncement that you can grab them by the pussy. One of the residues of this cultural and familial male prerogative is an uncertainty within one's female self, an uncertainty and discomfort about responsibility: whose is it – and what are the limits?

2

On the night of my husband's book party, people arrived in what seemed unusually good spirits. The table was set with food prepared by a young woman and her partner; music played, candles were gleaming. We were at home. A man walked in, a colleague, and looking around, asked me had I made the food – I rather happily replied no, none of it, though of course I had arranged for all of it and was pleased with what now appeared. Well, then, did you help with the books? No, I laughed. Then what kind of wife are you, a terrible wife – and then, as if the words tumbled from his mouth, he said, "You must be a great fuck."

I think my jaw literally dropped. I was momentarily thrown off my effort at social grace. He said, "What? Was that a bad thing to say?" "Well, yes," I said and eased myself away. I think I didn't smile. I think I might have smiled at some other point in my life, with the overriding effort to protect the other from myself. I didn't smile, but neither did I speak.

But the moment stuck, the feeling stung, the lingering question to myself, why did I not say something more definitive, clearer, reproachful?

Why did I not take the moment in hand? Should I have asked him to leave? "What you said has crossed a line and I would like you to go" came to mind, later. But in the moment something ancient kicked in, something deeply habituated. My father grabbing my buttocks or my father calling to me when I came home from my first date (I was 14) asking, "Did you give him a blow job?"

Part of it I thought is the deep grip of something so ancient I don't even recognize its presence. Something so deep that I do not realize my own acquiescence to it. It is an odd kind of acceptance, really, because if you ask me, I would say, no, absolutely this is not something I or anyone should accept; in fact it is something we must fight against, and yet, in this most private, unarticulated zone of myself there is another tendency.

And isn't this the root of internalized misogyny anyway, this something so old and so deeply inside ourselves, that it functions practically as a reflex – only a reflex that instead of kicking outward, turns in, against ourselves? Or maybe it's that something internal recoils. Even at the word "Fuck." "A great fuck." To hear myself reduced to that makes me squeamish. For a second, my head kind of spins. Then it seems it is my problem to get it together.

My daughter, later, having overheard this exchange, challenged me. My daughter, then in her mid-twenties, was nearly in tears, outraged, upset, and shaken on my behalf. She felt keenly the degradation in the man's comment – she felt unambiguously his effort to make me feel small. Now I also had been upset, but the upset felt like mine to bear, mine to address, mine to recover from and turn into social and psychic equilibrium. This is one of the familiar social demands on women: to manage the unmanageable but remain gracious at all costs.

My daughter said something about how rude this man was, how out of line. She was crystal clear that what had happened was unacceptable, awful. I found myself thinking, then actually saying, "Yes, but what's the big deal? This is how my father treated me for years." As I said this, I noticed a feeling of strange self-worth, as though strength were accrued from being able to withstand a father for whom my body and inevitably my mind were up for grabs. This kind of self-regard is an illusion though, it's the same illusion that I held on to when I was a child, that the violence in my family would make me strong. I know it now to be a rationalization that both idealizes and manages away otherwise unmanageable experience.

But even as I thought it, and as I said it, I knew it *was* a big deal. That this man's mode of engaging me had been a sharp reminder of that feeling of being put in my place – or rather thrown off my place, if my place was to feel settled and well in my home, celebrating, and connected with my family and my husband, along with being a secure professional in my own right. He meant to undermine this place of satisfaction and to reduce it. It could all be reduced to "being a great fuck." And yet he did say *great* fuck, not a lousy fuck, and maybe that's supposed to be a compliment. It's part of what is confusing. That I am a great fuck undermines my composure. I then felt, in a way that was familiar to me, a wish to protect *him* and also his pride. I knew if I wanted to be wounding, it would be too much.

Although I believed that his comment represented a (perhaps desperate) effort to perform – to be a "bad boy," evocative and flirty, he is in reality an aging man with all the losses that aging entails.

He is also someone with a history of taking pleasure from putting the other person on the spot.

When this was infused with the sexually provocative it put me on the spot, but it also threatened to knock me off that spot, a spot which at that moment had been seeming pretty fulsome. The gesture leeches sadomasochism: it's the sadomasochism that drives a hook just there, just so, I feel it catch and not let go.

My daughter said, "But Mom how did you feel when he did that?"

It was now an action, no longer merely words.

As I grappled with how to answer my daughter, I sputtered and spoke of my father's way of crossing the line. My own instability with regard to holding this line, really knowing for myself what the line is. It's not that I don't actually know, but rather that all the while I might be holding a line, I am feeling uncertain that there isn't something wrong inside myself.

She ventured, "Is this why you let P stay over even when I told you he was touching me inappropriately."

Soon we were sitting on the floor, having a conversation that was at once deeply painful and awakening. We revisited a time from when she was sixteen and a friend, an esteemed colleague from out of town had come to stay at our house. Our daughter had come to us and said that this colleague – when saying goodbye – had hugged her, and then the hug moved its way down her backside until he was touching her in a way that made her uneasy. She was sixteen at the time and maybe just a bit dramatic, and I fear – I hate to say – I was dismissive. I cajoled, I reassured, but ultimately I dismissed. I basically communicated that her reaction was overblown, that he hadn't meant to make her uncomfortable, he was just being affectionate, that it wasn't as she saw it. I am uncomfortable now as I write this. As she told me again about this moment in her adolescence I could for the first time see it plainly. I was able to hear her, see this from her vantage, for the first time.

What I could see that night (and what has stayed with me since) is about transmission, something we bat around in psychoanalysis. Here I am the transmitter, the putter-into someone else of an unmistakable expression of misogyny, something unrecognized and therefore unchecked inside myself. This is a feature of how misogyny is communicated, and to recognize myself as a link in that chain of communication is at once obvious and disturbing.

Transmission is a complex psychological process. I cannot have transmitted without having had something transmitted into me. Transmission occurs verbally; it occurs silently. It is an accumulation of meanings that have gone unprocessed. I think of transmission occurring via projective identification which itself is an unconscious communication that puts into the other what one cannot face in oneself.

In my case, my father was a misogynist, glaringly, violently. He spoke degradingly about women, about my mother and, as I got older, also about me. But equally my mother was managing the force and weight of being a woman raised to "serve men" as she said. Her own lesson to me – explicitly stated and silently transmitted – was to submit. My father transmitted something by touching my body whenever he felt the need: bypassing any of my own sense of propriety, he pushed through, like when his heavy leg would pin me as he lay next to me while as a child I napped, when he would grab my head, because he liked to "smell my hair." Consciously, explicitly, I did and do contest this. I do recognize the damage and I do object. But with my daughter I fell into the unconsciously held idea that it's not so bad, that as women we don't need to take this too seriously, and that ultimately it is the man whom we protect.

3

"The Ego is first and Foremost a bodily ego" writes Freud in *The Ego and the Id.* (1923).

The ego is made permeable through its access by the body. The body ego is shaped, along with the mind, by the parent's explicit and ambiguous sexual messages. As repelled as I was by my father's crude gestures, there was always some part of me that wanted to love him, and somehow to understand him, and ultimately to forgive him, even as I squirmed or retorted or sometimes, simply, too overwhelmed, withdrew into long silence.

As my daughter and I sat up late into that night, this became searingly clear to me, not only what had been transmitted to me but, as is in the nature of unconscious communication, what I had passed along to my daughter. This is how it works. Something is taken in, absorbed, identified with, but it lies dormant, its presence uncalculated or unknown, perhaps it was too much in the first place to actually register, think about, face. Then, at a certain moment, there it is, being communicated, conveyed, often with no awareness that the passage has taken place. We rely on others to inform us about a part of ourselves that had been denied to consciousness.

Had I known what was underlying my response to my daughter at the time, I likely would have found another way. In most things in our relationship, I recognize her and affirm her. But this moment in her adolescence too closely dovetailed with a rote, unexamined, and frozen aspect of myself – an aspect that survived even through years of psychoanalysis, feminism, and what I would say has been a long-standing effort at being conscious. It had eluded me, this zone inside of capitulation, of dismissiveness toward myself and toward women, toward the need that we have as women to have boundaries of our own making around our own accessibility, of what is permissible. Clarity of mind and sanity themselves are bound up with caretaking that boundary.

To think that out of a rote responsiveness to a deep internal reality, I had actually counseled my daughter to minimize her own experience is now painful to me. But it also raises the question of what would I have liked to say to her. There has to be a place for unexcited, unexaggerated, direct confrontation, for drawing the line, wherever the line is. I think I would have liked to tell her that I would speak with our friend and tell him that his gesture was unacceptable and that it left her uneasy. I am not sure she would have let me. I think she needed to feel – first and foremost – that I validated her experience and was on her side.

I know that I am allergic to feeling like a victim. Maybe I am guilty about my father's impact on me. Maybe I worry that somewhere in being on the receiving end of unwanted sexual attention, there is inevitably an unwanted sexual response – and that this gets sewn into the response to men's violence. Where is it, what has happened to it, is it there, in some tucked away excitement that now registers as horror or other impassioned (yes, excited) declamations.

So if it's true that in our reactions to men's violence to women, there is, at least for some of us, a part of ourselves that has registered that violence, noninnocently, can we say, then, what does that do to our own reactions to standing strongly against any expression of violence toward women. Does this help me understand my own recoiling about impassioned responses – does it have something to do with the lingering and fraught, now transmuted expression of excitement?

4

I have been appalled and disquieted by white women's overwhelming support for Donald Trump during each of his two campaigns for president of the United States and through much of his term. The pull toward Donald Trump includes complicity with this man and his veiled dismissiveness and contempt toward women. As psychoanalysts, we can imagine how that comes to be. Take the outrage women expressed at Christine Blasey Ford when she testified against Brett Kavanaugh at his Supreme Court Confirmation hearings. Many women claimed that Blasey Ford was "unfair," which led to a broader claim that men are treated poorly by women in this country, that Donald Trump himself, misogynist and patronizing bully though he is, is the victim himself. In that turn, it is not men's violence toward women that is our object of concern – it is our violence toward men that we must atone for. Women vote for Donald Trump for many reasons. But one of them is a deep-seated internalized misogyny.

In trying to consider the workings of internalized misogyny – in response to Donald Trump in particular, I am thinking again about excitement, the kind that gets produced in our bodies, that agitates our minds – that arises from what in psychoanalysis owing to LaPlanche we commonly now think of as the enigmatic, that which doesn't quite take form but remains an ambiguous shadow presence in the mind. And how does internalized misogyny work, and in what ways does it show up in disguised and altered forms?

In watching the Kavanaugh confirmation hearings in the Fall of 2018 (which like so much of Trump's term in office slayed me for a week, once again the utter disregard for the truth, for Kavanaugh's distorted self-presentation, for the attack on women for telling their stories) . . . but something else also caught my notice.

When I would watch women, some women, convey their pain in an overtly distressed and outspoken way, maybe yelling or screaming in protest outside of the Capital building, I could feel in myself the usual cringy and critical (misogynist) response. The reaction inside myself was something like, "I wish she would tone it down, I wish she could be more measured." I agreed with the outrage in many cases but was uncomfortable with the mode of its expression.

Then I thought back to excitements. I wondered about the excitement now being conveyed by these women in the form and manner of their distress. Perhaps it is witnessing another's "excitement" now in the form of an emotional appeal that unsettles me. When I think about how this works, what the mechanisms are, I imagine various unconscious identifications that might be aroused. Perhaps I identify now with my father, a father who is indifferent to my distress, my urgings, my wishes for him to stop. And instead of taking my own side, perhaps bolstered as it could have been (but wasn't) by a maternal caretaker, I take his position, the father's position, and disidentify with myself, the child, the young woman, the woman with feelings of anguish, fury, feelings I can't quite say in a direct, calm way. This is a reflection of an internal object relationship that now makes itself known. In disidentifying from the women on my TV screen, I see my own distancing myself from myself in the scene. That is, in identifying with my father's critical and misogynist dismissal of me, I disidentify with my own cries, my own appeals, I look down on myself – seeing myself now through his eyes. As I am in identification at the moment with the man – the father, the patriarchy –I have disidentified from the woman's plaintiff position of needing to be heard. And I think this is what the women voters for Trump regularly do: hating a part of themselves, they disidentify from it, they identify with the man who hates them.

I suggest that we might at times all be prone to such cross-identifications. I/we identify with the strong figure, even the brutal figure, move into that position, attacking and demeaning the other, which is the position of our own vulnerability, our own disappointment, need, unease, despair, unmet longings, unmet aspirations, from which we disidentify.

And with misogyny in mind, then, it proceeds that I/we move into identification with a powerful, even hateful or tyrannical man, I assume his power, and I/we look down on myself/ourselves. I, in identification with him, discount, mock, deny their (mine, our) experiences.

5 Insidious excitement

When I was a little girl my father would drive very fast. This scared me, it seemed reckless and unsafe. I would ask him to please slow down. And rather than slow down he would speed up, veering in and out of traffic, with implausibly scant distance between us and other cars. He sped up because he knew it frightened me.

I take this as a paradigmatic moment of unbidden excess excitement in response to a sadistic provocation. That is, in his sadism (driving fast, in spite of my asking that he not, the pleasure he took in frightening me), his speeding up is not only sadistic in its own right, but it pushes his sadism into me, beckoning for a response from me. I contend that this moment enlists my own reactions which are split: fear on the one hand, upset, and somewhere, less conscious, an unbidden hidden excitement. As he disregarded my wish, it left an imprint of a sadomasochistic act, a kind of rape. An unknowable, unspeakable, really unthinkable thing . . . and yet I live with moments of unbidden excitement, indeed sexual excitement, that, because this excitement feels to be in the wrong place, I push out; in fact I turn away from it. And yet, I also must relate to it. Perhaps I find it being lived in other ways, in other domains, so that a woman's excess excitement is part of what I turn away from.

Sadism is itself an expression of an internalized object relationship and is reflective of an object-tie in which hate becomes inextricably intertwined with erotic excitement. As Ogden has expressed it:

> This combined state can be an even more powerful binding force (in a suffocating, subjugating, tyrannizing way) than the ties of love alone. In this sense, the sadistic aspect of the relationship of the critical agency to the split-off ego-identified-with-the-object might be thought of as a relentless, crazed stalking of one split-off aspect of the ego by another – what [we] would later view as the love/hate bond between the libidinal ego and the exciting object.
>
> (Ogden, 2002)

There is always an excess dimension to a parent's sexualized engagement with a child – I am not talking about sexual boundary crossing per se. I am talking about a father's (and it could be mother's, it could be any adult man or woman) everyday relation to a child's body-mind, the crosscurrents of the sexual and selfhood as they intertwine in development, the unconscious and conscious expressions of adult sexuality, whether in ordinary caretaking of the infant's body or the ways a parent exhibits her own body to her child. This might stay confined within the realm of the ordinary – or it may become an excess, something foisted on the child as the child contends with the development of her own sexual fantasy life and drive. This excitement is what I want to call insidious – the not so ordinary kind – that emerges in the excess pat, talk, look, probe, and in some instances, cruelty. I want to call this excess excitement insidious excitement: it gets inside. It becomes the stuff of what Ogden is describing as the "even more powerful binding force." Once inside, it perhaps remains sequestered. Silent or disguised, it will be aroused in unbidden, unconscious ways. I am linking for now this zone of excitement to what might be disowned in oneself and therefore subject to various psychic permutations: states of inexplicable arousal or disgust, moral judgments of various kinds, various kinds of identification and counteridentification including prejudices, unconscious projection, and projective identification.

6

The #MeToo moment in the United States convulsed in 2017 with Donald Trump as president. In response to the accusations of sexual violence in so many corners established a zero-tolerance reaction to sexual harassment at the same time that our president remained installed in power despite being a misogynist who stands accused of sexual violence toward dozens of women. We simultaneously live in a society that sequesters and/or condones Trump's violation of women at the same time that other men are losing their jobs and withdrawing from positions for the same and lesser charges. We have recently witnessed the appointment of Brett Kavanaugh to the Supreme Court in spite of (and perhaps because of) the accusations of sexual violence by several women. But at the same time, we are hearing a lot about women who disbelieve Kavanaugh's accusers, who can be whipped up into fury at her over "unfair treatment of men."

For weeks and months after Donald Trump was elected, I sat with an uneasy feeling. It was not only the terrible sadness and shame of electing an overtly corrupt white supremacist as president of our country; it wasn't only his dismantling of protections for our planet through his denial of the realities of climate change and his systematic attack on information, science, and fact-based learning; it was not only the explicit racialized violence that Trump has fostered, condoned, and seems to enjoy; it is not only the all-out assault on truth which at the time of this writing has led to, among other things, more than 300,000 dead people in the United States from COVID-19 with our numbers out of control and rising. All of this, all of this madness and destruction, links to Trump himself: crude, brash, solipsistic, racist, and misogynist, a man who takes no responsibility for his own actions but blames everything and anyone around him A man who lives in a world of his own design, whose chief mode of navigating is attacking reality, denying it with an absolutely straight and injured face, and exporting to us, the citizenry, an overload of bits and fragments of those truths that he cannot bear to hold. As with COVID-19 and his grave inability to confront the reality of it, Trump dispenses misinformation and lies based on a world he needs to inhabit. Trump's unruly, chaotic mind leads to what Roger Cohen calls "unleashing the barbarian" within each of us (Cohen). A man whose deep well of greed and perhaps disinterest in facing the world around him obscures any and all concern for the individuals or the country he is supposed to lead and licenses him to take in whomever he so choses in whatever way is most expedient to him. It is not only grabbing women "by the pussy." It now involves taking over the postal service and indeed the election to achieve his corrupt aims.

Since Trump's election, I have felt a revivication of my father's presence (though he has been dead for nearly thirty years). My father who also grabbed and took and spoke in crude ways about women and women's bodies. My father who when I was a young adolescent would tell me that my friends had "nice tits." My father who filled my being with a kind of deep and profound unease, a visceral unease, and hatred that inexplicably stirs insidious excitement.

Insidious excitement is terrible excitement: it gets into your skin, and while it is not exactly pleasurable, it is powerful; it disturbs, rattles, unsettles, riles up. "You must be a great fuck" reaches into the zone of such excitement.

Trump is a master of insidious excitement. He induces it. He plays on it. He mocks what is decent and whips people up into a frenzy, opening the gates of the sequestered, suppressed, most base aspects of ourselves, giving those aspects license to chant, to yell, to break rules, to body slam, to commit egregious acts of violence. When discussing this, as we are wont to do, we find ourselves excited – horrified yes, but in a state of excitement. This is the state that Trump has always meant us to occupy.

7

The day after the election in November 2016, Tessa, a woman in her late thirties, arrived for her session. The moment she lay on the couch she blurted out that she that she had voted for Trump. She confessed this now, feeling bad for it suddenly, because she didn't actually know why she had voted for him; she felt she did it because her husband had. Now as she was reading social media, she realized that for many women a vote for Trump was unthinkable, backward: Trump's misogyny was well-known and much discussed after all, and his administration would prove a threat to so much of what women have fought for. She expressed confusion because how was what he promoted really so terrible – isn't that just how men treat women? Is it so bad to be slapped on the butt, to be called a name; it's just in jest, maybe it's well intended? And anyway, it's the way men are.

The way men are. She then went on to describe her own father, who from the time she was young had been having an affair with another much younger woman and had confided this to her when she was thirteen, drawing a sharp wedge between herself and her mother. But it also drove a wedge between her and some aspect of herself, this sharp set of loyalties and division, the part of her that yearned for self-respect went underground, and a more brazen, ill defined, self-denigrating side took over, the part of herself that identified with her father – as a representation of all men. She started to fail in school; she started to spend time with a different group of kids; eventually the only time she felt happy was when she was getting high.

My patient's identification with the disregard of her damaging father – which coincided with a difficult and demeaning relationship with her mother – meant that *she lost track of herself* in foundational ways. Her allegiance to her father (an allegiance to a bad object) came at the cost of protecting herself, and for her this meant the cost of knowing her own mind and being able to use her mind. Her mind was disregarded by her father, the moment he began to fill her with descriptions of his sexual life with a woman other than her mother and to enlist her loyalty and care despite its variegated meanings for her as a young adolescent girl.

As an adult, Tessa had stopped working when she married a very wealthy man. But she was uncomfortable and unsatisfied with her life, feeling that there was something unrealized, even unidentifiable about herself. Her identities were more borrowed than owned, more facsimile than original.

Faced with this, and the difficulties presented by wading into her inner world, she often sought excitements in the world around her: distracting excitements. Drugs and alcohol were part of it as were powerful people and their intrigues – shopping and big plans for expensive parties, travel, horse shows. These manic excitements camouflaged the feeling of emptiness and dread, that at other times would surface, particularly when she would encounter someone, anyone who seemed to know her own mind – or to be living a more genuine life. Then she would succumb to what has to be described as hateful self-loathing and once again begin to seek some kind of excitement that would alleviate her bad feelings. Manic excitement transforms what might have at one point been a feeling of terrible disappointment with one's object – in Tessa's case, disappointment with her father, whom she preserves via a lifelong idealization. For Tessa, rather than confronting her feeling of pain at her father's treachery, via manic defenses she enters into a state resembling exaltation and heightened pleasure – until it dissolves, and she must repeat the cycle again.

It was once said to me that what psychoanalysis can offer is the ability to distinguish inside from outside – to begin to tell better what has been projected into oneself as distinct from what is oneself. The same can be said for sorting through identifications. Often, we identify with a figure expeditiously – that is, the identification helps to stave off a feeling of loss or psychic pain. To face the loss would be to realize the cruelty of the other and not to identify with it in oneself. Sorting out these identifications – and learning to face and tolerate psychic pain – is what psychoanalysis can allow us to do.

Tessa is not the only person I have treated whose father has elicited support and sympathy while having an extramarital affair. Excitement about being confided in overrides the reality of what is happening, the father's misuse of the daughter's sentiments, the misuse of the daughter's love and attention.

Helen was twenty when her father confided his long-standing affair with someone he was in love with. Helen who is now nearly sixty and single, still holds onto that encounter with her father as affirmation of her special tie to him, a tie she grabs onto as a lifeline, a signal of her superiority, even while she is alone and unable to sustain an ongoing relationship. The dynamics of this are extremely complex, but one aspect is the insidious excitement produced in Helen when her father enlisted her secrecy, her complicity, and along with it a numbing of her own mind. Again, there is the twofold response. On one level, I think she resented her father's calling upon her. On another level, the power of imagining and believing her extraordinary value to her father took hold. And in Helen's case, this is what she has maintained, albeit through a split-off fantasy picture of herself and her father, a fantasy that has been stoked and maintained all these years. In this fantasy, she is the woman in her father's life, she is central. Although she says that she wishes for an intimate relationship with a man, she is often drawn to sex with married men who ultimately are unavailable to her. The idea of her specialness to these men – that she is unforgettable to them is intoxicating, and it comes at a cost to her self-preservation. At the very same moment that she inquires of me, "Why can I not be as self-respecting as other women?" She maintains a very private picture of herself as having something more than these women – she has an "edge," is more desirable; she is unforgettable. She maintains this private zone of believing, a sort of erotic daydream, fueled by insidious excitement, yes, that fends off feelings of loneliness, and her fears of there being something unlovable about herself.

Insidious excitement, sequestered and private, is one level of my patient's experience. Another level, split off and denied, is a terrible feeling of being "disposable," the opposite of unforgettable. Ultimately, she felt disposable to both of her parents; she lives with the fraught determinants of loyalty, the unconscious meanings of having your father seemingly chose you when actually he implicates you, and when actually you aren't "chosen" at all, you are exploited, used. My patient is wrapped up in her insidious excitement that staves off psychic reality – it functions as gauze, or a cocoon. The excitement she feels, largely about her fantasied self, is addictive, it enthralls, thrills, and protects her, just as it works as a kind of counterdepressive stimulant to body and brain. That stimulant works for her much as it does for Tessa: it shields them from an underlying sense of isolation and despair.

8

When my father accelerated, I felt terrified and filled with hatred for him, who disregarded my feelings and seemed to be putting me in jeopardy. At the same time, there was something else, something even more disturbing. I would feel a sensation, absolutely unbidden, of what I think of now as maybe the first instance of the terrible excitement. What makes the excitement terrible is I didn't want it, I didn't enjoy its occasioning and do not want to abide by it. It was as if my body of its own accord responded to the sadistic provocation of my father. But I, as a person who also has a mind, must account for it.

When Helen's father confided in her about his affair with a much younger woman and enlisted her involvement and advice, she felt hatred but also an excitement about how special this must mean she was. Special because he had turned to her.

These are rogue bodily sensations. The sensible thing would be to get angry or turn away, to stand up for oneself. But when excitement obtains, it marks a triumph of the sexual over the self-preservative.

Freud describes a paradigmatic moment in the origination of the sexual drive. He says that the sexual leans on the self-preservative – and his example is the baby at the breast, who although no longer hungry continues to suck, in what he calls a moment of excess excitation. For LaPlanche, sexuality erupts in such a way as to constitute an attack on the ego – its effects are disorganizing and the effort to organize sexuality always bears the mark of this foundational antagonism (LaPlanche, *Life & Death in Psychoanalysis*). Ignes Sodre, from a Kleinian perspective, describes a similar process where, as a defense against terror, some people generate a world of excitement, perhaps in conjunction with a world of persons (as with Helen who became a drug dealer in college, defying what for most people would be very unsettling experiences of violence and threat), or by retreating into a daydream of fantasy where excitement can stave off the persecution of depressive feeling – sorrow, anguish, grief, guilt). Sodre describes how via a manic projective identification it becomes possible to create in the external world a reality that serves as a repository for internal damage – hatred, violence, and, I wish to add, the irreconcilable experience of terrible, insidious excitement.

9

Donald Trump broadcasts his presence. His speeches, rallies, tweets are projections that get inside of us, wreak havoc with our minds and our bodies. His communications seem to be masterful in generating their own brand of insidious excitement that weirdly leaves many of us addicted to wanting more.

I could turn the car radio off.

But instead, these last four years I have often turned it on (always when I am driving). I joke that I am getting my fix. But I do find this compulsive need to tune in, turn on the latest news, as though it is helping me make sense of things, as though I will learn something. Before I know it, I am in a state of hyperarousal, distraction, where I am overwrought, and perhaps less able to think. I am able to exclaim, certainly, and animatedly repeat what has become of a refrain of the Trump time in office: "Can you believe it?" And yet excitement of the kind Trump generates is actually meant to make perceiving, paying attention, and thinking impossible. We are meant to be swamped, worked up, agitated. And we are meant to be unable to effectively use our minds. We are meant not to know reality – to be as stirred up and confused about what is real as Trump is himself.

This reminds me – on a vastly larger scale, of course, of my two patients – who, gripped by the father's extreme actions, become unable to think. I want to suggest that insidious excitement represents to the mind an at-odds experience that torments and presses in upon the ego. This would be a form of persecution, in the sense that Klein means to suggest – an early experience of a bad object that one attempts to project, to be rid of, but that comes back to haunt and attack the ego and the mind. Sodre suggests that when the object cannot be made to die, when it continues to taunt and haunt the mind, the "ego resorts to drastic defenses which in some extreme cases can lead to effectively destroying part of the mind" (2015, 9).

But the fact is what Trump represents in America is becoming all too believable, too real, as the violence takes hold that Trump continues to deflect and deny. Trump is a symptom, which begins to make sense and locatable in the context of white supremacy, and within a history of authoritarian ploys, the denial of truth, the attack on the press, a penchant for absolute power that relies on the dismantling of law and order. As it becomes clearer what is happening, the excitement lessens as the reality settles in and becomes more disturbingly plain. With over 290,000 deaths from COVID-19 (as of this writing), and Trump's penchant for lying and misinformation, his failure of leadership becomes stunningly clear. When it fails to stave off reality, insidious excitement instead reveals a horrible truth. We are left with these truths now in the United States: a pandemic that has been appallingly mishandled and ill contained because it could not be faced and has thus sickened over six million people, the lasting ravages of racial inequality and police violence against Black people, a cynical dismantling of protections for the earth with a looming climate catastrophe, and a persistent attack on reality itself.

10

Now it's time to end, and I find myself not knowing how to write an ending. Maybe it's the sense that we don't know how this will end, that we don't know what we can count on to bring about an ending to Trump and what he signifies for us as people. At the time I am writing this, Trump has been defeated, and yet it seems there is no clear exit from Trump and what he has allowed to surface in America. But for me, as a psychoanalyst, the task has taken on somewhat of a different shape than it had three or four years ago. The task no longer seems to be thinking of my patients' minds as separate from the social world – but rather thinking about our minds in conjunction, intimately formed by the external world which we in turn inform. That the external world, whether it's our relationship to nature or sweeping socially structured hatreds like misogyny and racism, is foundationally part of how we have been formed, both as individuals and as a society. We have been formed, and we have been instructed, we have come to have beliefs based on how we have been formed and instructed. Ideologies take hold. Propaganda informs. We build walls, inside ourselves, in our minds, to protect us based on the beliefs and notions that we form. These beliefs and notions are always also social. My notion of myself as a woman cannot be separated from the fact of being brought up by a woman who herself was the product of 1950s' American values about femininity, and a father who was both deeply wounded by women and hateful and wanting to exact revenge. These are not just my parents but carriers of social meanings and imperatives that are always being transmitted. There is no end to that – but there can be consciousness: consciousness, and the capacity to think, to face both what is inside and outside, which is at the heart of being able to resist.

References

Freud, S. (1923). The Ego and the Id. *Standard Edition*, XIX.

Ogden, T. H. (2002). A New Reading of the Origins of Object-Relations Theory. *International Journal of Psychoanalysis*, 83(4):767–782.

Sodre, I. (2015). *Imaginary Existences: Psychoanalytic Exploration of Phantasy, Fiction, Dreams and Daydreams*. London: Routledge. (used with the permission of the author)

Chapter 5

A composite of King Kong and a suburban barber

Revisiting Adorno's "Freudian theory and the pattern of fascist propaganda"[1]

Samir Gandesha

There can be little doubt that today, after a long period of dormancy, authoritarian and, at times, perhaps downright fascistic elements have returned to public life with a vengeance, not just throughout Europe, the UK, and the United States but globally, most notably in Turkey, India, and Brazil. The most visually shocking image of such a return are the migrant detention centers that litter southern Europe and, more notoriously, those of neglected, terrified Central American children, allegedly subject to psychical and sexual abuse, housed in concentration camps on the United States' southern border with Mexico.[2] Today's fascism, however, for the most part, does not take the form of a mass movement geared to the violent overthrow of democracy, the installation of a one-party state, and the incarceration and liquidation of its "enemies." Rather, it entails the gradual but steady erosion of the institutions of the liberal-democratic order consisting of, inter alia, the rule of law, the separation of powers, and, in particular, the independence of the judicial branch, the freedom of the press, and the right to dissent. Taken together, such an erosion amounts to what has been called by both defenders and critics alike "illiberal democracy."[3] Against the backdrop of social and economic crises, such illiberal democracy is justified by supposedly strong leaders purporting to embody the will of an ethnonational "community" allegedly besieged by "floods" of migrants from below and a nefarious, abstract logic of finance from above. Occasionally, as in the case of figures such as George Soros, these two forces are sounded, in a paranoid key, as locked together in secret complicity.[4]

The return of fascistic elements to politics today within the context of a neoliberal capitalism, a social order in which the state has become fully marketized, in which the figure of *Homo politicus* has been eclipsed by

DOI: 10.4324/9781003214342-7

Homo economicus, requires some explanation. As Michel Foucault has shown in his lectures on biopolitics in the late 1970s, one of the dominant currents of economic thinking in the newly formed *Bundesrepublik* (Federal Republic of Germany) was the Ordoliberal economic doctrine of the Freiburg School. This doctrine held that the most effective way of preventing the return of the authoritarian state was by giving the rationality embedded in the market full reign, thus enabling it – in a kind of Keynesianism in reverse – to limit and regulate the state.[5] So how could it be that, rather than forestalling authoritarianism, neoliberalism has in fact created a salubrious environment for it to take root and flourish?

One way of explaining the relationship between authoritarianism and neoliberalism is through a reading of Theodor W. Adorno's essay "Freudian Theory and the Pattern of Fascist Propaganda" (hereafter "Freudian Theory"). While there is now a veritable "academic cottage industry" in studies on Trump and political authoritarianism,[6] such studies have largely failed, in my view, to connect their analyses with the larger problem of the specifically "damaged life" of neoliberal society.[7] The reason for this is that they focus rather too much on Trump himself – and figures like him – while overlooking the socioeconomic conditions that make such figures so attractive to a significant proportion of the electorate. This is precisely why Adorno's synthesis of socioeconomic and socialpsychological perspectives is so apposite and timely.

In "Freudian Theory," Adorno principally engages with two texts: the first is Löwenthal and Guterman's *Prophets of Deceit: A Study in the Techniques of the American Agitator* (1949),[8] and the second is Sigmund Freud's *Group Psychology and the Analysis of the Ego*, published one year before Mussolini's Partito Nazionale Fascista's March on Rome and seizure of power in 1922.[9] The first represents a content analysis of the speeches of "agitators" or far-right demagogues such as Father Coughlin and Gerald Smith, whom Löwenthal and Guterman situate in relation to a typology of responses to socioeconomic problems. The second seeks to show how the individual's orientation to the reality principle can be short-circuited via the sense of power and security afforded by virtue of membership in a mass.

How is it, as Adorno glosses Freud, "that modern men [and women] revert to patterns of behavior which flagrantly contradict their own rational level and the present level of enlightened technological civilization."[10] In order for such reversion, or *regression*, to be fostered, an *artificial* social bond must be created based upon the pleasure principle, which is to say, "actual or vicarious gratifications individuals obtain from surrendering to a mass."[11] Adorno highlights the way in which Hitler refers to the passive, feminine role of his followers at Nazi meetings, suggesting that, at least in part, unconscious homosexual desire, plays a role in the creation of the social bond. Later in the essay, though, as we shall see, Adorno will provide a somewhat different, more persuasive analysis.

Freud helps to *explain* what most other forms of social psychology merely *describe*: the potentiality for "short-circuiting" of the relation between "violent emotions" and "violent actions." The particular nature of the social bond, in Freud's view, enables the individual to throw off the "repression of his unconscious instincts."[12] Insofar as Freud points to the interpenetration of the archaic and the modern, the mythical and enlightened elements of social psychology, he anticipates the argument of *Dialectic of Enlightenment*. Archaic myth and modern enlightenment converge in the idea of *sacrifice*. The key difference is that the process of enlightenment through disenchantment and rationalization[13] entails the increasing "introjection" or internalization of sacrifice understood as "self-renunciation" or repression. This means that in order to survive, the individual must adjust to external imperatives and as a result renounce the aspiration to happiness (*Eudaimonia*).

It is, therefore, the civilizing process itself or "second nature" that produces the revolt of "first nature." In recent decades, Freud's supposedly "negative" account of repression has been challenged by such figures as Jacques Lacan, Gilles Deleuze, and Felix Guattari.[14] Nowhere has this account been more forcefully criticized, however, than in Foucault's introductory first volume of *The History of Sexuality*. Here Foucault takes Freud's "repressive hypothesis" to task as a purely negative account of power positing that social and historical forces restrict the expression of "instinct" or "nature" from a position exterior to it; implying that, for resistance, "nothing less than a transgression of laws, a lifting of prohibitions, an irruption of speech, a reinstating of pleasure within reality, and a whole new economy in the mechanisms of power will be required."[15] Adorno, in contrast, shows the way in which Freud's own account of repression is much more subtle and entails the interpenetration and mutual conditioning of nature and history in the very operation of psychical agencies. As

Adorno suggests in his gloss of *Civilization and Its Discontents*: "As a rebellion against civilization, *fascism is not simply the reoccurrence of the archaic but its reproduction in and by civilization itself.*"[16]

Returning to the question of the nature of the social bond, it seems doubtful, however, that an account of such a bond grounded in libido could provide a convincing account of Nazism insofar as Hitler replaces the *loving* with a *threatening* and *punishing* father. While there is a connection here to Freud's conception of the primal father in *Totem and Taboo*,[17] it is necessary to explain the nature and content of fascist propaganda which deliberately aims to reactivate the individual's "archaic inheritance"; that is, it is manufactured and constantly reinforced. If under modern conditions in which the guiding principle of public life is individualism, how is it that individuals can be induced to relinquish their own individuality and therewith their rational interests including, in extreme cases, their interest in *self-preservation* itself? This is a question that becomes especially pertinent under the hyperindividualistic conditions of the neoliberal order. Or, to reiterate: How do people become a mass?[18] The answer that Adorno provides, via Freud, is that this happens through the mechanism of *identification*.

This sits in some amount of tension with Adorno's earlier suggestion of the followers as occupying a passive position and, therefore, evincing homosexual *desire* for the leader.[19] Drawing on Erik H. Erikson's work, Adorno suggests that the agitator appears to be the "enlargement" of the subject's own personality rather than simply the image of the father whose authority had already started significantly to diminish in the interwar period.[20] Contemporary fascist leaders, then, are not simply the manifestations of an ambivalent image of the father or the domineering head of the "primal horde" who, through the threat of violence, establishes a monopoly on women but, rather, are what Adorno calls "great little men."[21]

The process of *identification* is inextricable from that of *idealization*. In *Prophets of Deceit*, the authors emphasize the way in which the agitator exploits the negative affects of his followers. Löwenthal and Guterman argue that "Unlike the usual advocate of social change, the agitator, while exploiting a state of discontent, does not try to define the nature of that discontent by means of rational concepts. Rather, he increases his audience's disorientation by destroying all rational guideposts and by proposing that they instead adopt seemingly spontaneous modes of behavior."[22] Adorno explains more specifically how these frustrations and anxieties emerge in the first place and how fascist propaganda exploits them by promoting identification through idealization.

In what is the crux of his argument, Adorno suggests that frustration has to do with the "characteristic modern conflict between a strongly developed rational, self-preserving ego agency and the continuous failure to satisfy their own ego demands."[23] In other words, the conflicts stem from the contradiction lying at the heart of bourgeois or liberal-democratic society between the *political* ideal of individual autonomy or self-determination through democratic institutions, on the one hand, and a purely negative conception freedom that characterizes capitalist relations of production, on the other. As Adorno presciently suggests in *Negative Dialectics*:

> The more freedom the subject – and the community of subjects – ascribes to itself, the greater its responsibility; and before this responsibility it must fail in a bourgeois life which in practice has never yet endowed a subject with the unabridged autonomy accorded to it in theory. Hence the subject must feel guilty.[24]

As a result of this contradiction between the *ideality* and the *actuality* of freedom, the promise of and failure to realize a self-determined life, the individual experiences frustration and discontent resulting from in the face of his own ego-ideal or idealized sense of self often deriving from the imago of a parent. Such a conflict constitutes a key aspect of the "damaged life" of late capitalist societies the anatomy of which Adorno lays bare in *Minima Moralia*.[25] "This conflict," Adorno argues, "results in strong narcissistic impulses which can be absorbed and satisfied only through idealization as the partial transfer of the narcissistic libido to the object."[26] The collective adulation and love of the leader is the way in which frustrated modern subjects overcome their negative self-images resulting from the failure to approximate their ego ideal – the gap between ego and ego ideal becomes, in other words, unbearable. The leader's aura of omnipotence, therefore, owes less to the "archaic inheritance" of the primal father and more to the individuals' narcissistic investment in collectivity resulting from this failure.

In order for such collective identification through idealization to be successful, the leader must be "absolutely narcissistic," that is, someone who *is loved but does not love in turn*. This is what explains the agitator's disinterest – in contrast to revolutionary and reformer alike – in presenting a positive political program outlining concrete policy proposals as Löwenthal and Guterman point out. In place of the latter, which would suggest some minimal concern for the needs of the followers, there is only the "paradoxical program of threat and denial."[27]

At the same time, the leader embodies a contradiction between, on the one hand, appearing to be a superhuman figure and, on the other, an average person – as Adorno puts it memorably, in reference to Adolph Hitler, "a composite of King Kong and the suburban barber."[28] This is key to understanding the psychological structure of fascism: these two dimensions mirror a split in the follower's narcissistic ego: one part of which attaches to "King Kong," the other, to the "suburban barber," and is retained by the follower. It is thus that the leader represents the follower, though, as his *enlargement*. Fascist propaganda is constructed around the basic concept of the "'great little man,' a person who suggests both omnipotence and the idea that he is just one of the folks, a plain, red-blooded American untainted."[29]

It is in this way that Adorno provides an account of the guiding concept of *The Authoritarian Personality*: that personality type characterized both by subordination to the "strong" (suburban barber) and domination over the "weak" (King Kong). In this, the structure of social character reproduces the contradiction lying at the heart of bourgeois society between the theory of autonomy or freedom and the practice of heteronomy or unfreedom. The image of the "great little man" therefore, according to Adorno, addresses the follower's:

> twofold wish to submit to authority and to be the authority himself. This fits into a world in which irrational control is exercised though it has lost its inner conviction through universal enlightenment. The people who obey the dictators also sense that the latter are superfluous. They reconcile this contradiction through the assumption that they themselves are the ruthless oppressor.[30]

This is perfectly expressed in Hitler's slogan, which lays bare the essence of the ambivalence of the authoritarian or sadomasochistic personality type: "*Verantwortung nach oben, Autorität nach unten* ["responsibility toward above, authority toward below]."[31] Or, as Adorno writes in Chapter 19 of *The Authoritarian Personality*, "The identification of the 'authoritarian' character with strength is concomitant with rejection of everything that is 'down.'"[32]

The more superfluous the idea of the dictator within formally democratic and egalitarian – though substantively unequal societies based on private ownership and control of the means of production – the more emphasis will be placed precisely on the dictator's *ersatz* quality. Such phoniness is maintained in the form of the hollow shell of the "artificial group" of the religious institution. The hierarchy of religion, stripped of its spiritual essence, is taken over by fascism, in particular its emphasis on the distinction between "sheep and goats," insiders and outsiders, and also, therefore, on its deployment of negative libido. In other words, the emphasis on love within the Christian religion, which was nonetheless also based upon hatred towards those who remained beyond the faith, is now, divested of even the appearance of *Agape* or fellowship, transformed into an almost exclusively *negatively* integrating function.[33] This enables fascism to play its "unity trick," which is to say, it elides differences *within* the group (other than the extant hierarchy) by emphasizing differences *between* the group and those who remain outside of it. Such a trick culminates in what Adorno terms a "regressive egalitarianism" – all members of the "national community" should *equally be denied* individual pleasures. The social bond is, as it were, solidified through a shared introjection of sacrifice or the renunciation of the aspiration to a sensuously fulfilled life. The Nazis' repeated and hyperbolic demands for sacrifice for the "Fatherland," which echo every form of nationalism particularly when it comes to war, bear this out.[34]

Adorno touches upon a key technique by which fascist propaganda emphasizes the difference between insider and outsider groups: namely the repeated use of images of lower animals such as insects and vermin to characterize foreigners, in particular Jews and refugees. Drawing not only on Freud but also on Otto Rank's observations that in dream symbolism insects and vermin signify younger siblings, in fact, babies, and such symbolism scarcely conceals negative cathexis. Yet, at the same time, such brothers and sisters have identified with one another through a shared love object, namely the leader, and therefore must direct or project this negative cathexis outward beyond the group.

Here, one might argue, as Horkheimer and Adorno suggest in *Dialectic of Enlightenment*, that it is not just the displacement of contempt experienced by the followers themselves that is projected outward in the image of lower animals but also a direct evocation in propaganda of powerful and affectively charged tropes of abjection. As Julia Kristeva suggests it has, ultimately, to do with the pre-Oedipal relation to the maternal body and, in turn, with the transgression of a boundary and the ensuing production of disgust.[35]

> But anything natural which has not been absorbed into utility by passing through the cleansing channels of conceptual order – the screech of the stylus on slate which sets the teeth on edge, the *haut goût* which brings to mind filth and corruption, the sweat which appears on the brow of the diligent – whatever is not quite assimilated, or infringes the commands in which the progress of centuries has been sedimented, is felt as intrusive and arouses a compulsive aversion.[36]

The abject and "compulsive aversion" it evokes has to do with a compulsive fear of self-dissolution.[37] This constitutes the drive to eliminate the nonidentical or that which cannot be conceptually grasped without remainder; in the attempt to bring nature under the sway of technical control and mastery, whatever residue of uncontrolled or uncontrollable nature remains elicits an automatic response of revulsion. The very signs of destructiveness that fascism itself substantively embodies is projected outward onto its victims; fascism, in this sense, is the paranoid performance of the victimizer who compulsively assumes the role of victim.

Abjection is employed as a propagandistic technique, in other words, to portray the other as a dangerous contagion who threatens the health and the very life of the body politic and must be both spiritually and physically excluded, by force if necessary. Traces of offensive yet secretly desired "nature" are projected onto the stranger which, as a result, becomes his stigma. Once so projected, the "other" can then be contained, excluded, and in extreme case, ultimately "liquidated" or "exterminated" like pests or vermin. Through the process, extirpating the nonidentical, the identity of the ethnonational "community" is confirmed and stabilized.

Adorno addresses the question of how the agitators came to such precise knowledge of group psychology without, themselves, having the intellectual wherewithal to access it? The answer is that, given the psychological identity between the leader and the led, the agitator accesses mass psychology through his *own* psychology. The key difference, though, is that the former evinces "a capacity to express without inhibitions what is latent in them, rather than by any natural superiority."[38] The authoritarian leader is an "oral" personality type that, according to Freud, seeks gratification through eating, drinking, and other oral activities including speaking. The *aggressive* oral type is hostile and verbally abusive toward others. The agitator evinces a "capacity to speak incessantly and to befool the other."[39] The incessant nature of such speech leads it to void itself of sense and becomes magical; it casts a spell over its listeners and plays on the followers "archaic inheritance." The power he exercises is, paradoxically, indicative of his powerlessness insofar as it intimates ego weakness rather than strength laying bare his unconscious drives. Yet this, at the same time, plays into the very image of the leader as the enlargement of the follower's own ego. "In order successfully to meet the unconscious dispositions of his audience," Adorno argues, "the agitator so to speak turns his own unconscious outward."[40]

The fit between the agitator's techniques and the "psychological basis of their aim" is assisted by larger transformations in society that also contribute to the increasing passivity of the individual, which is to say, the decline of her capacity for experience through the consolidation of the culture industry as a whole.[41] The standardization that lies at the heart of the culture industry harmonizes perfectly with a key attribute of the authoritarian personality, namely: "stereotypy" and "their infantile wish for endless, unaltered repetition."[42] The link between European high culture and the culture industry, for Adorno, can be located in the easily recallable *leitmotiv*, originated by protofascist composer, Richard Wagner, which he likens to "component parts of factory-assembled products: musical Fordism."[43] In order to mobilize the masses against their very own interests, fascist propaganda tends to circumvent "discursive thinking" and "mobilize[s] irrational, unconscious, regressive forces."[44] In this, it is aided greatly by the culture industry that already has greatly diminished the human capacity for autonomy and spontaneity.

What are we to make of Adorno's social psychological account of fascist propaganda today? There are broadly three areas in which Adorno's reflections are illuminating: (1) populism, (2) analysis of contemporary "agitators," and, finally, (3) the culture industry. Before addressing these in turn, however, it is important to consider the limitations of such reflections as well. As I have argued elsewhere, the sociological assumptions of Adorno's appropriation of Freud, specifically Pollock's concept of "state capitalism" – according to which the state's role is to manage the crisis tendencies of capitalism – must be rethought in the period characterized by the obsolescence of Keynesianism.[45] Moreover, Adorno's unmediated reliance on the orthodox Freudian account of drive theory and on the concept of the Oedipal conflict requires rethinking and reconstruction insofar as Freud's atomistic, Hobbesian ontology does not sit particularly well with a *social* ontology indebted to Hegel and Marx.[46] What remains of enduring importance, however, is Adorno's discussion of the basic contradiction lying at the heart of capitalist democracy and the way in which authoritarianism today reemerges as a powerful, if false, response to it in the face of a paucity of viable alternatives which comprises what Marcuse called one-dimensionality society.[47]

The objective condition for the stubborn persistence of authoritarianism is the contradiction lying at the heart of liberal-democratic society between the democratic principle of *egalitarianism*, on the one hand, and the liberal conception of negative freedom, on the other. The neoliberal, financialized form of capitalism, which has been in place roughly since the mid-1970s, has dramatically sharpened this contradiction insofar as the *citoyen* (Brown's *Homo politicus*) has become eclipsed by *homo economicus*, understood now as the "entrepreneur of himself."[48] The latter is forced to take more responsibility for herself, yet, at the same time, has access to fewer resources with which to *actualize* this responsibility in any meaningful sense. On average, rates of growth in high-income countries have dropped precipitously since the 1960s (4.3% p.a.) falling to 2.8% in the 1970s, 2.3 in the 1980s, 1.8% in the 1990s, and 1.2% in the 2000s.[49] Accordingly, since the 1970s, wages for the vast majority have remained stagnant, not even keeping pace with inflation,[50] while welfare state provisions have declined considerably and social services as well as higher education have become more costly. What has filled this vacuum is growing financialization and debt.[51] Individuals constantly fall short of their ego ideals, as a result of which there is a corresponding proliferation of guilt, anxiety, frustration, and ultimately anger.[52]

So, ironically, rather than forestalling authoritarian tendencies, as West German *Ordoliberalism* maintained it would, the advent of neoliberalism has proven to be particularly fertile ground for the germination of neo- and postfascist political movements.[53] In a way that echoes Moishe Postone's analysis of the implicit anti-Semitism at the heart of one-sided criticisms of finance capital (abstract labor) from the standpoint of the working class (concrete labor),[54] Neel argues that:

> As one of the poorest generations in recent history, debt and rent are the defining features of our lives. It is this fact that makes the current

incarnation of the far right an actual threat, because it increases the probability that some variant of present-day Patriot politics might actually find a mass base, as a program formulated specifically to oppose the extraction of rents from an unwilling population in the far hinterland is translated into a more general opposition of rents as a primary form of exploitation in contemporary capitalism.[55]

The contradiction between autonomy in the "political" realm or formal structures of representative democracy, as the citizen of a nation-state, and increasing heteronomy within the "economic" realm becomes evermore unbearable. As Adorno states in "The Meaning of Working Through the Past":

> Fascism essentially cannot be derived from subjective dispositions. The economic order, and to a great extent also the economic organization modeled upon it, now as then renders the majority of people dependent upon conditions beyond their control and thus maintains them in a state of political immaturity.

He goes on to argue:

> If they want to live, then no other avenue remains but to adapt, submit themselves to the given conditions; they must negate precisely that autonomous subjectivity to which the idea of democracy appeals; they can preserve themselves only if they renounce their self . . . The necessity of such adaptation, of identification with the given, the status quo, with power as such, creates the potential for totalitarianism.[56]

The idealization and identification with the aggressor can be regarded as a (false) solution to this contradiction. In the "great little man," the follower is mesmerized by an enlarged image of himself before which he bows down.

Populism emerges as a response to the ensuing legitimacy crisis of the neoliberal order.[57] Rather than dismissing and vilifying this political formation *tout court*,[58] it is worthwhile distinguishing between left and right versions of populism. Adorno helps us arrive at criteria that enable us to do precisely this by emphasizing that the process by which "people become a mass" is of vital importance, insofar as the foregoing discussion, as we have seen, is geared to understanding the role of the agitator in contrast with the reformer or revolutionary who, like contemporary left populists such a Jeremy Corbyn and Bernie Sanders, seek to genuinely outline concrete policy objectives and in the process respond to their followers' democratic demands, by specifically taking aim at *socioeconomic inequality*. In contrast, the agitators obviate such interests by emotional appeals to racist and exclusionary conceptions of the people and in the process transform them into a mass.[59]

Adorno's account of the mechanism of *identification through idealization* is especially helpful in understanding a host of right-populist leaders who appear to embody the oxymoronic idea of a "great little man" such as the Filipino President Rodrigo Duterte, Indian Prime Minister Narendra Modi, Brazilian President Jair Bolsonaro, and British Prime Minister Boris Johnson. But no one embodies this oxymoron more clearly than the former president of the United States. Donald J. Trump exemplifies the "great little man" and is consequently regarded by his supporters as a larger-than-life version of themselves. But could it be said their followers have internalized the logic of self-sacrifice or renunciation? Isn't it the case that they are aggressively standing up to the "elites" that have sacrificed them at the altar of globalization? Trump may not explicitly demand self-sacrifice but in supporting him most, though perhaps not all, of his supporters nevertheless sacrifice their own interest, for example, in the continued viability of the Affordable Care Act, at the altar of "Making America Great Again"? The massive tax cut for the ultrarich will materially harm them. To this one could add the opioid crisis that keeps deepening among poor whites and, as a result, their life expectancy is dropping rapidly.[60] Trump's supporters could be called "self-sacrificing" in a very literal way. Therefore, when the political establishment attacks him for his somewhat tenuous grasp of the English language, sartorial *faux pas*, gustatory blunders, fake hair, etc., it backfires and only reinforces the idea of the establishment's contempt not only for the president but for the "demos," the people who idealize and identify with him; it reinforces their identification with the aggressor. So, despite being presented with evidence that his presidency has harmed them materially, their support remains as more or less unabated.[61]

Trump is clearly an aggressive oral type who tweets incessantly, often issuing threats to his own political rivals such as Hillary Clinton ("Lock her Up")[62] or, perhaps more disturbingly, encouraging his followers at a recent rally to direct the chant "Send her Back!" at the Somali American Representative from Minnesota, Ilhan Omar, as well as Alexandria

Ocasio-Cortez, Rashida Tlaib, and Ayanna Pressley who were all born in the United States.[63] The incessantly contradictory nature of Trump's speech eviscerates language as the genuine medium of truth claims – this violence enacted on language itself is key to understanding our increasingly post-truth era perhaps even more than the rise of far-right media outlets such as Breitbart News. The slogan of "Make American Great Again," moreover, draws upon the rhetoric of an *authentic*, falsely concrete American life, liberated from frighteningly abstract, inscrutable, global processes signified by the barely concealed anti-Semitic trope of "the swamp."

The fetishization of the wall on the U.S. southern border with Mexico represents an extreme expression of authoritarian populism globally, manifesting a heightened hysteria directed at those driven to migrate by geopolitical and political economic catastrophes. Despite his claims that climate change is a hoax or conspiracy, Trump seems to be preparing for a worsening crisis of climate refugees. So people are transformed into a mass by virtue of a common object of affection that is inextricable from the negative libido generated by way of projection of strangeness, which is to say, illness, contagion, and ultimately danger (the abject), onto the outsider. Such negative libido is bolstered by references to "shithole countries" and statements that "all Haitians have AIDS."[64] Moreover, in addition to demonizing refugees as an "invasion," telling four nonwhite members of Congress to go back to the "broken and crime infested place from which they came,"[65] Trump referred to Baltimore, the home of Rep. Elijah Cummings (D-Md.) as "disgusting, rat and rodent infested mess" that was "far worse and more dangerous" than the conditions at the southern border.[66] French author Jean Raspail, who has profoundly influenced Trump's former advisor Steve Bannon portrayed a Europe in the near future overrun by the disposed of the Third World, symbolized by defecating and fornicating Indian migrants in his racist, dystopian novel *Camp of the Saints*.[67] One can see in Trump's rhetoric not only overt misogyny ("Grab 'em by the pussy") but also the hatred of ambiguity, which might explain the ferocity of attacks on LGBTQ+ communities, trans people in particular.

Perhaps most presciently, Adorno (with Horkheimer) draws attention to the elective affinity between the authoritarian personality and the culture industry. The condition for the possibility of people being transformed into the mass is the passivity that follows from the gradual but steady weakening of the critical function of the ego. In their account of the culture industry, Horkheimer and Adorno show the way in which the former replaces what Kant called the "transcendental schema," according to which the sensible manifold is related to concepts through the activity of the imagination, by:

> ready-made thought models, the termini technici which provide them with iron rations following the decay of language. *The perceiver is no longer present in the process of perception.* He or she is incapable of the active passivity of cognition, in which categorial elements are appropriately reshaped by preformed conventional schemata and vice versa, so that justice is done to the perceived object.[68]

Today, we can see this in the recent digitization of the culture industry in recent decades. The algorithm has come to replace the transcendental schema in organizing the manifold of sensible intuition. In place of Fordist mass production and standardization, it now generates difference and heterogeneity tailored specifically to the whims and tastes of each individual. Yet the algorithm is a code that also nonetheless locks into place a logic of repetition and stereotypy, often confirming, deepening, and reinforcing the subjective prejudices mentioned above through the creation of so-called "echo chambers" or unconscious manifestations of confirmation bias.

Just as twentieth-century fascists used radio and film to spread their propaganda, contemporary agitators evince a predilection for the use of Twitter, Facebook, Instagram and What'sApp which, amongst other things, enables them to effectively bypass the putatively rational and critical scrutiny of serious journalists, intellectuals, and academics and communicate often unconscious wishes and desires directly to their followers themselves. Of course, while social media has been taken up by progressive forces to organize and mobilize against authoritarian regimes, for example in Iran in 2009 and then subsequently in the Arab Spring and Occupy, it has become the means by which the far-right has successfully manipulated voters as the Cambridge Analytica scandal has shown, according to which this British consulting firm engaged in the mining by accessing millions of Facebook profiles to access personal data without their consent for the purpose of political advertising.[69] WikiLeaks' release of hacked e-mails in the final stage of the 2016 election, as the Mueller report has shown, was not inconsequential to its outcome.[70] Social media, moreover, has provided the infrastructure for right-wing populist parties and movements to spread fake news and misinformation. It could be said to create new types of what Freud called "artificial groups" that undermine the reality-testing capacity and therefore critical capacity of the ego.[71] It is both the medium and expression of a "turning outward" of the unconscious.[72]

Furthermore, online message boards such as 4chan and 8chan enable precisely the "short-circuiting" of the relation between "violent emotions" and "violent actions." Taking inspiration from the far-right mass murderers Anders Breivik and the Brenton Tarrant (the Christchurch mass murderer), copycat White Supremacists in Europe and North America, particularly the United States, have discussed and planned their attacks on this message board before executing them in the real world. Participants discuss topics such as "Target Selection" (most effective ways to maximize body counts), and the online group compares and celebrates the numbers of casualties from shooting to shooting in what *The New York Times* calls "a gamification of mass murder." Attackers often post manifestos and, indeed, in the case of Christchurch provide a live feed of the attack in real time. The aim is, of course, to appeal to the unconscious aggressive impulses of others who form part of the virtual artificial group.[73]

Adorno's examination of the stubborn persistence in the postwar period of the authoritarian personality type was oriented toward articulating "a new categorical imperative after Auschwitz" – that the Holocaust never repeat itself.[74] Key to this, for Adorno, was the Kantian idea of enlightenment understood as *Mündigkeit* which means political maturity or the notion that the citizen must be empowered to speak for herself as an *autonomous* subject.[75] This means having the capacity to break the compulsion to repeat embodied in the culture industry. The citizen is capable of speaking for himself, according to Adorno, "because he has thought for himself and is not merely repeating someone else; he stands free of any guardian."[76] *Mündigkeit* is vital, moreover, for the citizen's capacity to resist conformity to prevailing opinion and stands in a close relation to what Kant called reflective judgment. At the same time, Adorno emphasizes, with Nietzsche (and, later, Kristeva), that we are all "strangers to ourselves." This means that aspects of our experience, for example, pain, trauma, and suffering, can never be made fully transparent, can never enter into concepts without some excess or remainder escaping their grasp. In this, as the psychoanalyst Christopher Bollas has suggested, the genuine plurality of democracy, must echo the plurality within the mind.[77] Such a plurality, however, will not truly come into its own until the opposition between liberalism and democracy is transcended and overcome.

Notes

1. An earlier version of this chapter was presented at the Institute for Philosophy in the Academy of Sciences, Prague, Czech Republic in June 2019. I would like to thank Joe Grim Feinberg and Pavel Siostrzonek in particular for their helpful comments in that context. I would also like to thank John Abromeit, Ian Angus, Hilda Fernandez, Jay Frankel, Marty Jay, Am Johal, Claudia Leeb, and Jonathan Sklar for their very helpful comments on earlier drafts as well. Any errors of fact and/or interpretation are mine alone.
2. Mathew Haag, *Thousands of Immigrant Children Said They Were Sexually Abused in U.S. Detention Centres, Report Says*, February 27, 2019. Retrieved August 16, 2019, from: www.nytimes.com/2019/02/27/us/immigrant-children-sexual-abuse.html.
3. See Viktor Orban. Retrieved from: www.theguardian.com/commentisfree/2019/may/16/trump-orban-democracy-us-hungary Also Christopher Browning. Retrieved from: www.nybooks.com/articles/2018/10/25/suffocation-of-democracy/.
4. A good example of this is Hungary's antimigrant legislation called the "Stop Soros Law." Retrieved from: www.bbc.com/news/world-europe-44887638.
5. Michel Foucault, *The Birth of Biopolitics: Lectures at the College de France 1978–79*, trans. Graham Burchell (Basingstoke: Palgrave Macmillan, 2008), 129–184.
6. Richard Wolin, *Our "Prophet of Deceit": WWII Era Social Scientists Explained Trump's Appeal*. Retrieved from: www.chronicle.com/article/Our-Prophet-of-Deceit/238176 (Accessed July 13, 2019). See the section of The Frankfurt School and the New Right, *Logos Journal*, 16(1–2) (2017). Retrieved from: http://logosjournal.com/2017-vol-16-nos-1-2/ as well as that found in *Public Seminar* One of the best essays of the latter happens to be by Jay M. Bernstein in which he suggests that Adorno's "Freudian Theory" reads as "if it was written precisely in order to address the Trump phenomenon." Yet, what he tends to de-emphasize is that the Trump phenomenon is made possible by a distinctive set of socio-economic arrangements that are global. "Adorno's Uncanny Account of Trump's Authoritarian Personality," Public seminar, October 5, 2017. Retrieved July 23, from: www.publicseminar.org/2017/10/adornos-uncanny-analysis-of-trumps-authoritarian-personality/. See also *Authoritarianism: Three Inquiries*, and the excellent article by Claudia Leeb, A Festival for Frustrated Egos: The Rise of Trump from an Early Frankfurt School Critical Theory Perspective. In Marc Benjamin Sable & Angel Jarmillo Torres (eds.), *Trump and Political Philosophy: Patriotism, Cosmopolitanism and Civic Virtue* (Cham, Switzerland: Palgrave Macmillan, 2018), 297–314.
7. This has been recently described with tremendous eloquence and insight by Phil A. Neel in *Hinterland: America's New Landscape of Class and Conflict* (London: Reaction Books, 2018).
8. Prophets of Deceit, *A Study in the Techniques of the American Agitator* (New York: Norton, 1949).
9. Sigmund Freud, *Group Psychology and the Analysis of the Ego* (New York: W. W. Norton: 1990).
10. Bernstein, 121.

11 Bernstein, 122.
12 Bernstein, 122.
13 As, for example, analyzed by Max Weber in his *Protestant Ethic and the Spirit of Capitalism* (Oxford: Oxford University Press, 2010), his study of the crucial role of puritanism in the emergence of capitalism in western Europe.
14 See, for example, *Anti-Oedipus: Capitalism and Schizophrenia*, trans. Robert Hurley & Mark Seem (London: Penguin, 2009).
15 Michel Foucault, *The History of Sexuality Volume I: An Introduction*, trans. Robert Hurley (New York: Pantheon Books, 1978), 5.
16 Bernstein, 122; emphasis added.
17 Sigmund Freud, *Totem and Taboo* (New York: W. W. Norton and Company, 1990).
18 On this question, see Siegfried Kracauer's 1938 essay on fascism Siegfried Kracauer, Totalitäre Propaganda, ed. Bernd Stiegler (Frankurt: Suhrkamp, 2013), as well as John Abromeit, Siegfried Kracauer and the Early Frankfurt School's Analysis of Fascism as Right-Wing Populism. In Pierre-François Noppen, Gérard Raulet, et Iain MacDonald (eds.), *Théorie critique de la propagande* (Paris: Editions de la Maison des science de l'homme, forthcoming).
19 For example, in his classic account of the Oedipal conflict, the male child *identifies* with the father and hence wishes to supplant him on account of the boy's *desire* for his mother. Freud discusses this in a number of texts, but for our purposes the most important is *The Ego and the Id*, trans. Joan Riviere (New York: W. W. Norton: 1960), 33–34.
20 As Horkheimer, Marcuse, and Fromm had already suggested in their research on the family in the 1930s, and social psychologists such as Alexander Mitscherlich would subsequently emphasize in the 1960s *Society Without the Father: A Contribution to Social Psychology* (New York: Perennial Press, 1992).
21 This diminution of individual agency is accelerated through the war and is a phenomenon that can be understood today with transformations in the displacement of the industrial by service sector and the ensuing "feminization" of labor, leading to a profound crisis of heterosexual masculinity. Such a crisis is key to understanding the return of a misogynistic far-right today and the appeal of its spokespersons such as Carl Jung–influenced psychologist, Jordan Peterson. Retrieved from: www.nytimes.com/2018/05/18/style/jordan-peterson-12-rules-for-life.html. See also Harrison Fluss's critique in *Jacobin*. Retrieved from: www.jacobinmag.com/2018/02/jordan-peterson-enlightenment-nietzsche-alt-right.
22 Prophets of Deceit, 6.
23 Bernstein, 126.
24 T. W. Adorno, *Negative Dialectics*, trans. E. B. Ashton (New York: Continuum Books, 1981), 221.
25 T. W. Adorno, *Minima Moralia: Reflections on Damaged Life*, trans. E. F. N. Jephcott (London: Verso, 2008).
26 Bernstein, 126.
27 Bernstein, 127.
28 Bernstein, 127.

29 Bernstein, 127.
30 Bernstein, 127–128.
31 Bernstein, 128.
32 T. W. Adorno et al., *The Authoritarian Personality* (New York: Norton Library, 1950), 762.
33 In the *Genealogy of Morals*, Nietzsche saw this dynamic very clearly, referring to it as the *ressentiment* lying at the heart of the "slave morality" which Christianity took over from Judaism whereby the identity of the insider group is constituted by the pure negation of the outsider group.
34 While it would be mistaken to draw too close a parallel between fascism and contemporary identity politics of the Left, the "unity trick" can certainly be seen in the latter. See Samir Gandesha, Not Only the Difference Between Identities but the Differences Within Them. *openDemocracy*, November 19, 2018. Retrieved from: www.opendemocracy.net/en/not-only-difference-between-identities-but-differences-within-them/.
35 Julia Kristeva, *The Powers of Horror: An Essay on Abjection*, trans. Leon S. Roudiez (New York: Columbia University Press, 1982).
36 Max Horkheimer & Theodor W. Adorno, *Dialectic of Enlightenment*, trans. E. F. N. Jephcott (Paolo Alto: Stanford University Press, 2002), 147–148.
37 This lies at the heart of Theweleit's analysis of the writings of the members of the Freikorps in *Male Fantasies Volume 1: Women, Floods, Bodies, History* (Minneapolis: University of Minnesota Press, 1987); *Male Fantasies Volume 2: Psychoanalyzing the White Terror* (Minneapolis: University of Minnesota Press, 1989). See also Laura Marks' excellent discussion of this work in this volume.
38 Bernstein, 132.
39 Bernstein, 132.
40 Bernstein, 133.
41 While Adorno doesn't mention it, there was a direct line of transmission of psychoanalysis to the culture industry precisely through the figure of Edward Louis Bernays – Freud's nephew. Bernays was the originator of psychoanalytically informed propaganda techniques for modern industry. This propaganda was called advertising. See Adam Curtis's film *Century of the Self* (2002).
42 Bernstein, 133.
43 T. W. Adorno, *Essays on Music*, ed. Richard Leppert (Berkeley and London: University of California Press, 2002), 534.
44 Bernstein, 134.
45 Samir Gandesha, Identifying with the Aggressor: From the "Authoritarian" to the "Neo-Liberal" Personality. *Constellations*, 25(2018):147–164. See also John Abromeit, Frankfurt School Critical Theory and the Persistence of Right-wing Populism in the United States. In Jeremiah Morelock (ed.), *Critical Theory and Authoritarian Populism* (London: University of Westminster Press, 2018) in which he discusses in some detail the shift from the Fordist-Keynesian to the neoliberal period and how this has created conditions much more propitious for RWP.
46 See the work of Jessica Benjamin which challenges normative assumptions of the thesis of the "society without fathers" and, more recently, Chiara Bottici's

contribution to Public Seminar's Roundtable on "Freudian Theory". Retrieved from: www.publicseminar.org/2017/10/adorno-with-freud-adorno-beyond-freud/.
47 Herbert Marcuse, *One Dimensional Man: Studies in the Ideology of Advanced Industrial Society* (London: Routledge, 1991).
48 Foucault, 2008, 226.
49 Neel, 14.
50 See Thomas Piketty, *Capital in the Twenty-First Century* (Cambridge: Belknap Press, 2017) in which he shows that the average return on capital far outstrips the increase in the rise of wages leading to a logic of widening socioeconomic inequality, which reverses the anomalous trend of the *trente glorieuses*.
51 See Costas Lapavitsas, *Crisis in the Eurozone* (London: Verso, 2012); Maurizio Lazzarato, *The Making of the Indebted Man: An Essay on the Neoliberal Condition* (Cambridge, MA: Semiotext(e) Books, 2012); Maurizio Lazzarato, *Governing by Debt* (Cambridge, MA: Semiotext(e) Books, 2015).
52 As Jay Frankel and Lynne Layton have argued, this also leads to shame – a common response to trauma that results from the feeling that there is something wrong with oneself. See J. Frankel, The Persistent Sense of Being Bad: The Moral Dimension of Identification with the Aggressor. In A. Harris & S. Kuchuck (eds.), *The Legacy of Sandor Ferenczi: From Ghost to Ancestor* (New York: Routledge, 2015), 204–222.
53 On the idea of "post-fascism" see Enzo Traverso, *The New Faces of Fascism* (London: Verso, 2019).
54 Moishe Postone, Zionism, Anti-Semitism and the Left: An Interview with Moishe Postone. *Krisis*, June 27, 2010. Retrieved July 23, 2019, from: www.krisis.org/2010/zionism-anti-semitism-and-the-left/.
55 Neel, 44.
56 The Meaning of Working Through the Past, 98–99.
57 See Adam Tooze, *Crashed: How a Decade of Financial Crises Changed the World* (New York: Viking, 2018).
58 See the Eric Fassin's, *Populism Left and Right* (Chicago: Prickly Paradigm Press, 2019), which considers populism of both left and right to be fundamentally a politics of resentment.
59 Samir Gandesha, Understanding Left and Right Populism. *Zeitschrift für kritische Theorie* 46–47(2018):214–235. and reprinted in *Critical Theory and Authoritarian Populism*, ed. Jeremiah Morelock (London: University of Westminster Press, 2018), 49–70.
60 Josh Katz and Margo Sanger-Katz, *"The Numbers Are so Staggering": Overdose Deaths Set a Record Last Year*, November 29, 2018. Retrieved August 16, 2019, from: www.nytimes.com/interactive/2018/11/29/upshot/fentanyl-drug-overdose-deaths.html.
61 Trump's Core Supporters Are About to Be Handed the Bill for Tax Reform. *CNBC*, November 16, 2017. Retrieved August 11, 2019, from: www.cnbc.com/2017/11/16/trumps-core-supporters-are-about-to-be-handed-the-bill-for-tax-reform.html.

62 Uttered not just in the 2016 presidential campaign but reiterated in Trump's reelection announcement in Florida. Retrieved July 17, 2019, from: www.nytimes.com/2019/06/18/us/politics/donald-trump-rally-orlando.html.
63 Retrieved from: www.theguardian.com/global/video/2019/jul/18/crowd-chants-send-her-back-as-donald-trump-attacks-ilhan-omar-video.
64 *Atlantic Magazine*, January 13, 2019.
65 Jennifer Rubin, Trump's Speech Would Be Laughable If It Weren't so Infuriating. *Washington Post*, August 5, 2019. Retrieved August 5, 2019, from: www.washingtonpost.com.
66 Trump Calls Baltimore a "Disgusting, Rat and Rodent Infested Mess" in Attack on Rep. Elijah Cummings. Retrieved August 5, 2019, from: www.cnbc.com/2019/07/27/trump-calls-baltimore-a-disgusting-rat-and-rodent-infested-mess-in-attack-on-rep-elijah-cummings.html.
67 Jean Raspail, *Camp of the Saints* (Petoskey, MI: Social Contract Press, 1994).
68 Horkheimer & Adorno, 167, emphasis added.
69 See the *Guardian's* file here. Retrieved July 21, 2019, from: www.theguardian.com/news/series/cambridge-analytica-files.
70 Highlights of Robert Mueller's Testimony to Congress. *New York Times*, July 24, 2019. Retrieved July 24, 2019, from: www.nytimes.com/2019/07/24/us/politics/mueller-testimony.html.
71 Richard Seymour has this to say about the new Brexit Party led by Nigel Farage: "Unlike older party models, it doesn't invest in lasting infrastructure. It is nimble-footed, expert at gaming social media – the stock market of attention. It won the battle for clicks, and made a killing in this election. Such online frenzies are akin to destabilizing flows of hot money, forcing legacy parties to adapt or die. But when Parliament is so weak, its legitimacy so tenuous, they can look like democratic upsurge." Nigel Farage Is the Most Dangerous Man in British Politics. *New York Times*, May 28, 2019. Retrieved from: www.nytimes.com/2019/05/28/opinion/nigel-farage-brexit.html.
72 See the work of Christian Fuchs, in particular *Digital Demagogue: Authoritarian Populism in the Age of Trump and Twitter* (London: Pluto, 2018).
73 We Have a Nationalist Terrorist Problem. *New York Times*, August 4, 2019. Retrieved August 5, 2019.
74 Adorno, 365.
75 Immanuel Kant, An Answer to the Question: What Is Enlightenment? In *What Is Enlightenment? Eighteenth Century Answers, Twentieth Century Questions* (Berkeley: University of California Press, 1996), 58–64. This is also where I disagree with Vladimir Safatle's interpretation: autonomy in Adorno's sense has little if anything to do with the ego psychology of the neo-Freudian revisionists such as Karen Horney (the *bete noire* of the Lacanian school to which Safatle is sympathetic). In fact, Adorno had little more than scorn for such revisionism. Retrieved from: www.publicseminar.org/2017/10/adornos-freud-in-the-age-of-trump/.
76 Abromeit, 281.
77 Christopher Bollas, The Democratic State of Mind. In David Morgan (ed.), *The Unconscious in Social and Political Life* (Bicester: Phoenix Books, 2019), 27–39.

Part 2

The racialized object/the racializing subject

Chapter 6

On having Whiteness

Donald Moss

This is not a traditionally organized psychoanalytic text. No clear path links my argument to that of my predecessors. This formal peculiarity might be the product of my effort to braid together two incompatible voices, to write simultaneously from both inside and outside the affliction I mean to study. Each position – inside and outside – offers an irreducibly distorted view: the one by the limits of sincere introspection, the other by the limits of theorized observation. The two perspectives turbulently converged during a recent experience in South Africa, We dropped off a black woman hitchhiker at her ramshackle township home, one of hundreds we could see, all jammed together helter-skelter on a barren, cut-off, underserved piece of land – apartheid segregation still firmly in place. Back at the hotel, we spoke to one of the staff about how troubled we'd been by what we had seen. The young woman responded without hesitation. "Well," she said, "it's really simple: they have their houses; we have ours." She spoke with a serene confidence, pulling us in, indifferent to whatever resistance we, in our silence, might have felt. "They have their houses; we have ours" – that sentence, and especially that word, "we" – repellant and implicating – inspires, haunts, and deforms what follows.

I will focus on Whiteness as a condition one first acquires and then one *has* – a malignant, parasitic-like, condition to which "white" people have a particular susceptibility. The condition is foundational, generating characteristic ways of being in one's body, in one's mind, and in one's world. Parasitic Whiteness renders its hosts' appetites voracious, insatiable, and perverse. These deformed appetites particularly target nonwhite peoples. Once established, these appetites are nearly impossible to eliminate. Effective treatment consists of a combination of psychic and social-historical interventions. Such interventions can reasonably aim only to reshape

Whiteness's infiltrated appetites – to reduce their intensities, to redistribute their aims, and to occasionally turn those aims toward the work of reparation. When remembered and represented, the ravages wreaked by the chronic condition can function either as warning ("never again") or as temptation ("great again"). Memorialization alone, therefore, is no guarantee against regression. There is not yet a permanent cure.

Whiteness as a way of being and a way of knowing

In what follows, I will use "Whiteness" to signify parasitic Whiteness – an acquired multidimensional condition: (1) a way of being, (2) a mode of identity, (3) a way of knowing and sorting the objects constituting one's human surround. Whiteness should not be confused with whiteness, a commonly used signifier of racial identity.

Parasitic Whiteness infiltrates our drives early. The infiltrated drive binds id–ego–superego into a singular entity, empowered to dismiss and override all forms of resistance. The drive apparatus of Whiteness divides the object world into two distinct zones. In one zone, the Whiteness-infiltrated drive works in familiar ways – inhibited, checked, distorted, transformed – susceptible, that is, to standard neurotic deformations. In the other, however, none of this holds true. There, the liberated drive goes rogue, unchecked and unlimited, inhibited by neither the protests of its objects nor the counterforces of its internal structures.

Any infant is vulnerable to the parasite of Whiteness. The extent of the infant's vulnerability derives from how the infant is mapped, how it is positioned, where it is placed. All infants orient themselves in relation to a first, initial, mapping line. On this side of the line will live its familiars, us – while on that side will live its strangers, them. For every infant, this mapping line founds, delineates, and defines the place of the "stranger." As such, it marks the site of the first organized and enduring representation of an external source and cause of anxiety. Beginning with the onset of stranger anxiety, the infant, while working to find its place in the world, will perpetually aim for safety, avoiding, as best it can, any external object located on the dangerous/stranger side of the line. Parasitic Whiteness works to turn this foundational line into an impermeable wall, to permanently fix the place of the nonwhite stranger on the far side of the wall, there to be sorted and categorized, and eventually to be mastered.

Our merely unruly sexualities may exert a constant pressure to erotize the bodies and beings of strangers, transgressively aiming to defy the wall, to integrate those bodies and beings, to take them in. But the rogue sexualities of parasitic Whiteness add to that. They negatively erotize nonwhite bodies and beings. These objects, now marked, are wanted still but wanted not to be taken in but simply to be taken, not to be loved but to be hated. Holding these objects in place, inflicting pain on them – this (sadism) becomes the exquisite and economical solution to any apparent conflict between wanting and hating. Parasitic Whiteness further demeans its nonwhite bodies and beings by way of a naturalizing system of naming and classification. Once it has mapped and transformed its nonwhite objects into such a fixed taxonomical category, the rogue sexuality of parasitic Whiteness can expand its aim. It permanently maps them as external/away, and from there, wherever that is, these objects are available for limitless use – limitless labor, of limitless kind.

Parasitic Whiteness generates a state of constantly erotized excitement, a drift toward frenzy. Here is that frenzy revealed, a grounding frenzy whose resonances, though often much muted, continue to be communicated via Parasitic Whiteness: "AnAnglican missionary observed that the first toy given to white children in Jamaica was often a whip; the overseer Thomas Thistlewood, who managed forty-two slaves in St. Elizabeth Parish, kept a horrifying diary that describes how, in a single year, he whipped three-quarters of the men and raped half the women. When he moved to a different plantation, he threatened to dismember the enslaved men and women under his care, devising tortures and humiliations that included forcing some to defecate into other slaves' mouths and urinate in others' eyes, rubbing lime juice in their wounds after floggings, and covering a whipped, bound man in molasses while leaving him for the flies and mosquitoes. (Casey Cep, "The Long War Against Slavery," *New Yorker*, January 20, 2020; Vincent Brown, Tacky's *Revolt: The Story of an Atlantic Slave War*.)

Fix, control, and arouse; want, hate, and terrorize. Whiteness resides at this always volatile edge, in a state of permanent skirmish, always taking on the never obliterated resistances of its nonwhite objects. Opaque to itself and hyperconscious of those objects, Whiteness pursues the impossible, a stable synthesis, an end point. It can therefore never rest. Blindly, then, it continues forward, unendingly bent on conquering. There seems no backward path, no mode of retreat. It faces an interminable forward march. If only it could totally and permanently transform these objects, turn the once feared and unknown into the now reduced and measured; turn the once unique and overwhelming into the now fungible and the owned.

Whiteness originates not in innocence but in entitlement:

> And God said, Let us make man in our image, after our likeness: and let them have dominion over the fish of the sea, and over the fowl of the air, and over the cattle, and over all the earth, and over every creeping thing that creepeth upon the earth. And God blessed them, and God said unto them, Be fruitful, and multiply, and replenish the earth, and subdue it: and have dominion over the fish of the sea, and over the fowl of the air, and over every living thing that moveth upon the earth.

Whiteness, taking this injunction as its own, transforms it into an *epistemology of entitled dominion*, a mode of coming-to-know in which identity and entitlement are fused. We are, and therefore we are entitled to be, licensed at birth to find, capture, dissect, and overpower our targeted objects. As such, we will finally come to *know* and take *dominion* over them. Within the terms of the *epistemology of entitled dominion*, knowledge becomes both a sign of superiority and an instrument of power. The steps from knowledge to dominion are clear. The more We know, then, the more We can do; the more We can do, the more We can control; the more We can control, the more We can dominate; and finally, the more We can dominate, the more We are realizing our divine mandate to "have dominion ... over every living thing that moveth upon the earth." Triumphantly submitting to this mandate, Whiteness pursues a utopia of permanent satisfaction and assigns to its nonwhite peoples the task of being its ideal, infinitely need-satisfying object, there to service its voracious and uncheckable appetites.

Whiteness in action: inside and out

When targeting individuals, Whiteness opportunistically attaches to any psychic structure that maps self and object vertically. These vertical planes are ubiquitous and as such, provide an abundance of potential host receptors for parasitic Whiteness. Six separate, yet intersecting, such planes seem apt to keep in mind here. (1) The ego's foundation in a vertical split – pleasure inside, pain outside; good subject here, bad object there. The original object, then, is the bad object, the demeaned one, below and threatening, of whom Freud writes: "the ego hates, abhors and wishes to destroy." (2) The subject–object world of the paranoid/schizoid position.[1] The emerging subject here is in a constant struggle to maintain itself against threats emerging from bad objects, to withstand them, and, finally, to fix and locate them elsewhere enough, below enough, to settle in, to keep going. (3) The subject–object world of narcissism, of grandiosity and diminishment, of the master and the slave, of the all and the nothing, the highest and the lowest. (4) The subject–object world of perversion: of the user and the used, the person and the thing, the whole and the part, the owner and the owned, the dominator and the dominated. (5) The subject–object world of the Oedipal triangle – of higher and lower, of power and powerlessness, of having and not having, of being able to and not being able to, of satisfaction and despair. (6) The subject–object world of the authoritarian superego: we can listen to this representative example – "I was a decent person with her, with my dog Cleo. I was never sadder than when she died. . . . Stupid, fucking stupid. Shut up. Why'd I say that? Just blabbing. Get to work. What's a fucking dog got to do with anything? You fat piece of shit." The interior verticality is obvious, the severity, the top-down conviction, the malign domineering – the tyrannical accuser, the cowering accused.

Along each of these vertical planes, subject–object relations are defined by power and grounded in the fantasy of sovereignty. And along each of these vertical planes, safety, satisfaction, and pleasure are necessarily fragile and contingent. Everything I have, everything I am, can be lost: my strength turned to abjection, my inclusion to exile, my calm to terror.

This vertical fragility makes us all susceptible to parasitic Whiteness. Whiteness promises to turn anxious singularity into confident plurality, isolated frailty into collective might. Whiteness caresses its hosts with reassurances; "Never again," it can seem to murmur, "will you have to be alone." An always strained and always jeopardized "I am" will necessarily be susceptible to this preformed dream of an always empowered "We are."

But, of course, Whiteness does not limit its opportunistic work to individuals. It easily infiltrates even groups founded on the protection of individuals, on democratic principles, on a systemic concern for fragile singularities. But when this group contacts an ominous vertical plan, when, for example, it feels jeopardized by external or internal threat, its founding horizontal principles can suddenly seem naïve and dangerous.

Opportunistic Whiteness, then, can provide an instantaneous alternative, readily transforming the group's democratic impulses into nativistic ones. As with susceptible individuals, all parasitic Whiteness needs from its susceptible pluralities is a disruptive collision with verticality, a threat from "below." We can sense one such "threat" across the world now – refugees in need, demanding a place, and disrupting democratic assumptions of inclusiveness. Whiteness is always ready to respond to such a threat, to answer the call. Once installed, its epistemology of entitled dominion will license its host – individual or group – to power without limit, force without restriction, violence without mercy. Whiteness now enjoys the liberty to freely enact its foundational epistemology of entitled dominion. Entitled dominion not only defines its objects – we can "see" them gathering at our southern border – it also sets up the frame inside of which all definition is possible. Anything outside the frame is, by virtue of its outsidedness, both unreal and impossible. The voice of Whiteness's entitled dominion, inside or out, is firm and final:

> You are not a people; you are labor. You are not a person; you are a deviant. This is not desire; this is sickness. You are not in need; you are a failure. You are not your own; you are ours.

Personal reflections

The infiltration of Whiteness can begin modestly:

For two years, aged 3–4, Bobby was my best friend. Bobby had a speech impediment due to a severe cleft palate. I was the only kid on the block who could understand him when he spoke. I loved Bobby. When school started, though, I went to a regular school while Bobby was sent to one for disabled kids. That was the end of the friendship. We never spoke again.

I wanted no part of him now. Something was wrong, weak, and deficient about him. I wanted only to be with kids of my kind. Bobby was now part of Nature, part of what I would learn about. He was no longer, like me, one of those who would do the learning. No one told me to respond this way. No one told me not to. I had had what amounted to a revelation. I simply shunned him, turned away. That shunning, that act of mapping him now as an object, no longer a subject like me – this marked the site where Whiteness might begin its work.

I had drawn a line, established a premise. Whiteness could then opportunistically inaugurate a stepwise expansion of this premise, proceeding as though it were my ally. Together, we then sought and found more markers of deficiency, until finally we arrived at color. Color offers Whiteness, now firmly housed, an apparently limitless, instantly available field for expansion – providential and clear – an opportunity to realize itself, to arrive at its adult, fully developed form. Color provides a universe of suitable objects, placed there like gifts, to be captured and crushed, all at a whim, like, for so many Gulliver-ed children, ants are there to be crushed, butterflies to be locked in a jar. These crushed ants and suffocated butterflies – victims of a nearly cellular narcissism – offer Whiteness a platform on which to begin. Once begun, the rest can seem like simple common sense, the preservation of the host's proper place – somewhere near the apex – within the only proper and permanent Order of Things. But first, before arriving at its fully developed form, Whiteness has to begin – and for this, nearly anything – even a little boy's cleft palate – will do.

Whiteness began its work only after I had done mine. I had loved Bobby. I was a lonely kid, and he was the best thing I had. I was unprepared to lose him; in fact, not only unprepared but, in retrospect, unable. My fear, my sadness, my loss – Bobby and I would no longer be together – had been erased by my mapping revelation: his wound confirming my intactness. This seemed fair exchange for losing a friend. I was grateful to have escaped from an unbearable loss. The fragile attachment of love and friendship had been transformed into the robust attachments of hatred and revulsion.

All Whiteness needs for a receptor site is an original act of vertical mapping. Whiteness begins with this verticality. It then infiltrates you. You can feel it. It's like getting high: a new reality; an enhanced stature, a special community. You can breathe easier, feel protected and watched over. And then you can look down, below you, and you can see the others, others like Bobby, and they seem to be drifting ever further downwards, toward some bottom. And unlike you, they appear helpless and unprotected. They fade into the distance, further and further away, over there, permanently other now, permanently elsewhere. Parasitical Whiteness, in fact, functions as inherited property does. You have received your due. You simply claim what you suddenly realize is yours for the claiming. But with this comes a fear of a crash, of losing everything, of having it taken away. So parasitic Whiteness, bent first on dominion, now bends toward aversive, and then violent defense. Defense now a permanent necessity, safety turns into anxiety, freedom into paranoia, escape into entrapment. Parasitic Whiteness, promising health, delivers sickness.

I shunned the neighborhood's blind peddler; my beloved Aunt Bell suddenly became too fat; JT, the guy who taught me how to drink out of a Coke bottle, turned into the black guy whose bottles I ought to avoid; my immigrant grandparents became stupid peasants. But these were merely personal relationships, each one weighed down with meanings and histories, weighed down, in fact, by love. But once these fraught transformations were in place, once I was willing to accept them, there emerged the easiest and most global transformation of all. As though I were simply learning to name a natural feature of my new surround, "Negroes" had now become "Schvartzes." And with that, I was now mapped in the real world. I was no longer merely white; I was White. I had property and properties. And with this last malign turn, this turn away from mere locality and toward a place in the natural world, parasitic Whiteness had firmly established its place in a compliant host.

I knew the whole thing was a betrayal. Whiteness regularly leaves a little space like this for consciousness and memory, for the awareness of one's own treachery. Whiteness maps this awareness, though, this residue of an original innocence, as yet another object to dominate: an interior disability, and as such, a threat to the whole enterprise – weak, sniveling, and regretful – that must itself be kept ordered, maintained, hidden, and in effect, sent away to an interior "school", in which it too – this sliver of conscience – is mapped as a subapex object.

All of this came in the form of a terrible flash, more revelation than thought. Bobby and the blind man belonged with those others, in that "school," somewhere both far away and barren. Parasitical Whiteness works this way – by opening up and mapping a faraway territory – easy to populate, easy to mine, and easy to diminish – a territory capacious enough to hold all the creatures of the earth, while promising its hosts that only they, intoxicated by real privilege and imaginary wholeness, will maintain both the power and the right to remain safe and secure, right where they are.

A ghost of Bobby seems to have come back to me, in the person of a current patient of mine, also born with a speech impediment. As I listen to him, I can also see and hear Bobby, his tiny head, his nasal twang, not quite forgiving, but simply welcoming, no matter how long it's taken for me to get there, over to his side of the line, or, in what amounts to the same identificatory thing, to bring him over to mine. Not realizing the gift he's giving to me, my patient treats me like an intimate.

> I could disappear and no one would notice. I remember in kindergarten, I was taken out of class and walked down the hall to a very small room. Dark. Four of us. All of us with impediments. It wasn't the impediment, really, but the method of dealing with it. They took me away. I deserved less than others. Getting pulled out of class. Defining. It locates me in a deficient category. That feeling has never gone away. Must have been countless other moments. I tried to speak and they had no idea what I was saying. Was I at fault? Must have felt I was doing something wrong. I remember walking into the house with my dad. I was five. He was trying to get me to say "key" and I kept saying 'kay.' Back and forth, 'key' 'kay,' seems like 10–20 times. He couldn't stand me as I was. Somehow, I was doing something to wrong him. He was so dead set on me saying 'key.' I couldn't do it. It was somehow my fault. Very powerful emotion. Leave me behind; I'm not worth waiting for. Now that I've thought of that memory, the feeling that 'you're just worth abandoning' is really powerful. I'm just something worth putting up with, nothing more.

"He couldn't stand me as I was" – this might be the central anthem of entitled dominion's objects. Misplace his wallet, forget a word, arrive late for dinner, and my patient now will slam his head against a wall, bash his face with his fist, and scream at himself repeatedly, "You idiot, you idiot." As long as he's an "idiot," the world as mapped is a properly ordered one. Interfere with this self-directed violence, though, as the analysis occasionally does, and the patient is left feeling simultaneously homicidal and insane. The map, then, is calming, in spite of its devastating cost.

The map's workings: in the world and in the consulting room

First, to sense the map's working in the world, listen to Lawrence Summers, ex-president of Harvard, ex-secretary of the treasury, writing here in a confidential World Bank memo from 1991: "I think the economic logic behind dumping a load of toxic waste in the lowest-wage country is impeccable and we should face up to that . . . I've always thought that countries in Africa are vastly under-polluted, their air quality is probably vastly inefficiently low compared to Los Angeles . . . Just between you and me, shouldn't the World Bank be encouraging more migration of the dirty industries to the Least Developed Countries?"

Though we all might identify with the superficial and manifest logic of Whiteness here – number and equivalence, fairness and justice – we will refuse and resist both its explicit epistemology of entitled dominion and its covert and foundational logic of mapping. This mapping logic puts Summers – anxious, disenchanted, swaggering – on one side of a partition, the world as some combination of dump and zoo on the other. Summers is mapping reality by organizing it hierarchically. He is imagining the planet as conceived by an epistemology of entitled dominion, dividing a once single and unified sphere into two, Whiteness, clean and whole, here; its least developed objects, there, far away, near the "shithole."

Summers exemplifies the map's workings in the material world. The following clinical examples represent the map's workings at the psychoanalytic edge, the plane formed by the intersection of psychic and material realities.

Clinical work

In the anecdotes that follow, I mean to illustrate some of the map's workings as they emerge in two very different clinical situations. The first may exemplify a kind of remission, the other may point toward an effective method of treatment.

(1)

Mr. A has been told that he is one of two finalists for a position he applied to, out of an initial pool of 400 applicants. Mr. A has undergone three extensive interviews and has been told that he will be informed of a decision after the weekend. This, the first session of the week, takes place on Tuesday.

> They still haven't called me. It's such bullshit. Those imbeciles. It's not as though they are interviewing me for the Supreme Court. This is one level from the bottom. It's disgusting. The guy says he'll call on Monday. And then, to add to the humiliation, my answering service

fails on just that day. I have to call the fucking secretary and ask her if perhaps her toad of a boss has found the time and the inclination to have called me. Sorry to bother her but my answering machine isn't working – the lamest excuse in the book. I have to stoop to that; even if it's true in this case, they have no reason to believe me. To them, I'm groveling for their piece-of-shit job. It's outrageous. And still he hasn't called. He then calls me and says by today, he promises, by noon, and now it's after that and he still hasn't called. And all I can do is wait. I hate it. I hate them.

But, at a meeting just now, I almost lost it. I'm still worried about touching these people. I know you can't get HIV by touching, but still – small cuts, fingernails, there's always a chance. And these people are coughing, hacking things up, they're sick, and I don't want them touching me. And at the end of the meeting, this guy comes in late, very late, like he always does. He comes just to show up. He's not a real scientist. He's a fraud. Filthy, fucking n-word comes in and fakes his way into my meeting. Dirty, sick, lying n-word. And I'm there in the same place, maybe having to touch his hand. It's outrageous.

Mr. A's entire orientation to the world is vertical. I can practically feel the sweat pouring out of him as he desperately tries to hold on to his place on his subject–object world's sheer vertical wall. The racial epithet bluntly marks and maps that sheer verticality. It establishes a bottom, a floor, below which, under no circumstances, might Mr. A follow. Mr. A can fall only so far, can lose only so much, can be only so out of control. Mr. A maps the pejorative object beyond his limits; this object houses everything that Mr. A cannot bear to house. Listen to the intimacy, the certainty in his voice – the absolute conviction that he knows, beyond any doubt, the essential and particular characteristics of everyone on the map. Mr. A does no work; the map does it all. Verticality is omniscient – no questions, only answers.

Mr. A had sought me out because he had heard I was "the real thing." For some time, I could work with him, more or less effectively, by leaning on his idealization, by putting the vertical map to what I thought might be a benign use. I was at a loss, though, as to how his reliance on the map might be disturbed. A violent incarcerated father, an ineffectual mother with whom he had almost no contact, a steady use of cocaine, weekends punctuated by physical altercations – he said seeing me helped him "stay cool" and "out of trouble." The only intense emotion he expressed was rage, with attendant regret that he hadn't "killed" the offending party. Two years into the analysis, he bought a tiny dog toward whom he seemed to feel intensely loving and protective. He became preoccupied with the dog, and less so with all of his demeaned objects. Then a woman entered his picture. She moved in and suddenly it was the three of them, trying to set up a household. Nothing about him seemed to really change except his preoccupations. He wanted to "be good," occasionally saying, without much conviction, "be like you." But, with these manifest aspirational changes, he was no longer sounding anything like he had. He was busy with the woman and the dog, wanting to be good to both of them. He now needed money and therefore a job. The work he found was not particularly elevated and yet he put up with it. After a while, living what seemed to him a mediocre but decent life, he ended his analysis.

The whole treatment was a strange experience for me. I felt I hadn't done much except to put up with him, to neither join in with nor aim to end his Whiteness-fueled pejorative epithets, and his reliance on his steep vertical mapping. And yet, comparing how he was to how he became, I came to think that his time in analysis had been a success, that it had somehow turned out to at least resemble "the real thing." The vertical planes of his life had been added to, pushed aside for now, by his affections for the woman and the dog and maybe by his wish to become like me, whatever that may have meant. Horizontal planes had emerged in the midst of the vertical ones. Not a cure, certainly, but a valuable remission, generating a zone of possibility. I remain almost certain, though, that, given even slight provocation, parasitical Whiteness will recur; Mr. A will resume his racist rants, his violently imagined solutions.

(2)

A woman in analysis is speaking of her growing disgust at her male partner. She can barely tolerate his neediness, his insistence that they always be together. Increasingly restless and sexually unsatisfied, she has begun to threaten either having affairs or a breaking up. Her partner responds forcefully and repeatedly, with an image that has long been a presence in their relationship. He says to her: "This is not you speaking. I know you love me. It's the pink monkey you have inside you. That's what's talking. That monkey is crazy, wild. You can't control it. You need me to keep it under control." The patient has a history of profound psychiatric disturbance; the idea of losing control terrifies her. For years, terrified, she has joined with her partner in working to keep the "pink monkey" under control. The "pink monkey" – a dangerous animal, demeaned by color – names what she and her controlling partner agree is an invasive humanoid presence, the incarnation of a mad dysregulating primitivity, located not outside where it belongs but instead deep in her interior.

Long compliant, certain that he alone can keep her from falling apart, she stays with him and grows increasingly unhappy. At a crisis point in the relationship, she has a dream:

> I am with some people in a sexual situation. Not sure of anything. Who they are, what they want. One is a boy, or a woman. I can't tell. Then it's a woman, but she has a penis. It's a little boy's penis. I'm excited. Then it's a woman again. And I look at myself. Not sure what I have, what I am. A boy, a woman, whether I have a penis. I'm excited. Everything about it is exciting. Scary.

She begins speaking about the dream hesitantly, afraid it means she is becoming crazy again, perverse and sick. I say she seems to expect me to confirm that. "Isn't that what psychoanalysts do," she says. "Raul says I'm crazy and you don't? Aren't you a cop too?" She begins to laugh. "If that dream isn't sick, then what is it?" she asks. Laughing more, she exclaims: "It's the pink monkey. That's what it is. The pink monkey is a sex monster. Every possible part. Penis. Boy. Woman. Me. Not so bad. Really, not so bad. Really kind of cute. Don't you think so?"

Within weeks, she has found her way out of the relationship with Raul and soon meets a man whom she tells me is "not afraid" of what she wants. "No more pink monkey," she says, "just me, maybe pink, maybe a monkey."

Countering the epistemology of entitled dominion, the work of the patient and analyst here was informed by what seems to me an *epistemology of identificatory obligation*. I am obliged to the other as I am to myself. The strange has been reconfigured as the curious, the threat of disorganization has become the promise of surprise. Identificatory obligation promises the possibility of permanent erotic contact – ever possible and ever uncertain – that entitlement and dominion had moralistically foresworn.

The pink monkey has been transformed. The patient and Raul, via a shared and perverse epistemology of entitled dominion, had relegated the patient's desires to the status of a mad animal in need of a cage, mapping her as a kind of domesticated zoo animal, dangerous without her trainer. Putting her dream to excellent use, the patient has found a way to liberate the monkey, turning it into a blurred flurry of sexual parts, polymorphous, yes, but no longer frightening – instead a "cute" whirr of desire. She is now enchanted by, and identifying with, what had once frightened her. In effect, in the dream the monkey speaks, essentially seducing her, winning her over, showing his "cuteness," making it clear that he need not be looked up, kept on a chain, suppressed.

The voice of Perversion had banished the woman and her primitive pink monkey to a psychic version of the walled-off faraway territory. Her partner's control was a non-negotiable condition of her release. A shared fear of the pink monkey's unruly desires bound this perverse couple. Those desires marked a threat to order. Entitled dominion here camouflaged itself as benevolent protection against the recurrence of psychic breakdown, which had long ago disfigured her, just as it was the voice of order and protection that had marked and mapped Bobby as disfigured.

But here, first the dream, and then the patient's work on the dream, counter the perverse partner's epistemology of entitled dominion. The patient, trying to figure out what she can actually claim to know, joins her analyst in an epistemology grounded in uncertain, tentative, experimental interpretation. The work of trying to come to know takes place right on the borderline. Patient and monkey speak to each other. Both begin in states of false erudition, internal representatives of the false vertical dichotomy, defining civilization here and the pink monkey – barbarism – there. The patient, though, is not actually civilized, the monkey not actually barbaric. Both terms are, in fact, entirely imaginary. Any identificatory epistemology engenders the possibility of a linking encounter across this imaginary divide. Enchantment is merely one means of eroding vertical disidentification. There are many others. Identification, looking for and finding likeness – this is the central clinical and social move that eradicates verticality and turns fixed hierarchy into mobile difference.

This kind of clinical work, dismantling perverse structures organized around an epistemology of entitled dominion, turns interior vertical maps into interior horizontal ones. As such, this work eliminates at least one psychic receptor site for parasitic Whiteness. Replace repulsion by desire and fear by delight, and a portion of the once perverse map turns horizontal – the once reviled monkey now dazzles, now an icon of vital possibility instead of devitalized excess. And with that transformation, parasitic Whiteness loses some access to a now less susceptible host.

Epistemologies of identificatory obligation aim to reverse Freud's famous axiom and to arrive, finally, at this: Where ego alone once was, there id too must also be.

Psychoanalytic work, then, need not properly target Whiteness itself here. Instead, it can effectively target the psychic receptor sites that provide Whiteness with the interior vertical mapping on which it depends. The vertical map disrupts the identificatory bond that might have once bound subject to object. The bond persists, though, reshaped and hardened now into a vertical format. Identification morphs into disidentification; similarity into difference, affectionate care into sadistic cruelty. Diminish the spread and influence of these interior vertical receptor sites, and, indirectly, the parasite of Whiteness is dislodged, loosed, itself becoming susceptible to exposure, as a differentiated and alien presence. Psychoanalytic work, in its most radical, fundamental, and finally neutral forms, targets any and all of the effects of vertical mapping. Where verticality was, there horizontality will be.

Concluding note

Where to stand? On what stable platform? To turn Whiteness into an object for thought, one must first look for a point of stillness. This point actually does not exist. There is no stillness to be found since Whiteness, in its mature form, generates a volatile totality, from which there is no clear exit, no clear escape. The pursuit of that exit, the hope for both escape and thought, depends, I think, on first locating others who can function as a beacon, imaginary or not. Then, I think, the working toward an exit turns feasible. Psychoanalysis provides a template for such work, a theoretical/technical structure to at least temporarily count on as we try to achieve the requisite conceptual, emotional, and personal nimbleness to grapple with Whiteness.

Note

1 Here is a clear and representative Kleinian conceptualization of the vertical plane: "[D]isillusionment opens up a gap between the self and the object; a gap that to start with, is filled by Chaos, leading to panicky feelings of falling into a terrifying unknown. Normally the mother's love saves the day, since it creates a link and is felt to rescue the baby from the abyss. But if this fails and the

pain, humiliation, and fear are unbearable, the 'horizontal' gap, between self and breast becomes a 'vertical' gap, with only two positions, triumph or humiliation. The longing for love is then replaced by a longing for power. The patient inhabits an up and down universe in which strength fuelled by hatred is idealised and love is seen as weak and contemptible. The patient is seduced by the belief that to become 'Big' via massive Projective Identification with the Idealised Bad Object takes seconds, whilst growing up, is always partial, insecure and takes time and hard work." Sodre (May 2012) personal communication.

Chapter 7

"When reparation is felt to be impossible"

Persecutory guilt and breakdowns in thinking and dialogue about race

Jane Caflisch

> Guilt is unbearable when reparation is felt to be impossible.
> – Ignes Sodre, 2015

> Not everything that is faced can be changed. But nothing can be changed until it is faced.
> – James Baldwin, 1962

"It starts to feel like everything in my life is built on crime," says a patient, a young white woman, politically progressive, thoughtful, starting to reckon with her own relationship with whiteness and its history in the United States.[1] "And my guilt is useless."

In this chapter, I take seriously the ways in which this perspective on whiteness and white guilt – which I have heard echoed by many other liberal and progressive white people[2] (the group I address here as "we," as detailed in the chapter), not only patients but also colleagues, friends, activists, scholars, and writers – is both accurate and necessary. Among other reasons, this perspective serves as a needed corrective to white liberal self-idealization, to the idea that racism and white supremacy are located "out there," in others and in the past, rather than in our own daily lives, to their foundations (e.g., Sullivan, 2014). Historically and into the present, it is true that much of what white Americans have – materially, and in terms of opportunities and unearned privilege – has been gained through violence, both physical and structural (e.g., Coates, 2014). As people of color have told us repeatedly and over time, this is part of the reality of being white in this country, painful but essential to face.

I also take seriously the ways in which, when well-meaning white people begin to recognize these realities about ourselves and our histories, we

DOI: 10.4324/9781003214342-10

can be left with a sense of these harms as, to some extent, irreparable. As I will argue here, this sense of the irreparable is, in part, simply a statement of fact, given the sweeping scope and depth of racism and its impact. In this context, the wish, among white liberals, that this depth of harm could be repaired completely can function, at times, as a defense to protect our sense of our own goodness, a fantasy of erasure of debt, and a type of manic reparation (Klein, 1935, 1940). At the same time, when reparation seems foreclosed, I believe this can result in a relationship to our own guilt that can lead to breakdowns in thinking, self-reflection, and dialogue (e.g., Bonilla-Silva, 2003; Davids, 2011; DiAngelo, 2018; Esprey, 2017), which can make change even harder to envision and practice.

My argument here is grounded in the contemporary Kleinian tradition, drawing especially from the Kleinian concept of *persecutory guilt*. Persecutory guilt – guilt in the paranoid-schizoid position or at the threshold of the depressive position – contrasts with reparative guilt in the depressive position (e.g., Klein, 1935, 1940) and describes the form guilt can take "when reparation is felt to be impossible" (Sodre, 2015).

The majority of the Kleinian literature referenced here – aside from Davids's (2011) essential work on internal racist organizations, which addresses different states of racial guilt and their implications – was not formulated with issues of race in mind. Yet I see this Kleinian theoretical framework as uniquely useful for understanding the ways in which our capacities to reflect, mourn, and engage can break down in the face of recognizing harm to others that may feel irreparable; as well as for considering what a more constructive relationship to our own guilt might entail.

Also drawing from a Kleinian perspective, I am interested in the ways in which white liberal self-idealization and self-reproach can function as two sides of a coin, grounded in splitting (Klein, 1946) and in divergent yet related forms of exceptionalism. I could summarize these positions as "This is not who we are" – a common refrain among white liberals in the United States, with each breaking news story illustrating our society's racism – and "This is all that we are." In other words, self-concepts either as completely innocent or completely corrupted. Both can be limiting and counterproductive as stances from which to approach racial justice and can block access to the kind of depressive guilt, responsibility, and concern that might, in fact, be generative and lead to reparative action.

A note on address and on centering whiteness

This chapter examines a tendency among white liberals and progressives to oscillate, when confronted with the realities of white racism, between negating our own guilt and projecting it into "other, bad" white people, while idealizing ourselves as virtuous and good; and at the other extreme, seeing everything we have and are as "built on crime," with little possibility for repair.

It is this group that I am addressing here when I write "we": namely, well-meaning, liberal white people who, at least consciously, hold ideals of racial justice as valued – even idealized – aspects of our identities, yet whose subjectivities have been shaped in the context of a society where whiteness confers power, and who continue to benefit from structural inequalities based on race. In other words, white people who feel guilt about the ways in which our histories and actions fall short of our ideals of racial justice yet who are unsure how to address this guilt. I include myself in this group and believe it also describes many white psychoanalysts and clinicians, though certainly not all.

Likewise, when I write "they," I am referring to people of color. I do not mean this to distance nonwhite readers but instead to describe a group that I don't, myself, belong to. In addition, while many of the examples here refer specifically to anti-Black racism in America, and the concept of reparation holds a particular meaning in this context, I also do not mean to overlook the experiences of non-Black people of color or of people of color outside the United States. The American tendency to construct race in binary terms can at times obscure the experiences of other people of color or falsely reify whiteness and Blackness as dichotomous (e.g., Eng & Han, 2019). Because I grew up in an American context, this dichotomous view has shaped my understandings of race in ways I am still uncovering. But I hope aspects of the dynamics I describe will also resonate beyond this context.

One concern I have about situating white people as the subjects of this chapter – and about antiracist writing on whiteness, generally – is that this may reproduce societal dynamics in which white people's experiences are centered at the expense of the experiences of people of color, rendering white people's subjectivities with nuance and leaving what it means to be an *object* of white racism overly abstract. This is an important debate that is still evolving, within psychoanalysis and elsewhere, and that I want to name, despite not having a clear sense of how to resolve it.

Another concern surrounds the implications of writing in theoretical language about a topic that touches on acutely painful aspects of lived experience for white people but, more importantly, for people who have been objects of white racism. I also realize that having the space, as a white person, to reflect on these dynamics through the lens of theory, at some remove from an experience of daily personal threat, may seem like a luxury born of privilege – which it is.

At the same time, I believe in the usefulness of theory to help us think about, understand, and engage differently with parts of our lives and relationships that can become stuck in an impasse, stalling both personal and societal change. It is with this in mind that I wrote this chapter, alongside an awareness of its limitations and my own. I hope it will be useful as one small piece of a much larger conversation.

The problem of white guilt

In her 1981 essay "The Uses of Anger: Women Responding to Racism," Audre Lorde describes white guilt about racism in the following terms:

> Guilt . . . is a response to one's own actions or lack of action. If it leads to change then it can be useful, since it is then no longer guilt but the beginning of knowledge. Yet all too often, guilt is just another name for impotence, for defensiveness destructive of communication; it becomes a device to protect ignorance and the continuation of things the way they are, the ultimate protection for changelessness.
>
> (Lorde, 1981/1984, 130)

This nuanced view of guilt – as a potential force for change that, when diverted from this goal, can also lead to paralysis and communication breakdowns (e.g., DiAngelo, 2018) – is strikingly resonant with the Kleinian view of guilt I am drawing from here, especially as it applies to guilt about racial injustice. It also crystalizes what I see as the problem of white guilt: that in different manifestations, it can both foster and hinder efforts to take responsibility for racism.

The counterproductive aspects of white guilt are likely the associations that come to mind first when we hear this term. An object of critique and caricature on both the right and the left, deployed by the alt-right to portray white liberals as weak, and by progressives to differentiate truly antiracist whites from the self-indulgent and hysterical, "white guilt" is not a term I think any of us would willingly use to describe our own attitudes toward racism and whiteness – although others might describe us this way, likely causing us to cringe and feel ashamed.

This cringe reaction isn't without reason. There is much about white guilt that is worthy of skepticism. Like the "guiltiness" described by Mitchell (2000) in contrast to reparative guilt, white guilt can be performative and excessive (e.g., Harris, 2012). There can be "something self-indulgent in (its) self-mortification" (Mitchell, 2000, 726).[3] It can lead to a confusion between who, in fact, is the subject versus the object of harm, "psychically colonizing" the suffering of the other and claiming it as our own (Eng, 2016; Hartman, 1997; Zeavin, 2018). It can get stuck in a melancholy space where sorrow is romanticized but responsibility is deferred (e.g., Harris, 2007). It can be used to cover over rather than address our aggression, can lead us to demand comfort and forgiveness from those we have harmed in a way that perpetuates these harms, and can mimic but in fact block genuine remorse and efforts at repair (Harris, 2012). It can lead white people to abdicate our sense of moral agency out of a belief that only people of color possess moral authority. It can be used to preserve a sense of omnipotence, through a wish that our guilt could purify us of racist badness (Benjamin, 2002).

Even just writing this account of how white guilt can go wrong and perhaps also reading it, a feeling of futility – and maybe also of shame[4] and difficulty thinking – creeps in. Our guilt *itself* may start to feel "built on crime," corrupted and worthy of suspicion. As I will elaborate in this chapter, I see this as a state of persecutory guilt, which can mobilize paranoid anxieties that interfere with self-reflection. This is one of the dilemmas of writing and thinking about white guilt – namely, that recognizing its presence and impact can also *evoke* it in ways that shut down thinking rather than fostering it.

These risks are real and have genuine consequences. At the same time, I also see guilt as an appropriate response to considering the vast, ongoing racial inequities that exist in our society, as well as the overwhelming debt, emotional and material, that white people owe for these inequities. As Eula Biss observes in her essay "White Debt," in German the words for guilt and for debt are the same: *Schuld* (Biss, 2015). Our guilt, in this way, is matter-of-fact, pointing to a debt that is concretely real and that requires action as well as reflection.[5]

By invoking this debt, I refer not only to direct legacies of slavery and overt racial violence but also to the more subtle yet pervasive daily circumstances that shape our lives in ways that are colored by racial difference, including the networks of social, educational, professional, and economic access we receive by accident of our birth, where we send our children to school, where and with whom we practice and for what compensation, etc.

When we are functioning within depressive rather than paranoid-schizoid states of mind, in addition to its many possible pitfalls I believe there is also potential for our guilt about these realities to serve as a compass of sorts, guiding us to take responsibility for the debts we owe (e.g., Klein, 1940).

At least in theory (which I recognize can diverge greatly from lived experience), depressive guilt is painful but can also be hopeful in that it points toward aspects of ourselves and our society that can and should be changed. Again, ideally, it is grounded in an acknowledgment of our own aggression and destructiveness, without collapsing into a view of ourselves as irredeemably harmful or broken and, in respect and concern for those we have harmed, maintaining an awareness of their separateness rather than identifying with their suffering in an appropriative or masochistic way (e.g., Berlant, 1998; Eng, 2016; Hartman, 1997). And, at least as I see it, it is grounded in an understanding of reparation – at an interpersonal level and also, I would argue, at the societal, political, material levels – as something we are responsible for, even when the breadth of repair is beyond what we, as individuals, can bring about on our own.[6]

Yet this reparative guilt can often become diverted to an internal experience focused more on the self than the other, inspiring ways of thinking and acting that – like the defensive moves described by DiAngelo (2011, 2018) as *white fragility* – have less to do with repair than with protecting ourselves from a sense of persecution, by others and by our own thoughts and feelings.

Guilt can take on this persecutory tone when we see ourselves and the world in starkly divided terms, as all good or all bad. In this split state of mind, the presence of guilt may be felt as a total threat to the self's goodness – a persecutor threatening to spoil our sense of ourselves as clean or worthy, which needs to be warded off. We may then experience our guilt less as a feeling from within, inspiring concern and repair, and more as a threat or injury from without, from which we need to defend ourselves.

Kleinian and contemporary Kleinian concepts of persecutory and reparative guilt

The preceding descriptions of persecutory and reparative guilt are woven together from my own understanding of Kleinian and contemporary Kleinian theories of guilt in the paranoid-schizoid and depressive positions, applied to white liberal guilt. I will pause, here, to elaborate on the theory I am drawing from in order to build this account.

Melanie Klein's writings about guilt locate it mainly as belonging to the depressive position, with its capacities for integration, concern and repair (e.g., Klein, 1935, 1940); yet she also alludes to experiences of guilt characterized by splitting and paranoia (e.g., Klein, 1932, 1957).

In her earlier work, she discusses this in relation to the early superego, composed of relatively unintegrated idealized and persecutory internal objects (e.g., Klein, 1932). She later refers to this as the "envious superego," which she argues is "felt to disturb and annihilate all attempts at repair and creativeness" (Klein, 1957, 213). According to Klein, when a person is unable, either in a transient or more enduring way, to bear depressive guilt, "the object that rouses guilt is turned into a persecutor," and guilt itself can be "felt as persecution" rather than as an opportunity for repair (Klein, 1957/2002, 194).

The concept of persecutory guilt grew out of Klein's work and was explicitly formulated by other Kleinian analysts such as Money-Kyrle (1952) and Grinberg (1964), who first used the term to refer to guilt in the paranoid-schizoid position. Money-Kyrle draws on Klein's earlier work to propose "two types of conscience," depressive and persecutory. Grinberg similarly distinguishes between depressive and persecutory guilt, with the former characterized by sorrow, remorse, concern, and responsibility and the latter by resentment, despair, fear, and self-reproach (p. 368). In Grinberg's view, persecutory guilt can be experienced as an attack on one's idealized sense of self, interfering with both mourning and reparation.

Several contemporary Kleinian writers have built on these ideas in ways I find useful for understanding white liberal guilt, although aside from Davids (2011), issues of race are not their focus. Among these are Rosenfeld (1962) on the "persecutory superego"; O'Shaughnessy (1999) on the "pathological superego" and its attacks on our capacities for thought, reflection, memory, and understanding; and Steiner (1990, 1993) on pathological organizations and psychic retreats as defenses against unbearable guilt. More recently, Davids (2011) has described the workings of internal racism from a Kleinian perspective, and Sodre (2015) has explored manic defenses against guilt "at the threshold of the depressive position." While a detailed discussion of these ideas is beyond the scope of this chapter, I will introduce a few main themes that I see as particularly salient for understanding persecutory guilt about racism among white liberals.

Central among these is the idea that guilt is experienced as "unbearable" and persecutory *"when reparation is felt to be impossible"* (Sodre, 2015, 24; italics mine) and that experiencing guilt as "unbearable" and irreparable can lead to a shift from depressive to paranoid-schizoid states of mind in which thought and reflection break down (Davids, 2011).

When I refer to "unbearable" guilt or anxiety (a common term in the Kleinian literature), I do not mean this as a plea for sympathy for white people's distress at facing our complicity in racial harms or as an attempt to center white subjectivity at the expense of attention to racism's impact. I also do not mean to compare the experience of facing guilt about racism to the daily, often unbearable reality of being an *object* of racism. I am instead using the word "unbearable" less in terms of its causes and more in terms of its consequences. Specifically, I am using it to refer to experiences that are felt to apply strain or pressure to our minds in ways that shut down our capacities for thought and understanding (e.g., Bion, 1959), resulting in states of white fragility (DiAngelo, 2011, 2018) and "defensiveness destructive of communication."

In other words, as Davids (2011) argues in his work on internal racism, "Guilt felt to be unbearable cannot be processed mentally" (p. 50). It can lead, instead, to concrete repetition rather than reflection (p. 225), as well as a reliance on pathological organizations and psychic retreats (Steiner, 1990, 1993) – a network of defenses built to avoid emotional contact with painful aspects of both inner and outer reality – as a refuge from facing guilt and responsibility (Davids, 2011, 205).

Persecutory guilt is seen as "unbearable" in this way because the possibility of reparation – which makes reparative guilt ultimately bearable and usable, though painful – seems foreclosed. This can give rise to projection of our guilt and aggression onto others in an attempt to protect ourselves from persecutory anxiety, leading to a confusion between subject and object in which the harmed other and the fact of their suffering come to be experienced as a threat to the idealized self.

Rosenfeld (1962), Steiner (2011), and Sodre (2015) have each described this experience in terms of facing the "accusing eyes" of the injured object, either in external reality or as represented internally, and have sketched nuanced accounts of the aggression (Rosenfeld, 1962), retreats from emotional contact (Steiner, 1990, 1993), and manic defenses (Sodre, 2015) mobilized to defend ourselves from recognizing responsibility for harm.

For example, when something we have said or done is described as "racist," we may feel attacked in a total way, to our core, and may perceive whoever was hurt by our words or actions – with their "accusing eyes" reflecting back an image of ourselves that we don't want to acknowledge as true – as the *actual* persecutor. When this happens, we lose our ability to make reparative use of our guilt because it has now been projected and disowned (e.g., Davids, 2011; Rankine & Loffreda, 2016).

Davids (2011) makes the essential point that relying on these types of defenses against facing racial guilt, which he refers to as "internal racist organizations," can lead to a vicious cycle of escalating harm, guilt, and retreat from contact with reality. The more we use these defenses – especially if we are aware, on some level, that their use harms others who, at least consciously, we do not want to harm – "the more guilt there is to face, making the burden (of guilt) more unbearable, and the more in need we are therefore of the [racist] organization as a refuge" (p. 51).

So if I, as a liberal white person, don't *see* myself as someone who would respond to a statement that something I said or did was racist by feeling persecuted, but I nevertheless *do* respond this way, then recognizing the dissonance of this response with my idealized sense of self may cause even *more* guilt. If I then struggle to face this guilt, perhaps because of a fear that I won't be able to repair it, I may get stuck in a loop where I oscillate between a sense of myself as irredeemably bad, and a conviction that I am in fact innocent, that all the aggression belongs to the person who "accused" me (Davids, 2011, 48) and not to me. In both these positions, concern for the other gets lost, and so does the possibility of repair.

This is essentially how Sodre (2015) describes persecutory guilt: as a "constant shifting backwards and forwards from 'It is my fault' to 'It is not my fault'" that leads to splits in the mind. Struggling to avoid both a loss of self-idealization and a dawning awareness of responsibility for harm, the superego is split into idealizing and persecutory parts, and the ego is also split such that "the internal observer, the ego's capacity to know itself, is attacked." "Violence," she continues, "is therefore directed not only against the persecuting object and the persecuting superego, but also against the functioning of the mind" (pp. 25–26).

I will return shortly to this argument about the impact of persecutory guilt on the functioning of the mind, as this affects thinking and dialogue about race. Because persecutory guilt is catalyzed by a sense of harm as beyond repair, however, I will first consider some of the factors that contribute to this sense of the irreparable with regard to racial injustice.

Race and the irreparable

To shift for a moment from the internal world to the political and historical: in "The Case for Reparations," Ta-Nehisi Coates (2014) argues in favor of H.R. 40, the "Commission to Study and Develop Reparation Proposals for African Americans Act," while also suggesting that a full repayment for the harms of slavery is likely impossible.

"Perhaps after a serious discussion and debate – the kind that H.R. 40 proposes – we may find that the country *can never fully repay* African Americans" (italics mine). He writes:

> But we stand to discover much about ourselves in such a discussion – and that is perhaps what scares us. The idea of reparations is frightening not simply because we might lack the ability to pay. The idea of reparations threatens something much deeper – America's heritage, history, and standing in the world.
>
> (pp. 200–201)

I find this resonant on multiple levels, including the recognition that white Americans are responsible for irreparable harms, that reparation is nevertheless essential, despite its incompleteness, and that engaging in efforts at necessary yet incomplete reparation involves relinquishing an idealized view of our own goodness and exceptionalism, as individuals and collectively.

Whether we are thinking about reparation in political, material, and economic terms or at the more intimate scale of interpersonal relationships, the idea that some racial harms may be irreparable, or at least may appear this way, is crucial for understanding white liberal guilt. I will consider several reasons this may be the case.

First, when we speak about racism and its impact, we are speaking not only about the present but also about history. This includes violence that unfolded over centuries and can't be undone, even if its active reproduction in the present is radically altered. Facing this scale of harm that is irreparable because it is past, though ongoing, can lead to states of persecutory guilt, as can reckoning with the paradox of a country (in this case, the United States) founded on ideals of liberty but materially "built on crime" – on slavery and genocide (e.g., Anderson, 2017; Coates, 2014; Jones & Obourn, 2014).

Second, white supremacy as a system – of ideals, political and economic policies, and ways of relating with ourselves and others – is bigger than any of us as individuals, and as such, is beyond what any of us as individuals can fully repair. To imagine we could is essentially a white savior fantasy, cathartic but naïve and counterproductive. But to engage anyway, despite our relative smallness in relation to a problem of this scale, requires a level of internal structure, tolerance of frustration, recognition of our own limits, and ability to collaborate with others without centering ourselves that can sometimes elude us as white people, through lack of practice and, as DiAngelo (2018) has argued, lack of stamina in addressing issues of race.

Third, because of their scale, issues of race and racism often evoke intense group process and a "first person plural" voice (Moss, 2001) prone to splitting, projection, and basic assumptions (Bion, 1961) that can make it very difficult to think or to work effectively. I will discuss this further in this chapter, regarding breakdowns in thinking and dialogue about race in our field and elsewhere. This group process and the rifts it can both cause and expose may themselves seem irreparable at times because they can take hold so quickly and so intensely.

On a more intimate scale, racial reparation may seem elusive if we are thinking about racial privilege and oppression solely as abstract phenomena rather than also as forces that shape our own daily lives with people we love. I believe this disconnect can be heightened when, as white people, we live lives that are relatively segregated, with few close relationships with people of color, and beyond this, when we are socialized not to even recognize this segregation as a *loss*, which impoverishes our own lives as well as those of others (e.g., DiAngelo, 2018). This interpersonal distance – coupled with a failure to see and feel the loss this distance entails – can make reparation seem even more out of reach because reparative guilt tends to grow out of intimacy, not abstraction.

When we stop relating to racism as something abstract and outside ourselves and begin to reclaim some of our own projections, another possibly irreparable fact emerges: namely, that the history and present-day realities of racism are inscribed in our own minds, permeating and shaping our thoughts, feelings, perceptions, and relationships, at times outside our conscious awareness or at the edges of this awareness (e.g., Davids, 2011). In this regard, feelings of the irreparable around racial guilt can resemble feelings of the irreparable that we experience when any area of our minds that is dissonant with our ideals yet that we feel unsure how to change is first exposed.

Finally, even when we acknowledge the realities of racism in our own histories, inner worlds, and present-day actions and commit to repairing what we can, grounded in this awareness, we may begin to notice the places where we hesitate at the threshold of even *possible* repair. We may notice that, for example, even after identifying things we have that aren't rightfully ours, we all, at times, still cling to them fiercely.

This dynamic is captured evocatively by Harris (2012), who describes her relationship with a collection of Haida objects passed down through generations in her family. She travels to visit a Haida village in Canada and meets the people to whom these objects once belonged. She is moved to tears when hearing about a museum returning their artifacts to the tribe from which they were taken. She reflects on the ways in which her possession of the Haida objects she has come to cherish is based on a "delusion of ownership" (p. 205). Yet she also reckons with a growing recognition that, despite all this, she doesn't want to give these objects back.

Harris uses this story from her own life to reflect more broadly on experiences of guilt and "guiltiness" about what we don't actually own yet want to keep as white people. Suchet (2007) likewise examines this grasping relationship we can have to our own privilege, even as we try to disown it, which she describes as "this deep, visceral refusal to let go" (p. 881). This applies not only to "possessions" as specific as particular objects but also to a wide array of privileges, social, economic, institutional, and otherwise, that we come to see ourselves as owning – including, as Cheryl Harris argues in her classic paper "Whiteness as Property," whiteness itself (Harris, 1993).

In other words, some things may feel irreparable not because they *are* but because they involve giving something up that we have grown attached to and don't want to relinquish, even when this goes against what we see as our ethics and our politics (e.g., Harris, 2012).

Recognizing these truths about ourselves can evoke intense guilt and shame. It can also lead to breakdowns in thinking, as we outwardly express antiracist ideals yet internally contend with a realization that, in many areas of our lives, we are clinging to things that are "built on crime" but that we don't yet want to part with (D. Frank, personal communication, December 2018). This dissonance may not be fully resolvable. Yet acknowledging these sites of "refusal to let go" can be profoundly useful because they point toward forms of repair that *could*, in fact, be possible – beginning in our own daily lives and expanding out to larger structural issues that reflect the same dynamics.

I will return shortly to some implications of these dynamics for how we might understand and engage with reparation. But first I will consider the breakdowns in thinking that I believe can result from these states of dissonance and persecutory guilt. I see these thinking breakdowns as important both because they are one common, outward manifestation of the internal dynamics I have been describing and also because, when they occur, they can cause our reparative efforts to grind to a halt and our discussions to get lost in confusion.

Fragile talk and breakdowns in thinking

I am in the audience at a panel at a psychoanalytic conference.[7] The theme is racism in America. I assume that everyone present chose to attend this panel, at least on a conscious level, because we see racism as an urgent issue that we want to address – personally, politically, and as clinicians. I also assume that, at least consciously, we do not want to do harm, either in our work or through our participation in this conversation.

Yet when the session is opened for commentary from the audience, things quickly start to unravel. Many comments from white audience members are difficult to follow because they seem to start going in one direction and then reverse course, as though suddenly there is danger – from outside or inside, it isn't clear – that needs to be dodged from all sides. Many of these comments converge around split positions, with refrains of "This is not who we are" – racism exists outside this room, and belongs to others, whom we can judge and feel united in judging – and "This is all that we are" – we are bad and broken, and there isn't much we can do about this except hope to be absolved and forgiven. As white participants, in other words, we quickly find ourselves in a paranoid-schizoid place, dominated by splitting and a sense of threat and suspicion.

I don't mean to single out other white audience members for criticism. I feel these pressures, too, and partly as a result, decide not to speak, which isn't a constructive solution. I have trouble formulating what *would* be a constructive way of engaging. This conversation starts to feel increasingly hopeless and confusing, and as I'm trying to gather my thoughts – as I imagine many others are too – more harmful things are being said and enacted that make it even harder to imagine how, as a group, we might repair the damage we are doing in the moment, let alone the damage we are speaking about.

This is one example of what I mean by breakdowns in thinking around sites of persecutory guilt about racism. These are moments when our capacities for self-reflection become fractured; our speech stops making sense; we try both to communicate and to hide at the same time (D. Frank, personal communication, December 2018), attempting to preserve an idealized self-image while recognizing traces, in ourselves, of its opposite, and we become deeply confused about who is causing harm to whom.

A number of psychoanalytic thinkers have identified this phenomenon as occurring specifically in the context of conversations about race. Leary (2000) has observed that talk about race can be "extremely fragile and easily subject to collapse" (p. 642). Esprey (2017) has discussed "thinking-thwarting enactments" around race, dominated by "mindlessness and non-thinking" (pp. 20–21). And Davids (2011) has captured the tendency, among white liberals speaking about race, for there to be "an atmosphere . . . in which all [are] on the right side, but the capacity to think [is] utterly paralyzed" (p. 99).

This precariousness in white thinking and dialogue about race has been described with nuance, outside psychoanalysis, by DiAngelo (2011, 2018) in her work on white fragility, which she defines as "a state in which even a minimum amount of racial stress becomes intolerable" (or, in the language of this chapter, unbearable), triggering feelings of being under attack, interpersonal defensiveness, and increasing verbal incoherence (2011, 54). She especially observes this among white liberals because of the dissonance evoked when we consciously hold one set of ideals about race but find that our thoughts and actions reflect something else altogether.

Sociologist Eduardo Bonilla-Silva's studies of "colorblind racism" (Bonilla-Silva, 2003) also document the incoherent talk that can result from living within a dominant culture that, in his words, "forbids the open expression of racially based feelings, views, and positions" (ibid., p. 91) but that nevertheless allows the *power* relations that proceed from and inform these racial views to remain intact.

In other words, if we relate to racism as a form of impurity that must not be spoken about or exposed, which characterizes the "colorblind" worldview (Bonilla-Silva, 2003; DiAngelo, 2018), we become paranoid towards our own thoughts about race, and our thinking breaks down. Our speech may become a kind of purity ritual (e.g., Shotwell, 2016) aimed more at reassuring ourselves and others that we are "clean" from the contamination of racism than at actual thought and communication. As a result, as we lose our ability to think clearly and openly, we lose access to the kind of reflection that could lead to change.

Many psychoanalysts of color (e.g., Holmes, 1999; Leary, 2000) have observed similar processes at play in their clinical work with white patients, especially liberal white patients, describing the ways in which these patients' thinking and speech can unravel when issues of race come up in their presence, or even when these issues *don't* come up directly but are evoked simply by the fact of speaking with a person of color and fearing that some racist thought or feeling will be exposed.

This is essentially a paranoid-schizoid stance: fearing exposure of something "bad" in the self – a part of the self that feels "built on crime" – while also experiencing the other as fundamentally threatening, simply for witnessing and holding a mirror to our internal process (e.g., Rankine & Loffreda, 2016). We may respond by trying to hide these parts of ourselves, both from ourselves and others, and by feeling wronged when they are noticed anyway. Or we may respond by defensively idealizing the other, in the hope that an idealized image of ourselves will be reflected back in turn. But when we engage with others in this way, grounded in splitting and suspicion, communication and emotional intimacy become increasingly out of reach.

I believe similar dynamics can arise in white liberal clinicians' work with patients of color, as well as in our interactions with colleagues of color – at conferences, in training institutes, on listservs, and in supervision. If, in their presence, we are in the paranoid state of mind that comes with persecutory guilt, even if we are not directly discussing race *at all*, our abilities to think, understand, and connect will be damaged by our fears of exposure. We may feel pulled to obscure areas of internal racism by, for example, relying on excessive idealization without actual depth (e.g., Straker, 2004; Suchet, 2007), which can be used defensively both in treatment and in dialogue among colleagues, creating a superficial atmosphere of harmony at the expense of engaging with another person in their complexity. Or we may place unfair claims on patients or colleagues of color to affirm us as "good" white people, to be our teachers when that is not their role, and/or to be our judges, handing out punishment or absolution – each of which can be burdensome in its own way.

These dynamics can also arise in white liberal clinicians' work with other white people and in our interactions with white colleagues. We may think of racism as situated entirely outside ourselves, in other white people – including, potentially, white patients and colleagues – and project our own racism into them, rather than recognizing it as something we, too, have "an ongoing struggle with" (Davids, 2011, 101). In other words, we may take a stance that "This is not who we are," despite evidence to the contrary and, by disidentifying in this way, damage our abilities to understand others or ourselves (e.g., Moss, 2001). At the other extreme, we may insist that "This is all that we are," a way of relating with other white people that may begin with a desire to take responsibility but that can end, instead, by evoking states of persecutory guilt that shut down reflective space.

At a fundamental level, whether we are working with people who share or diverge from our own racial backgrounds, as clinicians we work with our minds, and we can't do so effectively unless we can face and bear what we find there. An ability to reflect and communicate openly about race is not, in itself, reparative, but it is a beginning, and very little is possible without it.

Reparation

I have been considering two, perhaps on the surface contradictory ideas about racial reparation, as this relates to white guilt. One has to do with what can't be repaired, at least not fully and with how we might remain engaged without shutting down our reflective capacities when this is the case. The other has to do with what I will refer to, here, as the ordinary and what is in fact within reach for meaningful, though incomplete change.

From the first perspective, I have been arguing for the importance of recognizing that some of the harms caused by racism and white supremacy *are*, in fact, irreparable; that some of the privileges we hold as white people are "built on crime" in an indelible way; and that the guilt and even the moments of hopelessness that this reality can evoke for liberal white people are things we need to learn to sit with and bear without looking for the relief of reparation to make it go away.

This stance is captured evocatively in an exchange from Claudia Rankine's play *The White Card* (2019). In it, a liberal, white male art collector, deeply invested in being perceived as a "good" white person on the side of racial justice but hesitant to look at the ways in which he is also implicated in racial oppression, is speaking with a Black female artist whose work he wants to acquire. As she urges him to recognize his own participation in the white supremacist system he critiques without rushing to cast himself as a white savior, he laments: "That is so hopeless."

"Go further into that hopelessness," she replies, "and then we can begin to really see each other" (p. 87).

Sometimes trying to move immediately to reparation, in other words, can cause us to avoid the kind of internal reckoning and interpersonal understanding that we need in order to engage, deeply, with the realities of racial injustice and our role in it.

The second perspective, which I see as complementary, is that some of the harms of racism may seem irreparable not because they *are* but because of how we relate, as white people, to what reparation is and should be, which in turn deeply affects how we relate to racial guilt.

As liberal white people, we may imagine reparation not in the sense Klein intended, which involves an acknowledgment of loss and of our own limits; but instead as a fantasy of omnipotence and erasure known in Kleinian theory as "manic reparation" (Klein, 1935, 1940; Mitchell, 2000; Sodre, 2015). In other words, a desire "to repair the object in such a way that guilt and loss are never experienced" (Segal, 1973, 95).

This manic approach to racial reparation – described by philosopher Shannon Sullivan (2014/2017) as a "desire to pay off and thus sever [our] connections with white history" (p. 70) and a wish to be "a different kind of white . . . expunged of some of the guilt and shame of whiteness" (p. 50) – is ultimately more about establishing our own exceptionalism than about meaningful repair.

The problem, however, isn't only that thinking about reparation in this way – as something cathartic that will erase what we owe and restore ourselves to an idealized state of "goodness," debtless and clean – is essentially a narcissistic goal, though I believe it is. The problem is also that it is an *impossible* goal.

And because a cathartic, self-idealizing kind of reparation is, in fact, impossible, thinking about it in this way makes it nearly *inevitable* that we will experience our guilt as persecutory, with all the breakdowns in thinking and relating that come with this.

I want to argue instead, then, that we think about reparation within the realm of the ordinary. An ability to accept ordinariness, within oneself and others, is seen as a central goal of psychoanalysis within the Kleinian tradition – an idea I have found both moving and grounding and that I also see as deeply relevant to social as well as psychic change.

When I refer to the ordinary, I mean a stance of accepting our own ordinariness: understanding ourselves, as white people, neither as exceptionally good nor as exceptionally broken, and giving up the excitement, self-idealizing or masochistic, that can come with either view. I also mean, following Davids (2011), coming to recognize the ordinariness – the full complexity and humanity, beyond denigration or idealization – of people of color, rather than demanding, as the internal racist organization does, that "s/he *is not and must not be an ordinary person*" (p. 47, emphasis added). And I mean a stance of accepting the ordinariness of our efforts to repay our debts: understanding that these efforts will be neither futile nor absolving, just *necessary* and real despite their limits.

Outlining what these efforts might entail is beyond what I can address here,[8] but I do want to stress that they may involve loosening our hold on privileges we have been clinging to, also within the realm of the ordinary: for example, within the field of psychoanalysis, the assumption that what we learn and teach about human experience will in fact be structured, by default, around white experience (e.g., Ahmed, 2007). This implicit assumption shapes much of our literature and the structure of our training institutes. It determines who holds power within these institutes. It shapes our notions of what constitutes universal human truths. It influences our sense of who is an authority and why (e.g., Swartz, 2018). Our efforts to shift these underlying assumptions and structural issues will likely be messy and incomplete. But I see our willingness to engage with them as crucial to the ethics of our field, as well as the continuing relevance and vitality.

Davids addresses this reality when he reflects that "doing something about racial injustice in the world, rather than turning a blind eye to it, does not abolish one's inner racism but it does mitigate guilt and allows one to live more easily with it." He continues:

> There is a dialectical relationship between engagement and internal racism. Failure to engage allows the internal racist organization to claim that to do so would be just impossible, and its protection is therefore the only way. Engagement, on the other hand, shows the task to be not impossible, but . . . just very difficult, at times.
> (Davids, 2011, 227)

The gap between impossible – or unbearable, or irreparable – and "just very difficult, at times" may seem modest but is actually vast. This, too, has to do with the ordinary, and our ability to recognize and pursue the ordinary yet meaningful possibilities for repair that present themselves constantly in our lives as citizens, friends, clinicians, colleagues, and across the many different roles we occupy. As DiAngelo (2018) has argued, as we engage in this way, our sense of what is bearable begins to expand, and more engagement becomes possible – the opposite of retreat.

This is one of the insights that psychoanalysis has to offer, in the sense that its goals have to do, essentially, with giving up fantasies of exceptionalism, innocence, and control and with facing realities that may at first feel unbearable, in a way that allows us to continue to think, to take responsibility for ourselves and our histories, and to act with integrity in both work and love. All of these are among our tasks, as white people, if we want our guilt to be useful, and our efforts at reparation to have meaning for anyone beyond ourselves.

Notes

1 This is my country of origin and the context I am most familiar with in terms of history and dynamics around race and racism, but I hope aspects of the ideas here may also resonate with colleagues from other parts of the world.
2 While I am using these terms (liberal and progressive) somewhat interchangeably for the purposes of this chapter, I do not mean this to obscure the real political differences they imply.
3 Mitchell was not writing about race or white guilt here, but about "guiltiness" more generally. Harris (2012) later used his concept of "guiltiness" to reflect on the more problematic aspects of white guilt.

4 While a detailed discussion of white shame is beyond the scope of this chapter, I believe there is some overlap between shame and persecutory guilt, in the sense that both can be evoked in moments of exposure that threaten an idealized sense of self. See Watkins, 2018; Grand, 2018, for more extended discussions of shame in the context of whiteness.
5 For example, the cost of reparations for slavery in the United States has been estimated at between $5.9 and $14.2 trillion (Craemer, 2015), and the racial wealth gap continues to grow (Chetty et al., 2020).
6 As many writers and activists of color have argued, sometimes reparation may also involve white people ceding aspects of our own power and privilege in order for others who have been marginalized in leading.
7 This is a composite of my experiences at a number of psychoanalytic events on the topic of racism.
8 Recent work by Lynne Layton and others aimed at involving American psychoanalysts in dialogue and activism related to reparations for slavery serves as one meaningful example.

References

Ahmed, S. (2007). A Phenomenology of Whiteness. *Feminist Theory*, 8(2):149–168.

Anderson, C. (2017). *White Rage: The Unspoken Truth of Our Racial Divide*. New York: Bloomsbury.

Baldwin, J. (1962). As Much Truth as One Can Bear. *The New York Times Book Review*, January 14.

Benjamin, J. (2002). Terror and Guilt: Beyond Them and Us. *Psychoanalytic Dialogues*, 12(3):473–484.

Berlant, L. (1998). Poor Eliza. *American Literature*, 70(3):635–668.

Bion, W. R. (1959). Attacks on Linking. *International Journal of Psychoanalysis*, 40:308–315.

Bion, W. R. (1961). *Experiences in Groups*. London: Routledge.

Biss, E. (2015). White Debt. *The New York Times Magazine*, December 2.

Bonilla-Silva, E. (2003). *Racism Without Racists: Color-Blind Racism and the Persistence of Racial Inequality in America*. Lanham, MD: Rowman & Littlefield.

Chetty, R., Hendren, N., Jones, M. R. & Porter, S. R. (2020). Race and Economic Opportunity in the United States: An Intergenerational Perspective. *The Quarterly Journal of Economics*, 135(2):711–783.

Coates, T. (2014/2017). The Case for Reparations. In T. Coates (ed.), *We Were Eight Years in Power*. New York: One World.

Craemer, T. (2015). Estimating Slavery Reparations: Present Value Comparisons of Historical Multigenerational Reparations Policies. *Social Science Quarterly*, 96(2):639–655.

Davids, M. F. (2011). *Internal Racism: A Psychoanalytic Approach to Race and Difference*. New York: Palgrave Macmillan.

DiAngelo, R. (2011). White Fragility. *International Journal of Critical Pedagogy*, 3(3):54–70.
DiAngelo, R. (2018). *White Fragility: Why It's So Hard for White People to Talk About Racism*. Boston: Beacon Press.
Eng, D. (2016). Colonial Object Relations. *Social Text*, 34(1):1–19.
Eng, D. & Han, S. (2019). *Racial Melancholia, Racial Dissociation: On the Social and Psychic Lives of Asian-Americans*. Durham, NC: Duke University Press.
Esprey, Y. (2017). The Problem of Thinking in Black and White: Race in the South African Clinical Dyad. *Psychoanalytic Dialogues*, 27(1):20–35.
Grand, S. (2018). The Other Within: White Shame, Native American Genocide. *Psychoanalysis, Culture and Society*, 54:84–102.
Grinberg, L. (1964). Two Kinds of Guilt – their Relations with Normal and Pathological Aspects of Mourning. *International Journal of Psychoanalysis*, 45:366–371.
Harris, A. (2007). Discussion of "Unraveling Whiteness". *Psychoanalytic Dialogues*, 17(6):887–894.
Harris, A. (2012). The House of Difference, or White Silence. *Studies in Gender and Sexuality*, 13(3):197–216.
Harris, C. I. (1993). Whiteness as Property. *Harvard Law Review*, 106(8):1707–1791.
Hartman, S. (1997). *Scenes of Subjection: Terror, Slavery and Self-Making in Nineteenth Century America*. New York: Oxford University Press.
Holmes, D. E. (1999). Race and Countertransference: Two "Blind Spots" in Psychoanalytic Perception. *Journal of Applied Psychoanalytic Studies*, 1(4):319–332.
Jones, A. L. & Obourn, M. (2014). Object Fear: The National Dissociation of Race and Racism in the Era of Obama. *Psychoanalysis, Culture & Society*, 19:392–412.
Klein, M. (1932). *The Psychoanalysis of Children*. London: Hogarth Press.
Klein, M. (1935). A Contribution to the Psychogenesis of Manic-Depressive States. *International Journal of Psychoanalysis*, 16:145–174.
Klein, M. (1940). Mourning and Its Relation to Manic-Depressive States. *International Journal of Psycho-Analysis*, 21:125–153.
Klein, M. (1946). Notes on Some Schizoid Mechanisms. *International Journal of Psycho-Analysis*, 27:99–110.
Klein, M. (1957/2002). Envy and Gratitude. In M. Klein (ed.), *Envy and Gratitude and Other Works: 1946–1963*. London: Vintage.
Leary, K. (2000). Racial Enactments in Dynamic Treatment. *Psychoanalytic Dialogues*, 10(4):639–653.
Lorde, A. (1981/1984). The Uses of Anger: Women Responding to Racism. In A. Lorde (ed.), *Sister Outsider*. Berkeley, CA: Crossing Press.
Mitchell, S. A. (2000). You've Got to Suffer If You Want to Sing the Blues. *Psychoanalytic Dialogues*, 10(5):713–733.

Money-Kyrle, R. E. (1952). Psychoanalysis and Ethics. *International Journal of Psychoanalysis*, 33:225–234.
Moss, D. B. (2001). On Hating in the First Person Plural. *Journal of the American Psychoanalytic Association*, 49(4):1315–1334.
O'Shaughnessy, E. (1999). Relating to the Superego. *International Journal of Psychoanalysis*, 80(5):861–870.
Rankine, C. (2019). *The White Card*. Minneapolis, MN: Greywolf Press.
Rankine, C. & Loffreda, B. (2016). Whiteness and the Racial Imaginary. In C. Rankine, B. Loffreda & K. Cap (eds.), *The Racial Imaginary: Writers on Race and the Life of the Mind*. New York: Fence Books, 13–22.
Rosenfeld, H. (1962). The Superego and the Ego-Ideal. *International Journal of Psychoanalysis*, 43:258–263.
Segal, H. (1973). *Introduction to the Work of Melanie Klein*. London: Hogarth Press.
Shotwell, A. (2016). *Against Purity: Living Ethically in Compromised Times*. Minneapolis: University of Minnesota Press.
Sodre, I. (2015). *Imaginary Existences: A Psychoanalytic Exploration of Phantasy, Fiction, Dreams and Daydreams*. London: New Library of Psychoanalysis.
Steiner, J. (1990). Pathological Organizations as Obstacles to Mourning: The Role of Unbearable Guilt. *International Journal of Psychoanalysis*, 71(87):87–94.
Steiner, J. (1993). *Psychic Retreats: Pathological Organizations in Psychotic, Neurotic and Borderline Patients*. London: New Library of Psychoanalysis.
Steiner, J. (2011). *Seeing and Being Seen: Emerging from a Psychic Retreat*. London: New Library of Psychoanalysis.
Straker, G. (2004). Race for Cover: Castrated Whiteness, Perverse Consequences. *Psychoanalytic. Dialogues*, 14:405–422.
Suchet, M. (2007). Unraveling Whiteness. *Psychoanalytic Dialogues*, 17(6):867–886.
Sullivan, S. (2014). *Good White People: The Problem with Middle-Class White Anti-Racism*. New York: State University of New York Press.
Swartz, S. (2018). *Ruthless Winnicott: The Role of Ruthlessness in Psychoanalysis and Political Protest*. New York: Routledge.
Watkins, M. (2018). The Social and Political Life of Shame: The U.S. 2016 Presidential Election. *Psychoanalytic Perspectives*, 15(1):25–37.
Zeavin, L. (2018). Discussion of *Race, Ghosts and Reparation*. Panel at Division 39 Spring Meeting, New Orleans, LA, April.

Acknowledgments

My best path through breakdowns in thinking has been through dialogue. I want to thank the many people who have been in conversation with me over the past few years either directly about this chapter or in general related to the internal and external realities it describes, including Han Yu,

Lynne Zeavin, Donald Moss, Danielle Frank, Ben Kafka, Claudia Rankine, David Eng, June Lee Kwon, Annie Lee Jones, Alexandra Woods, Gloria Ellis, Suheyla Zubaroglu, Forbes Singer, Melanie Suchet, Cleonie White, Sue Grand, Judy Roth, Lauren Levine, Ryan Kull, Hannah Wallerstein, Cassie Kaufmann, Erin Jeannette, Stephen Anen, Lara Sheehi, Callie Watkins-Liu, Yi-Ping Ong, Katie DiSalvo-Thronson, Patrick Blanchfield, Sowjanya Kudva, Sarah Shapiro, Karen Taylor, and many others. Earlier versions of this chapter were presented at the spring conference of Division 39 in New York City, June 2016; at On Whiteness: A Symposium, organized by the Racial Imaginary Institute, in New York City, June 2018; and at Psychoanalysis on Ice in Reykjavik, Iceland, July 2018.

Chapter 8

Murderous racism as normal psychosis[1]

Alan Bass

"[P]sychology ... is a Jewish invention, and does nothing but invent diseases and tell people they have problems when they don't" (cited, Sack and Blinder). This sentence is taken from a statement written by Dylann Roof, who in 2015 killed nine people in a black church in Charleston, South Carolina. He said that he wanted to start a war between a white race threatened by the black race. Roof published the statement about Jewish psychology after the guilty verdict at his federal trial, for which he faced the death penalty. His lawyers wanted to avoid a death sentence with an insanity defense. Roof dismissed them. He considered that he had no significant problems and that "psychology" was invented by the other enemy of the white race, the Jews.

My aim here is to use this quote as a framework for thinking about murderous racism and even genocide from a psychoanalytic point of view. While Roof might be considered a "lone shooter," his intent to start a "race war" was itself genocidal. Schabas, a genocide scholar, writes: "[A]n individual acting alone, without any state involvement, may still perpetrate the crime of genocide, provided that he or she intends to destroy a protected group in whole or in part" (p. 98).

It would be foolish, if not unethical, to use this case simply to develop psychoanalytic insights about this most terrible topic, with its destruction of millions and millions of lives. The only justification for my approach is to see whether it is possible to think practically about the prevention of murderous racism.

Prevention, not elimination. In *The Prevention of Genocide*, Leo Kuper lists three theories about why genocide is ineradicable: the invention of weapons removes inhibitions against aggression, so that one can kill impersonally; the new brain, the neo cortex, has not established proper control of the old brain, the seat of archaic, emotion-based beliefs; the

DOI: 10.4324/9781003214342-11

belief that one can avoid death by sacrificing others (pp. 195–196). Kuper then writes:

> It is clear that we cannot hope to restructure the human psyche in the foreseeable future . . . Hence, the theoretical problem is transposed to a different level of analysis, that of the conditions under which the destructive impulses in man find expression in genocidal massacre. . . . Nevertheless, these theories . . . suggest that genocide is not an aberrant pathological phenomenon but close to the nature of man.
>
> (p. 196)

Kuper sees that prevention of genocide has to entail understanding what is intrinsic to the human psyche but includes nothing psychoanalytic. I do think that there are specific psychoanalytic resources for understanding why genocide is ineradicable. And I also think that details of the Dylann Roof case offer a window into some of the most difficult questions about murderous racism as intrinsically genocidal, about law, and about the death penalty.

Whatever information I will present about Roof is not intended to "psychoanalyze" him and to reduce his actions to individual psychodynamics. Rather, it will be a question of using what is known about him to delve into the unconscious forces at work in murderous racism itself. Because of extensive media coverage of the case, and much investigate reporting, there is an enormous amount of information about Roof online. Crucially, the hearing to determine his competence to represent himself when he dismissed his lawyers, which includes competing mental health evaluations from the defense and the prosecution, is also available online.

A brief sketch of the details of the case: on June 17, 2015, in Charleston, South Carolina, Dylann Roof, then 21 years old, shot ten people in the Emmanuel African Methodist Episcopal church, killing nine. Not everyone in the church at the time was shot – there were survivors. Roof was the product of an unhappy marriage – he was born after his already divorced parents had temporarily reconciled; they then separated again. He was largely raised by his stepmother. It is worth noting that he lived in integrated neighborhoods and had black friends early on. However, he did not attend school after ninth grade and was quite isolated, spending his days alone in his room online. By Roof's own account, he was radicalized by the Trayvon Martin case, in which the unarmed black teenager was killed by George Zimmerman, who was subsequently acquitted at trial. Roof thought that Zimmerman was clearly in the right and began to read racist and neo-Nazi websites, focusing on black on white crime. Roof had already had minor encounters with local police. According to the FBI itself, a background check should have prevented his purchase of a handgun – but did not.

Roof was convinced that black on white crime threatened the very existence of the white race. He felt that white supremacist and neo-Nazi groups were only talking. Someone had to be brave enough to take decisive action. He deliberately chose a well-known Black church because he thought that a killing there would receive the most publicity. He consistently expressed no remorse for his actions and vehemently rejected the idea that there was any psychiatric, pathological motivation for them. He did plead guilty at his state trial to avoid the death penalty, but at his federal trial refused an insanity defense and was sentenced to death.

After outlining a basic psychoanalytic theory for understanding murderous racism, I will turn to important aspects of the hearing to determine his competence to represent himself at sentencing.

Hatred, self-preservation, reason

I have deliberately chosen a limited number of concepts from Freud, Klein, and Bion to develop my argument, because I think them fundamental. Many other resources in the psychoanalytic literature are applicable here. For example, in an important book Weisband develops a Lacanian perspective on this topic. Hopefully, a large, integrative psychoanalytic contribution to this issue will be elaborated, if indeed genocide is "close to the nature of man" as Kuper says.

In "Instincts and Their Vicissitudes" (1915), before the introduction of a death instinct, Freud has important things to say about hate, culminating in the famous statement, "Hate, as a relation to objects, is older than love" (p. 139). Why does Freud say this?

The assumption, as always in Freud, is that our minds operate to avoid unpleasurable stimulation. The early ego can find pleasure in itself, autoerotically. But self-preservation, the *need* to be fed, introduces a necessary relation to objects in the external world (p. 135). Freud is often misunderstood on the question of primal object relatedness, because his theory says that infantile *sexuality* is autoerotic, with a contingent relation to an object. However, in the *Three Essays on the Theory of Sexuality* (1905), Freud had already said, as he does here, that in relation to self-preservation there is always an object (p. 222). The necessary difficulty is that one has to conceive an early psychic organization that is *both* autoerotic and object related. On one hand, the early ego takes into itself all sources of pleasure and "expels whatever within itself becomes a cause of unpleasure" (1915, 135). (In other words, if I, the baby, feel hungry, and experience unpleasure, I attribute that hunger to something outside of me.) The ego "has separated off a part of its own self, which it projects into the external world and feels as hostile" (p. 136). On the other hand, as per the idea that there is always an object of self-preservation, it is reasonable to think that the ego projects unpleasurable stimulation into that object, which is then felt as hostile. The projected part of the ego becomes conflated with the needed object: "We do not say of objects which serve the interests of self-preservation that we love them; we emphasize the fact that we *need* them" (p. 137; my emphasis).

Once the needed object"

> is a source of unpleasurable feelings, there is an urge which endeavors to increase the distance between the object and the ego and to repeat in relation to the object the original attempt at flight from the external world with its emission of stimuli. We feel the "repulsion" of the object, and hate it; this hate can afterwards be intensified to the point of an aggressive inclination against the object – an intention to destroy it.
> (p. 137)

The result:

> The ego hates, abhors and pursues with intent to destroy all objects which are a source of unpleasurable feeling for it, without taking into account whether they mean a frustration of sexual satisfaction or of *the satisfaction of self-preservative needs*.
> (p. 138; my emphasis)

Thus, hate as a relation to objects older than love "derives from the narcissistic ego's primordial repudiation of the external world with its outpouring of stimuli. As an expression of the reaction of unpleasure evoked by objects, *it always remains in an intimate relation with the self-preservative instincts*" (p. 139; my emphasis). This is a fundamental point – there is an urge to destroy a needed, self-preservative object.

Murderous racism is always linked to the compulsion to establish an externality free of another kind of unpleasurable stimulation, the unpleasurable stimulation of the racial other. Keval, in *Racist States of Mind*, calls this the yearning to "return to an imagined and idealized state free from *intrusions* such as the minor differences that ethnicity brings forth" (p. 18; my emphasis). (In *Group Psychology* [1921] Freud too had said that ethnic difference provokes primal, murderous aggression; more on this in this chapter.) But we must add that this means the destruction of an object conflated with projected unpleasurable tensions from within oneself. If the "racial other" is hated because it is experienced as both an intrusion and as the recipient of projected unpleasurable tension from within oneself, then hatred of the racial "other" would be primally related to what Freud called the "unpleasure evoked by objects." Even the hatred of a needed, self-preservative object. (Imagine a baby capable of murdering the needed object of self-preservation conflated with unpleasurable tension.) Later development can add the "intrusive" tension of ethnic difference to this structure.

Here another clarification of the nature of the original object of self-preservation is necessary. At the end of his life, Freud said that for the baby, "'The breast is a part of me, I am the breast.' Only later: 'I have it' – that is, 'I am not it'" (1938, 299). In other words, one is originally identified with the object of self-preservation. It is both other and oneself. While Freud had always said that in the oral phase love is incorporative, identificatory, one also has to take into account the projection of unpleasure into the external world. There is then a complex process of expulsion of, and identification with, the hated object of self-preservation. (The relation of this idea to Kleinian thought will be discussed later.) The intent to destroy the needed object of self-preservation conflated with unpleasurable tension is then an attack on oneself. We arrive at an essential paradox: murderous racism itself is an attack on one's own self-preservation. Who needs the "racial other" more than the murderous racist, if he or she is to be saved from uncontrolled self- and other-directed aggression?

A nonpsychoanalytic genocide scholar, Holslag calls this process "baby grammar." He starts from the idea that we create an identity by creating an "Other" that is a reverse mirror image of *ourselves* (p. 96; my emphasis).

If I am good, the other is bad; if my need for the other is unpleasurable, then the other embodies that unpleasure. So, like Freud, Holslag imagines a primordial murderousness: "violence is the ultimate method of making baby-grammar physical, tangible, visible . . . it is the physical outcome . . . of reverse mirroring" (pp. 103–104). Just as being the breast is primordial, so the creation of a reverse mirror image creates an "Other" who is the reflection of oneself. Holslag says that this "subconscious" process makes killing the Other "a communal duty to the dominant culture group" (p. 109). As part of the dominant cultural group, one is also protecting oneself – but by killing the reverse image of oneself, hence, unconsciously destroying oneself. Again, this is why the murderous racist above all *needs* the "racial other" to prevent self-destruction. We will see this played out dramatically by Dylann Roof.

Self-preservation itself is always linked to the capacity to tolerate tension rather than project it into the other. Toleration of tension is the essence of the capacity to think, a secondary process. In "Formulations on the Two Principles of Mental Functioning" (1911), Freud proposed that secondary process is grounded in an *unconscious* origin of the capacity to think: "Restraint upon motor discharge . . . was provided by means of the process of thinking. . . . Thinking was endowed with characteristics which made it possible for the mental apparatus to tolerate an increased tension of stimulus. . . . It is probable that thinking was originally unconscious" (p. 211). The "unpleasure evoked by objects" can be so extreme that there is no "restraint upon motor discharge." Hatred becomes uncontrolled aggression, which is then justified because the object is conflated with a threat to self-preservation, e.g., a white race threatened by a black race. If one is threatened, it is reasonable to defend oneself. The result is that "non-thought" – the discharge of aggression, murder, genocide – becomes "reason."

This is why Keval links racist murder to reason, the possibility of thought: "how to continue *thinking* in a way that accommodates the other when the very existence of the other is the grievance? Murder is then felt to be the only solution" (pp. xxiv–xxv; my emphasis). The very existence of the racially designated other is an "intrusion" and hence a "grievance," a threat to self-preservation, but such an overpowering threat, such an overwhelming intrusion, that it cannot be thought. Or rather, it *can* be thought if thought itself becomes murder as "reason," reasonable self-protection. But to return to the paradox, when racist murder becomes reasonable self-protection, one must also think about the attack on one's own self-preservation.

Narcissism and destruction

Self-preservation is necessarily narcissistic. Freud directly addresses the questions of narcissism, racial difference, and destructiveness in *Group Psychology and the Analysis of the Ego* (1921).

> [T]he South German cannot endure the North German, the Englishman casts every kind of aspersion upon the Scot, the Spaniard despises the Portuguese. We are no longer astonished that greater differences should lead to an almost insuperable repugnance, such as the Gallic people feel for the German, the Aryan for the Semite, and the white races for the colored. . . . In the undisguised antipathies and aversions which people feel towards strangers with whom they have to do we may recognize the expression of self-love – of narcissism. This self-love works for the *preservation of the individual* and behaves as though the occurrence of any divergence from his own particular lines of development involved a criticism of them and a demand for their alteration [or even destruction; my addition]. We do not know why such sensitiveness should have been directed to just these details of differentiation; but it is unmistakable that in this whole connection men give evidence of a readiness for hatred, an aggressiveness, the source of which is unknown, and to which one is tempted to ascribe an elementary character.
>
> (pp. 101–102; my emphasis)

Is the source really unknown? Is it not, at least in part, the need to destroy the external object equated with unpleasurable tension from within oneself? Keval had equated Freud's logic of the primordial ego's wish to repudiate the stimuli of the external world with "intrusions" of the kind of ethnic differences Freud speaks of here. Narcissism intensifies this paradox of self-destructive self-preservation. One maintains an idealized sense of narcissistic integrity by destroying the (needed) object (the "reverse mirroring" of Holslag's "baby grammar"). Genocide itself is always carried out in the name of a return to an idealized purity free of ethnic difference. One must also factor in that this idealized state is "delusional" (Keval, p. 9), as delusional as the fantasy that one can free oneself of the external world of needed/hated self-preservative objects. From within the delusional belief of possible freedom from the external world of ethnic difference and the remaking of the world in one's own idealized image, it only makes sense to do everything possible to attain that state. But the inevitable twist, again, is that in destroying the ethnically different other, one is also destroying the needed object of self-preservation and thus destroying oneself. Roof stated that he left one bullet in his gun in order to kill himself after his murders. Although he did not do so, he seems to have enlisted South Carolina's death penalty to do it for him.

Life and death

This emphasis on self-preservation and self-destruction necessarily leads to Freud on the life and death drives. In *Beyond the Pleasure Principle* (1920) Freud extended his basic idea that there is a fundamental unconscious tendency to reduce tension (the pleasure principle) to its ultimate point: the drive to reduce *all* tension, a drive to death. The death drive extends the understanding of self-destruction, making it a primal unconscious force. Other directed aggression is the projection of the death drive. Looking back to "Instincts and Their Vicissitudes," one can link the projection of unpleasurable tension to this self-destructive force. But Freud also introduced the counterpart to the death drive, a life drive, Eros, that operates to increase tension, the tension necessary to life itself, and to the possibility of thought. Significantly, Freud amalgamated self-preservation and libido, which previously had been opposed in his theory, under the heading of the life drive. The newly understood life drive simultaneously integrates with the external world, raises tension levels, and introduces what Freud calls "fresh vital differences" into the psyche (p. 55). The essential point here is that the ethnic differences that Freud spoke about in *Group Psychology*, which Keval called "intrusions," can also be understood as psychically *vital*, necessary to life. But then, from the point of view of the death drive as the fundamental tendency to reduce tension, the life drive is what Freud called in *The Ego and the Id* (1923a) a "mischief maker" (p. 59). This is another way of conceptualizing why the racial other is a "grievance." Because it is different, it raises tension, is a "mischief maker."

The implication is that the conflict between the life and death drives necessarily produces a tension-reducing, dedifferentiating attack on differentiating, tension-raising self-preservation. To the extent that dedifferentiation is equated with a return to a delusionally ideal narcissistic state, we again have the paradox of self-destruction equated with self-preservation. And again, we come back to the question of need. Life, Eros, libidinal self-preservation *is* the need for the different other. If the needed different other becomes the embodiment of unbearable, destabilizing tension, it has to be destroyed in the name of dedifferentiating tension reduction. The libidinal tie to the other is split from self-preservation, which then operates in the service of the death drive. Thus self-destructive, suicidal self-preservation. Murder as reason.

Delusion

But with regard to reason in the support of the delusion of an idealized state of ethnic purity, Freud's late theory of delusion is crucial. In "Neurosis and Psychosis" (1923b) he says that when the ego finds some aspect of external reality unbearable, it detaches itself from that piece of reality. But another "reality" has to be put in its place. This is always a fantasy applied like a "patch" over the apparently lost reality (1923b, 150).

In order to maintain the belief that this fantasy *is* reality, the delusional person always seeks to find perceptions that seem to support this belief (1924, 185). For Freud this is a defensive process. Since reality cannot actually be eliminated, it always presses on the delusion. Because murderous racism is an attempt to buttress the delusional belief in a state of racial purity, the racist analogously has to find perceptions that support this belief. Such a "patch," placed over the need for the differentiating other, creates what one might call perverse reason.

Keval comes to a similar conclusion. The subtitle of his book is *Understanding the Perversion of Curiosity and Concern*. Speaking of expressions of racism in treatment, he writes:

> The capacity to obstruct or pervert a knowing that a development of curiosity and concern might bring forth creates a *fraudulent* state of affairs that takes precedence over an awareness of the *real complexities of life*. . . . [C]oncrete features such as skin color or

ethnicity are sometimes used as an opportunistic vehicle by the patient to project the intolerable feelings that a different viewpoint might engender.

(p. 23; my emphasis)

The "intolerable feeling" that I have been emphasizing is the unbearable tension of the need for the differentiating other. Keval's point is that if this other embodies the "real complexities of life," the "curiosity and concern" that complexity might engender have to be eliminated so that "concrete features" like skin color are used in the service of creating a "fraudulent," perversely simplified, delusional reality. Any alternative viewpoint can be so intolerable that murder becomes more reasonable than concern.

Considering the "arduous task of giving up grievances and taking responsibility for destructiveness to others and to the self" (p. 24), Keval says that

> the most vulnerable part of the [racist] patient is trying to keep sane but is easily led by a more destructive aspect with which there is an unconscious alliance . . . a combination of enthrallment and helplessness . . . that is idealized in a chilling way.
>
> (p. 25)

This is a precise description of Roof, whose nonchalance about his actions was observed by all. It is readily observable on the YouTube tape of his confession to the FBI.

The attack on one's own mind

Klein and Bion offer important ways of thinking about Keval's point that the racist attempt to remain sane produces an unconscious alliance with destructiveness (or the dedifferentiating death drive). Klein herself grounded her theorizing in Freud's statement about hate as a relation to objects older than love and in the necessary projection of the death drive. Her theory of the paranoid-schizoid position is that the early ego incorporates the object which is the recipient of projected self-destruction. This is close to the idea that the baby can identify with the hated object of self-preservation because the baby "is" the breast. Klein introduced projective identification as an extension of her theory of the paranoid-schizoid position, emphasizing that it is "the prototype of an aggressive object relation" (p. 183). Certainly, it seems that the murderous racist depends upon projective identification. As in Freud's description of splitting off unpleasurable internal tensions and projecting them into the external world, racist projective identification entails splitting off hated parts of oneself, and in fantasy inserting them into the ethnic other ("reverse mirroring"). The ethnic other then becomes a dangerous persecutor whose destruction is a necessary act of self-defense. This is yet another way of understanding that destruction of the other is destruction of oneself: again, the other is the hated part of oneself. Klein says that the dominance of such mechanisms not only leads to a distortion of reality but also to an omnipotent denial of psychic reality (p. 182). For the murderous racist there is no question of one's inner life, one's conflicts, vulnerabilities, fantasies, and needs. Indeed, any possible understanding of this process comes from the racially designated other – "psychology is a Jewish invention."

Bion took all this further in his fundamental essay on psychotic and nonpsychotic parts of the personality. Extending Klein on projective identification, splitting, and the attack on one's own mind, Bion speaks of "a minute splitting of . . . that part of the personality that is concerned with awareness of internal and external reality, and the expulsion of these fragments so that they enter into or engulf their objects" (p. 266). The factors that predispose to such splitting are

> a preponderance of destructive impulses so great that even the impulse to love is suffused by them and turned to sadism; a hatred of reality, internal and external, which is extended to all that makes for awareness of it; a dread of imminent annihilation.
>
> (ibid.)

Bion here offers a good description of murderous racism, which is always rationalized in terms of a dread of annihilation, e.g., Roof's conviction of the imminent annihilation of the "white race."

Following Freud's late thought that even in the most severe psychosis there is never an absolute break with reality, Bion says that:

> contact with reality is masked by the dominance in the patient's mind and behavior of an omnipotent phantasy that is intended to destroy either reality or the awareness of it, and thus to achieve a state that is neither life nor death. . . . On this fact, that the ego retains contact with

reality, depends the existence of a non-psychotic personality parallel with, but obscured by, the psychotic personality. . . . [T]he withdrawal from reality is an illusion, not a fact, and arises from the deployment of projective identification against the mental apparatus.

(p. 267)

Projective identification against the mental apparatus itself produces psychotic and nonpsychotic parts of the personality – sanity *and* madness, normality *and* psychosis. Throughout the hearing to assess Roof's competence to represent himself, participants were repeatedly confounded by just this issue. On the one hand, Roof's act seemed utterly insane; on the other, there was no way to demonstrate that he was insane. In the face of Roof's adamant refusals of an insanity defense that might have saved his life, Judge Richard Gergel repeatedly reminded him that this was a capital case, with a mandatory death penalty if no mitigating factors were found. But the judge finally found no way to demonstrate Roof's mental incompetence and had to rule in favor of his self-representation. Roof then presented no self-defense. This is fundamental to murderous reason as self-destructive self-preservation, as the normal psychosis that is the suicide of genocide.

No descriptor for it

This is where aspects of the hearing to assess Roof's competence to defend himself and to dismiss his lawyers are essential. Roof was represented by David Bruck, a well-known opponent of the death penalty, who had filed a brief claiming its unconstitutionality. This brief was dismissed, and so Bruck had to rely on an insanity defense to prevent a death sentence, using testimony from mental health experts to make his case. The question is not the accuracy or the inaccuracy of the diagnoses presented by the defense in order to plead insanity. Rather, the contradictory nature of the testimony for the defense and the opposing testimony presented by the prosecution addresses the essential paradox that there can be both psychotic and nonpsychotic parts of the personality and that this is the very structure of murderous racism – and even genocide itself.

John Robison, the psychologist for the defense, who assessed Roof as both autistic and psychotic, reviewed Roof's online writings after his self-reported radicalization by the Trayvon Martin case. Robison said that he:

> found it very interesting that Mr. Roof wrote many pages of diatribe about the evils of black people, yet he does not have any anecdotes

of any blacks harming him. It's as if he absorbed the idea of a "black threat" without any real awareness of the humanity of black people. This corroborates his statement to the FBI in which he said he never suffered harm from a black person.

(*Transcript*, p. 12)

To which one has to add a startling fact. Roof spent about 45 minutes with the Emmanuel A.M.E. Bible study group before opening fire on them. An all-Black group of what Roof himself called "good people" followed their principles and welcomed him. This is where I risk one speculation about Roof because it goes to the heart of the incomprehensibility of genocide and speaks to its unconscious dynamics. During those 45 minutes, Roof witnessed a nonjudgmental acceptance that he *needed*. This is need in the sense of the relation between the needed object, self-preservation, and self-destruction. When Roof spends time with an all-Black group that did not reject him because he is white, he is poised between self-preservation and self-destruction. He encounters what he needs, an alternative to murderous racism, just as he is on the verge of it. According to survivors' accounts he did argue with the church pastor, but even this takes time. But the unconscious force of having to destroy the other *as* destruction of oneself made the benevolence Roof encountered in the church intolerable.

Robison reports that Roof said to him: "'That's why I had the last magazine [in the gun]. It was not to shoot cops, you see. It was to shoot myself'" (*Transcript*, p. 13). Robison testified that "the arguments for the Charleston church shootings being an incomplete murder/suicide are very strong" (ibid.). Robison links Roof's statement to the self-directed violence one often finds in autism in order to support his assessment. One does not need a questionable diagnosis to support Robison's logic. Rather, it speaks directly to the self-destruction within the destruction of the needed other as "normal psychosis." Donna Maddox, the forensic psychiatrist who also testified for the defense, gave a detailed account of Roof's somatic delusions, which are often associated with psychosis. These were mainly associated with his belief that testosterone "pooled" in the left side of his body, and that the right side of his body was "feminine," or a "eunuch" (*Transcript*, pp. 16–17). One can consider these delusions in terms of the sexual conflicts of a disturbed adolescent and indeed in terms of the unconscious sexual aspects of racism, which are not the subject of this chapter. But they also present the picture of a mind at war with a body, of a self-hatred then conflated with a hatred of the racial other.

Roof's statement that "psychology . . . is a Jewish invention, and does nothing but invent diseases and tell people they have problems when they don't" is, then, a direct echo of Klein's and Bion's idea that projective identification not only attacks external reality but is also an attack on one's mind conflated with the racial other. In other words, Roof has reincorporated the murderous forces that he has "projectively identified" into the other. Roof's racist dismissal of "Jewish psychology" is in fact the delusional patch over what he knows but cannot tolerate: Jewish psychology is something else that he *needs*, just as he needed the nonracist benevolence he found in the church – a need so intense it has to be killed off. This kind of understanding is what the entire hearing to determine his competence to represent himself also needed, instead of questionable psychiatric diagnoses. Although Robison did argue that Roof's actions were suicidal, he could not really explain why. And this left Judge Gergel in the impossible position of complying with Roof's racist *and* suicidal attack on his own mind by having to impose the death penalty.

James Ballenger, the court-appointed psychiatrist who interviewed Roof several times for the prosecution, testified that Roof consciously chose to kill "the best people" because it would be "more outrageous; therefore more newsworthy" (*Transcript*, p. 27). Ballenger went on to say, "All of that is understandable, predictable, and logical – logical, if I can put it in quotes" (ibid.). Judge Gergel then asked Ballenger:

> As I understand what you are saying, the difficulty that you, and I think others . . . have, is the incomprehensibility of his racial views [that] leads people to want to project mental illness on him. Is that fair?

Ballenger responded:

> Yes. I put it in my report because it was so astounding. In one of our last conversations he [Roof] said, "I think there is a lot of projecting going on here," and he said, "Doctor, do you know what projection is?"
>
> (*Transcript*, p. 28)

Astounding: like Roof's having sat for about 45 minutes with a Bible study group before killing nine of them. The judge finds Roof's racial views incomprehensible – but this is the very incomprehensibility of genocide. How can innocent people be killed because of their race? It seems insane, so one wishes to explain it by psychosis. But then one finds that the perpetrator himself not only understands this point – "'Doctor, do you know what projection is?'" – but is willing to die for it. This too seems insane. It is precisely the normal psychosis of murderous racism. The nonpsychotic part of a personality or of an entire nation that engages in racial murder justifiably rejects that he or it is psychotic in order to protect the psychotic self- and other-destructiveness of racial murder. Judge Gergel had to find Roof competent to represent himself in the sentencing hearing because there was no question about a nonpsychotic part of Roof's personality. But in doing so, Gergel had to cooperate with the psychotic part of his personality which was seeking his own death in the name of *logical* racial hatred.

The mind-boggling nature of all this came up very clearly in the testimony of Father Parker, a priest who had visited Roof in jail many times. He told the court:

> Dylann said to me recently. . . "I don't hate black people. I hate the things that they do" . . . Your Honor, it just doesn't compute. . . . The point that I was trying to make with that is what I would have pictured in my mind about a person who was capable of doing – not only capable, but having done such a thing, would not be the person – would not be a person like Dylann as I have experienced my visitations with him over this time period. Cold-hearted, angry, I don't – I don't know what other words to say about that. Please understand what Dylann did was heinous. I have expressed that to him many, many times . . . I'm simply saying that my pastoral relationship to him has involved – I can't understand how A connects to B. . . . The only way I can explain it is mental illness.
>
> (*Transcript*, pp. 175–181, passim)

Returning to Roof's statement that he does not hate Black people but only the things that they do, Parker quotes him as having said, "'I could even sit down and have a meal with families of the surviving family members.'" Parker then comments:

> For me as a pastor and a human being, there are only – in my mind, there are only two ways that that can be true: On the one hand there

has to be some unexplainable mental condition that I'm not qualified to name, but – but I can't put my finger on it, or you are an irredeemable monster.

(*Transcript*, p. 190)

Prosecutor Nathan Williams, cross-examining Parker on this point, commented

You had said in your direct testimony that you thought there were two options, mental illness or . . . irredeemable monster. I'm trying to determine whether there would be a third option which is this defendant, who you've never seen somebody like before, and maybe you just don't have a descriptor for it.

(p. 195)

Murderous racism and the death penalty: psychoanalysis and deconstruction

The third option between insanity or monstrosity, for which there seems to be no descriptor, is murder as reason, as self-destructive self-preservation, as normal psychosis. This kind of phrasing combines opposite terms in order to describe "third option" phenomena that exceed our usual categories. Deconstruction is the mode of thought that provides the means to understand such third options and, with psychoanalysis, the apparently most incomprehensible ones, for instance genocide, murderous racism. And in the case of Dylann Roof, the relation to the death penalty.

In his seminar on the death penalty, Derrida wrote:

[T]he death penalty claims to put an end . . . to some life. Whence the seduction that it can exert over fascinated subjects on the side of the condemning power but *also sometimes on the side of the condemned* [my emphasis]. Fascinated by the power and the calculation . . . it affirms its power over time; it masters the future; *it protects against the irruption of the other* [my emphasis]. In any case, it *seems* to do that. . . ; it only seems to do that, for this calculation, this mastery, this decidability, remain phantasms. It would no doubt be possible to show that this is even the origin of phantasm in general.

(2014, 257)

Derrida here speaks of the death penalty as imposing a phantasmal mastery over the end of life, a phantasmal mastery which "protects against the irruption of the other." This phantasmal mastery exerts its compelling influence on both the condemning and the condemned. Dylann Roof believed it necessary and reasonable to impose the death penalty on Black people and simultaneously sought to have it imposed on himself – via rejection of "Jewish psychology." Roof was compelled to protect himself against the irruption of the racial other and the irruption of any otherness in himself. Again: the attack on his own mind as self-destructive self-preservation, normal psychosis.

Here there is another psychoanalytic/deconstructive question. Roof assigned himself the necessary right, the sovereignty, to impose death on a specific racial group, like a genocidal state. In "Psychoanalysis Searches the States of Its Soul," Derrida made the point that "[t]he first gesture of psychoanalysis will have been to explain this sovereignty" (2002, 244). (Freud's most basic idea is that where I believe I am making conscious, even self-preservative decisions, unconscious forces are acting to compel something other, which I then delusionally, phantasmatically believe is my conscious decision.) But, says Derrida, psychoanalysis itself

> has not yet undertaken and still less succeeded in thinking, penetrating and changing the axioms of the ethical, the juridical, and the political, notably in those seismic places where the theological phantasm of sovereignty quakes and where the most traumatic. . ., the most cruel events of our time are being produced.
>
> (ibid.)

And if psychoanalysis is to intervene in the phantasm of sovereignty which produces "the most traumatic events," he goes on to say, it "must remain within the neutrality of the undecidable. . . . It is in . . . the space of undecidability . . . that the transformation to come of ethics, law and politics should *take into account* psychoanalytic knowledge" (2002, 273–274; author's emphasis). This is the undecidability that prosecutor Williams encounters when he speaks of a third term for which there is no descriptor. It is the undecidability that *is* the self-destructive self-preservation of murderous racism, of genocide. And it is the undecidable complicity between Roof's attempt to begin a race *war*, a sovereign declaration of independence of the white race against its enemy, the black race, and the state sovereignty that he knew very well would sentence him to death.

Derrida gives further elaboration of the undecidability between the commission of murder and the death penalty, which can be extended to genocide, when he writes:

> If I know why I kill, I think I am right to kill and this reason that I give myself is a reason that one must be able to argue for rationally with the help of universalizable principles. I kill someone, and I know why, because I think that it is necessary, that it is just, that whoever found himself in my place would have to do the same, that the other is guilty toward me, has wronged me or will wrong me, and so forth. So, even if a court as such has not heard the case, I kill by condemning to death as regards universal law, at least potentially. And therefore, given that the crime is meaningful, deliberate, calculated, premeditated, goal oriented, it belongs to the order of penal justice and is no longer dissociable from a condemnation to death, to a properly penal act. At that point the distinction between vengeance and justice becomes precarious.
>
> (2014, 230–231)

Roof believed he was justified in "taking the law into his own hands." This is always the case with what is called vigilantism and underwrites the entire history of unpunished racist murder. But one must say more about the unconscious-political forces at work. If the state gives itself the power either to commit genocide or to condemn to death, if both are done in the name of what Derrida calls "universalizable principles," then the state or the individual vigilante also unconsciously, lawfully condemns him- or itself to death. Was not the secession of the Southern states, their sovereign declaration of independence to protect slavery, suicidal? Is not Roof suicidal in his phantasmic attempt to start a race war, according to the universal principle that one has the right to protect oneself from the "enemy" who wrongs one?

Psychoanalytically, Klein's point about projective identification as the prototype of an aggressive object relation, in which aggression against the other *is* aggression against oneself, and Bion's subtle point about projective identification directed against one's own mind extend this thinking. One finds the psychoanalytic/deconstructive version of all this when Derrida writes:

> [T]he death penalty is always, by definition, death that comes from the other, given or decided by the other, be it the other within oneself. The possibility of the death penalty – this is too obvious but what we have here is an obscure obviousness that one must begin by recalling – the possibility, and note I say the *possibility*, of the death penalty begins where I am delivered into the power of the other, be it the power of the other in me. . . . To have done with it, one would have to have done with the other; and perhaps those who commit suicide, or those who run toward the condemnation to death as toward suicide want first of all to have done with the other, before finishing themselves off.
>
> (2014, 250)

This is why Roof gives us a window into genocide. To have done with the racial other is to have done with the other in oneself. In similar vein, Laplanche (1999) has written:

> In the face of the alterity of the other, the methods of defense are immutably the same: attempt at assimilation, denial of difference, segregation, destruction. . . . [W]hat is lacking in all the analyses of 'racism' is any consideration of the internal split inherent in the other himself: it is this internal alterity which is at the root of the anxiety provoked by external alterity; it is this that one seeks to reduce at any price.
>
> (p. 230, n. 21)

To which one has to add that the attempt to destroy the internal alterity of the other *is* the attempt to destroy the internal alterity in oneself. And to do so according to legal, universal principles. The protocols of the Wannsee Conference, at which Nazi officials decided on the "final solution," are replete with legal reasoning. Whether it is Roof planning to incite race war or the Nazi government legally planning the final solution, any observer must wonder: how can you not understand what you are doing and the inevitable consequences for yourself? How can you not see that your reasonable, murderous self-preservation is inevitably self-destruction? Foucault characterized Nazi Germany as "an absolutely racist State, an absolutely murderous State, and an absolutely suicidal State" (p. 260).

Derrida makes analogous points about the death penalty. The:

> suicidal truth of the death penalty is unavoidable. . . . [I]t is structurally implied by the logic of the verdict. Insofar as the latter claims to be grounded in law, in reason, in a juridical rationality that is supposed to be universally shared, the guilty one . . . must acknowledge his judges and thus his executioners to be right. . . . [I]t is as if he were committing suicide, as if he were executing himself. . . . But from the moment that he acknowledges his judges and his executioners to be in the right and symbolically transforms hetero-punishment into auto-punishment . . . he . . . ends up no longer really believing in the reality of the death of which he remains the master, a death that he gives himself instead of having it inflicted on him. He believes it without believing it, whence the feeling of fictional or theatrical unreality.
>
> (2014, 67)

Derrida here describes the logic of disavowal, in which the ego splits itself by rejecting a piece of reality, replacing it with a fantasy taken to be reality, and then oscillates between the two states. Recall that Derrida had also spoken of the "madness" of the death penalty grounded in a phantasmal mastery over death, time, and the other as the origin of phantasm in general. For the executors of genocide or Roof himself, there is phantasmal mastery over death by deciding upon the death of the racial other and unconsciously over one's own death. When Roof spends *time* with his intended victims, he is poised to question his own murderous racism and self-destructiveness. But he has to master that time phantasmatically by imposing the death penalty on them and himself. The result is precisely what Derrida describes: the unbelievable scenes of both mass murder and the usual judicial proceedings against it. On the one hand, there must be such judicial proceedings. But, on the other, unless they include an understanding of a "third option" for which there is "no descriptor" such proceedings too will participate in a structure of disavowal which leaves nothing changed.

(Im)possible prevention

If there is any justification to this psychoanalytic/deconstructive analysis, it reemphasizes why racist murder, genocide, cannot be eliminated. Thus, any discussion of prevention must take this terrible truth into account. I will list some possibilities.

(1) As counterintuitive as it sounds, the elimination of the death penalty in places where racism is rampant – particularly in the United States – might have an effect. Historically the application of the death penalty to a majority of Black prisoners has gone hand in hand with racist murder. While Germany, Cambodia, and Rwanda, to name conspicuous examples of twentieth-century genocide, have eliminated the death penalty for all crimes, and Turkey has eliminated it for "ordinary crimes," all had a death penalty in place during their genocidal periods. Whether or not countries that maintain the death penalty are particularly prone to racist murder, or even genocide, cannot be answered definitively but must be considered. (The attack on the mosque in New Zealand is a conspicuous counterexample.) The most recent history of the United States is particularly chilling, as I believe the case of Dylann Roof illustrates. Nor does the elimination of the death penalty by most countries in the world guarantee the prevention of racist murder. It is also worth considering whether the elimination of an insanity defense for "hate crimes," especially racist murder, might help. Because any racist murder is undecidably "normally psychotic," the legal application of the insanity defense obfuscates all the complexities of the relations between reasonable madness and sovereignty. Israel Charny, another noted genocide scholar, came to a similar conclusion in what he called his "requiem" statement about prevention. Addressing the question of genocide as both destructive of others and oneself (p. 114), Charny wrote:

> One can murder millions while looking and acting super competent and therefore, in current language, as if one were quite mentally healthy, and only later in the process of the madness of power and destruction of life do symptoms of personal disorganization and self-hurting appear, but in my view the disturbance was there from the beginning of hurting others.
>
> (ibid.)

His conclusion is that "there can be no resort to a defense of psychological illness and the perpetrator must face criminal charges" (ibid.).

(2) Therapeutic engagement with racism is essential. Keval makes an essential point here:

> When there is an insistence that people must change and learn how to get along better, racist fantasies and ethnic conflicts become more volatile. . . . The challenge of psychoanalysis is to square up to the many faces of racism, and to do so not with the aim of eliminating this type of cruelty but to interrogate the psychic investments and the complex alliances that exist between the forces of reason and racism.
> (p. 120)

To speak of murder as reason, of self-destructive self-preservation, and of normal psychosis aims to demonstrate why Keval is right. So then the question is how to engage, how "to interrogate" "psychic investments" and "complex alliances." For psychoanalysis this means keeping to a rigorous psychoanalytic perspective, i.e., understanding that racist murder and even genocide are the products of powerful unconscious forces, which no good will can ameliorate. As Keval says, such a perspective makes things worse because it disavows the cruelty and "sovereign" reason that produce the worst racist crimes. Derrida says that cruelty and sovereignty are the issues psychoanalysis has to bring to law and ethics *and* to psychoanalytic practice itself. While it is unlikely that a member of a racist group would seek treatment for his or her beliefs, it is possible that such a person would seek treatment for other reasons. (Imagine Dylann Roof in treatment for his very real psychological problems as he is developing his racist beliefs.) The clinician would then have to have the forbearance to deal with these other issues, while also understanding that the patient's racism is an unconscious use of fantasy and delusion to defend against intolerable need for the racial other via self-destruction and the attack on one's own mind. Racist beliefs must be considered very serious symptoms. Clinicians must be educated about this. Individual racism will certainly not be ameliorated by assuming that if other problems have been resolved, racist beliefs will disappear. Rather, the complex psychodynamics of murderous racism or really racism itself demands the kind of prolonged attention psychoanalytic therapy should always entail.

(3) Racist groups are potentially murderously suicidal. (Was not Nazism suicide for Germany, as Foucault said?) In the United States, free speech is constitutionally guaranteed. But this does not have to imply that speech is only speech. In fact, law enforcement should be educated to understand that racist speech is an expression of an ineradicable murderous or even genocidal impulse. When Roof lamented that the racist groups he found online were "all talk and no action," he correctly understood an implicit call to "race war." If law enforcement is to protect citizens, it must be very vigilant about the possibilities of racist violence. (One can only wonder whether the police in Charlottesville were even thinking about this.) The recent designation of white supremacist groups as terrorists could help, but only if law enforcement itself does not consciously, or especially unconsciously, collude with their thinking. Certainly, the spate of murders of Black people by police in the United States and the lamentable record of nonprosecution take one back to the unconscious forces that can unite racist murder with law itself. The "final solution" was to be carried out legally. Hence, the police and military who murdered were carrying out the law. Can one think of a more extreme example of "normal psychosis"? In the face of endemic racism in police forces, a movement to address "implicit bias," i.e., nonconscious racism in police officers, has begun in several cities, including New York. While this may prove to be helpful, if the "complex alliances" between "reason and racism" (Keval) and between self-destructive self-preservation and racism as law are not addressed, there is little chance that things will change.

Note: As of January 2020, a new team of Roof's lawyers are appealing his death sentence with an insanity plea.

Note

1 This is a revised version of a paper that was presented at Second Story, New York City in January 2019; at the National Autonomous University of Mexico, in Mexico City in November 2019; and at IPTAR in February 2020. These dates make clear that the chapter was written before the current racist murders in the United States. The final point about the dangers of continued police murders of Black people stands as originally written.

References

Derrida, J. (2014). *The Death Penalty*, trans. P. Kamuf. Chicago: University of Chicago Press, vol. 1.

Derrida, J. (2002). Psychoanalysis Searches the States of Its Soul. In P. Kamuf (trans.), *Without Alibi*. Stanford: Stanford University Press.
.Freud, S. (1905). Three Essays on the Theory of Sexuality. *Standard Edition*, 7.
Freud, S. (1911). Formulations on the Two Principles of Mental Functioning. *Standard Edition*, 12.
Freud, S. (1915). Instincts and Their Vicissitudes. *Standard Edition*, 14.
Freud, S. (1920). Beyond the Pleasure Principle. *Standard Edition*, 18.
Freud, S. (1921). Group Psychology and the Analysis of the Ego. *Standard Edition*, 18.
Freud, S. (1923a). The Ego and the Id. *Standard Edition*, 19.
Freud, S. (1923b). Neurosis and Psychosis. *Standard Edition*, 19.
Freud, S. (1924). The Loss of Reality in Neurosis and Psychosis. *Standard Edition*, 19.
Freud, S. (1938). Findings, Ideas, Problems. *Standard Edition*, 23.
Keval, N. (2016). *Racist States of Mind*. London: Karnac.
Laplanche, J. (1999). *Essays on Otherness*, ed. J. Fletcher. London: Routledge (*Transcript of Competency Hearing Before the Honorable Richard M. Gergel*. (2017). District Court of the United States, Charleston Division).

Chapter 9

Hunting the real

Psychosis and race in the American hospital

Hannah Wallerstein

Over the last three decades, it has been consistently observed that black Americans[1] receive psychotic disorder diagnoses at higher rates than white Americans (Olbert et al., 2018; Schwartz & Blankenship, 2014; Anglin et al., 2010). While this finding has proven robust across time and setting, with other demographic variables accounted for, reasons for the disparity remain obscure. Here I will briefly outline possible explanations, and then turn to a framework for thinking about the relation between race and psychosis that I find particularly productive. I will argue that elevated rates of psychosis among black Americans may reflect the catastrophic experiences carried by black people that have been disavowed in the social inscription of American history and that a clinical approach sensitive to historical and political factors may be critical to recovery.

One explanation for the link between black race and psychosis in America is clinician bias. Research has pointed to clinicians' mistrust of African American patients (Barnes, 2008; Eack et al., 2012), the underdiagnosis of mood disorders in African American populations and the misinterpretation of socially disruptive behavior (Schwartz & Blankenship, 2014) as potential mediators to the disproportionate diagnostic patterns. Even when using structured interviews with clear-cut diagnostic criteria, race has been shown to influence clinicians' diagnosis of schizophrenia, independent of symptoms (Neighbors et al., 2003).

But reasons for the disparity also surpass individual prejudice. In his book, *The Protest Psychosis* (2010), Jonathan Metzl charts how the very diagnostic classification of psychosis has shifted historically in response to anxieties in the medical establishment inspired by black liberation, beginning with slavery and the protest thereof by black slave leaders and others.

In 1851, American surgeon and proslavery defender Samuel Cartwright developed two categories of insanity specifically for slaves. The first, Dreptomania, described the "symptom" of attempting to run away, and the second, Dyaesthesia Aethiopis, described the "rascality" and "disrespect for the master's property" that resulted when slaves did not have white men overseeing their every action (30). The "treatment" Cartwright recommended was, not surprisingly, brute violence: "whipping, hard labor, and in extreme cases, amputation of toes" (30).

Cartwright's work influenced early twentieth-century researchers, who argued that rates of insanity rose dramatically in black Americans after emancipation, a supposed but demonstrably false relationship. For instance, in 1913 psychiatrist Arrah Evarts wrote an article in the *Psychoanalytic Review* in which she linked psychosis in "colored" patients to the pressures of freedom: "This bondage in reality was a wonderful aid to the colored man. The necessity of mental initiative was never his, and his racial characteristic of imitation carried him far on the road. But after he became a free man, the conditions under which he must progress became infinitely harder" (in Metzl, 31). The association between blackness and dementia precox (a biological category for psychosis at the time) was further used by the Eugenics movement as justification for sterilization. A key advocate was eugenicist and Chief Justice Harry Olsen of the Chicago municipal court, who argued that American society deal with the "defective insane" via "race betterment . . . segregating and sterilizing defective stocks so that they may not reproduce their kind" (in Metzl, 33–34). Put simply, the medical treatment of psychosis is directly tied to the cruelest aspects of our racial history.

Metzl documents how shifting trends within mental health over the following decades along with anxieties consequent to a changing racial climate led to a reorganization of the diagnostic category of schizophrenia. As psychoanalytic conceptions of psychosis and its treatment came into fashion in the 1930s and 1940s, the diagnosis schizophrenia became associated primarily with upper-middle-class white housewives; black Americans suffering from psychosis during these decades were in large part diagnosed as antisocial. Legal and medical innovations in the 1950s (such as the increased use of insanity as a defense in criminal court and advancements in the chemical treatment of psychosis), along with overcrowding in asylums, then led to a shift from treating asylum patients to suppressing and controlling them. With this turn towards coercion, and concurrent with the rise of militant racial justice movements, came a reorganization of the category of schizophrenia in the DSM-II to address primarily aggressive black men.

Where the DSM-I had considered schizophrenia a "reaction," suggesting an "individual extension of normal personality," the newly introduced DSM-II named schizophrenia an "exogenous disease" (96); it began using male pronouns to describe its subject and highlighted hostility and aggression. Medical research on schizophrenia began focusing on black subjects for the first time, and associating schizophrenia with Black Power. The most egregious example, and Metzl's title, came from psychiatrists Walter Bromberg and Frank Simon, who described a new form of schizophrenia called the "protest psychosis": "a condition in which the rhetoric of the Black Power movement drove 'negro men' to insanity" (in Metzl, 100). Similar arguments appeared in various forms in many mainstream research articles in the 1960s and 1970s.

Over the next several decades, deinstitutionalization further produced black men as psychotic subjects par excellence. Metzl writes:

> The process [of de-institutionalization] did not only dictate which patients the state set free, it also determined which patients it held on to. The later and much smaller group – most all of whom were men – [were argued to have] suffered from a particularly violent form of schizophrenia, one that required their continued incarceration. . . . As a result, these men became the institutionalized bodies that de-institutionalization left behind.
>
> (136)

In short, both the diagnostic categories and the clinicians who implement them associate psychosis with blackness, and more specifically with black people fighting for freedom.

While much of the correlation between blackness and psychosis can be explained by clinician bias and structural racism within our diagnostic categories, recent empirical research pushes our thinking further. Using nuanced techniques such as race-blind symptom descriptions, newer studies suggest that a relation between black race and risk of psychosis may exist in America, even with individual and structural biases accounted for (Bresnahan et al., 2007; Arnold et al., 2004). Rates of psychosis do not appear elevated in black populations outside of the United States and Europe (Anglin et al., 2010),[2] suggesting a correlation between the experience of being black in America and elevated expression of psychosis. This chapter aims to provide a psychoanalytic and historical framework for thinking about this correlation. Instead of dismissing black liberation as insane or dismissing the elevated rates of insanity amongst black Americans as mere racist fabrication, I propose to listen to what speaks through insanity, for what it may reveal about the historical and present realities of being black in America. To do so, I will first outline Francoise Davoine and Jean-Max Gaudilliere's framework for thinking psychosis alongside historical trauma and then turn to my experiences on internship at a city hospital in the Bronx.

In their book, *History Beyond Trauma* (2004), Davoine and Gaudilliere theorize madness not as a flight from reality (as it is commonly framed) but as an investigation of aspects of reality that have been subject to erasure. Focusing primarily on war trauma, they elaborate a type of catastrophic experience at the edge of the personal and historical that is mis- or disremembered by an entire society, often for political reasons. For Davoine and Gaudilliere, such events and their continuous erasure erode the fundamental securers of social and subjective existence. This on two registers. First, there is a "rupture of the symbolic order, of the place in which alliance, the guarantee of promises and treaties, and hence the social link, is founded" (45). Normal modes of trust and relationality have been destroyed, leading language and history to falter in their anchoring functions. Second, there is a "disorganization of the orientation points of the Imaginary" (45). Time and space fall into disarray, destroying the capacity for "specular identification" through which one comes to have a self (45).

Madness, for Davoine and Gaudilliere, becomes then both the effect and the expression of a horror that has been forgotten: "What we are dealing with . . . is a normal craziness that bears witness to a normality that is crazy, trivialized, dehistoricized, and denied" (47). They continue:

> In the gap opened up by those patients who rightly lament that they have no self, no 'me,' . . . [t]hey . . . bear witness to the stories that have been erased from history . . . whose disaster they reveal at the price of their own identity.
>
> (xxi–xxii)

For Davoine and Gaudilliere, this witnessing of a failure to inscribe historic catastrophe points the way towards resolution: "In speaking to the wall, to the TV, or the universe, madness challenges its interlocutor to find the place of otherness to which it can speak" (7). The analyst's role, then, "far from diagnosis of deficit," becomes to "bring into existence zones of nonexistence wiped out by a powerful blow that actually took place" (xxvii). Davoine and Gaudilliere articulate this project as a battle, and one that does not leave the analyst unscathed: "the analytic act in cases of madness may be compared to an arrow of language repeatedly shot at the Real Thing in order to force it to enter the realm of speech" (206). More specifically, they argue that such patients find resonances in our own histories and make use of them to locate points of overlap from which experience without witness can find the other necessary to be spoken and, even more importantly, to be heard.

Using Davoine's and Gaudilliere's model, I turn to my experiences as a psychology intern on the inpatient psychiatry units of a city hospital in New York, where I treated primarily poor and working-class men of color experiencing psychosis. As I was able to witness only momentary glimpses into the breakdowns patients were experiencing and giving voice to, my presentation will be associative, drawing from literary and historical references. My goal is not to offer a conclusive elaboration of what psychosis can tell us about blackness in America but simply to point to a way of listening that may allow us to take seriously a form of expression often dismissed as nonsense and medicated into silence.[3] I will present my observations in three parts, relating themes in the order they returned to memory.

I Destruction

It is difficult to reenter the hospital – to walk myself through the two double doors to which I held the key, never knowing what I would find inside. Swallowing fear every time, because no kind of safety was ensured. The day I left the inpatient units, I dreamed of a mass murder I had barely escaped, leaving many to die. When I think of the hospital, it is the threat of destruction pulsing through the halls that first returns.

This seems multiply determined. Current qualifications for inpatient hospitalization make acts of violence or violent urges close to mandatory for admission. Insurance-driven short stays then created more acute patient populations, less stability, and less relational trust within the unit. A deprived environment exacerbated tensions, as well as symptoms. Lastly and perhaps most insidiously, little containment was offered. The hospital did not supply staff who could intervene upon violence on the unit – instead when violence erupted, there would be a "blue light," and support staff would show up minutes later, after enough time for significant damage to have occurred. The responding staff were often police officers who were unfamiliar with the unit and could be aggressive themselves, making matters worse. In addition, the limited containment possibilities that did exist (blue lights, physical and chemical restraints, and confinement) were recorded, and affected the hospital's reputation, creating pressure to abstain from intervening with an escalating patient until the situation was already out of hand.

All this contributed to a sense of destructiveness that often paralyzed the unit. Staff hated patients for threatening their safety. Patients hated staff for threatening theirs. Attention went towards suppressing anger on all sides, getting rid of it, expelling threats, often loading projectively into the bodies of black men. (We would sometimes count the days until a particularly terrifying patient was off the unit). What was eclipsed was any space to listen to what the destructiveness had to say.

Winnicott writes of destructiveness as primary to human subjectivity (1989), not opposed to creativity, love, and life, but rather one and the same, an inherent drive toward engagement with the world. He points to the baby's first kick at the uterine wall and the infant's "spontaneous gesture" as earliest examples. What develops out of this primary destructivity is, for Winnicott, completely dependent on how it is received: "The fate of this unity of drive cannot be stated without reference to the environment. The drive is potentially 'destructive' but whether it is destructive or not depends on what the object is like" (245). If the environment is able to meet the child's intensity, receive his destructiveness and provide opposition that contains while registering his power, the child can discover what is "me" and what is "not me" and, through this experience, both himself and his environment as real and usable. Alternatively, if the environment cannot tolerate the destructiveness natural to existing, if instead it retaliates or collapses, the process of discovering "me" and "not me," fantasy and reality, is foreclosed. Instead the child becomes either compliant or unable to contain destructive aggression within fantasy.

One does not have to look far to see evidence of the particular refusal of black destructiveness in the United States, from the pathologization of militant Black liberation movements discussed previously, to the countless shootings of black people assumed to be a "threat" simply by going about their daily lives. Perhaps nowhere is this more starkly rendered than in the recent backlash against the Black Lives Matter movement, where even fighting for the right to live has been condemned as hostile, dangerous, and unacceptable.

In *Beloved* (1987), Toni Morrison writes of white terror of black destructivity and its consequence:

> White people believed that whatever the manners, under every dark skin was a jungle. Swift unnavigable waters . . . red gums ready for their sweet white blood. In a way . . . they were right. The more colored people spent their strength trying to convince [white people] . . . how gentle they were, how clever and loving, how human, the more they used themselves up to persuade whites of something Negroes believed could not be questioned, the deeper and more tangled the jungle grew inside. But it wasn't the jungle blacks brought with them to this place . . . it was the jungle white folks planted in them.
>
> (234)

Here it is white fear and refusal of black destructivity that creates a "jungle," demanding a compliance insidious to subjective life. Returning to the hospital with this framework in mind, the level of violence on the unit can be understood as a hopeful, although tragically unmet, communication – an attempt to fight for something, which is always on some level a fight for life, and to find an environment that can receive, clarify, and take seriously the matter at hand.

One black Guyanese American patient I'll call Loki brought to us a particularly tragic history of foreclosed destruction. Loki arrived agitated, violent, and high on K2; a constant trickster, his initial pranks suffered from his level of intoxication. In our first meeting he "pretended" he was open to talking with me, followed me into a meeting room and then began laughing at my having fallen for his interest. I told him I supposed I'd fall for that one every time; he thought this was hilarious and decided now to try to trick me every day. Mostly this consisted of attempting to manipulate me into buying him a snack.

One day, Loki performed a darker prank. Staff on the unit were gathered in morning report, and Loki was very angry – his psychiatrist was refusing to meet with him due to threats Loki had made early on in his stay, and Loki knew he would not be able to leave until this circumstance was remedied. Our staff meeting was held behind a large glass window, and Loki screamed on the other side. He finally yelled, "If you do not talk to me I will bash my head into the window!" and with this, he ran at the glass, at what seemed like full speed, and slammed his head. I was hysterical, thinking he was going to snap his neck. He then did it again, screaming, "Look what you are making me do! Look what you are making me do!" The most disturbing aspect of this event, as we waited for the police to arrive, was witnessing the nursing staff on the other side of the glass standing by and simply watching Loki hurt himself. He was a small man, easily containable, and yet no one stepped in. In hindsight, I imagine the nurses were enraged at him, having dealt with his mischief and yelling for days, maybe also furious with the mostly white medical staff on the other side of the glass for leaving them with the mess; perhaps they enacted their anger by letting Loki attack himself.

Later that day, when talking with Loki about what had transpired and the terror it evoked, he smiled at me and said, "You shouldn't have worried, didn't you think I would use my head to hurt my head?" He explained that as he was acting out a suicidal act, he was in reality making sure his head and neck were safe (apparently he had put his hood up a certain way, and used his shoulders to protect his spine).

A couple of days later he asked me if I wanted Kool-Aid.

"Kool-Aid?"

He started laughing, "You know my father was killed in Jonestown, right?"

I hadn't. I looked it up.

I was aware that there had been a mass-murder-suicide in Guyana in 1978, in which 918 people had died, most from drinking cyanide-laced Kool-Aid at the command of cult leader Jim Jones. What I had not known was how linked this horrific event was to racial politics in the United States at the time. White American Jim Jones founded the People's Temple in Indianapolis on an activist platform, dedicated to racial justice. The church moved its headquarters to Oakland in the 1970s, where Jones's focus on social welfare programs, housing and health care attracted a largely black followership. Jones repeatedly declared his own blackness, emulated black preachers, and offered a vision of racial utopia free from white supremacy, segregation, and oppression. The move to Jonestown in Guyana was the culmination of such a vision – the desire to escape all the hate, injustice, and danger and find a place where finally there would be safety and freedom.

In reality, the racial oppression and antiblack violence imagined to be left behind by the move ran a particularly devastating course. Beneath the illusion of racial equality, Jonestown was run almost exclusively by Jones and white women, demanding total submission from a majority black followership. The act of murder-suicide, presented as a necessary response to the threat of racist annihilation, in fact annihilated roughly 600 African Americans.

And then I hear the echoes: "Look what you are making me do! Look what you are making me do!" Loki screams at the white male attending, a man in power professing to help but instead keeping him captive. "Look what you are making me do!" as he pretends to commit suicide at the hands, at the command, of the "White Knight" (Hutchinson, 2017) in charge. In tricking us, he also flips positions – commandeering his captives to bear the terror of a suicidal rage they are both complicit in and cannot contain. Playing all parts, Loki performs a history of violent deception – the seductive offering of a utopia free from racial oppression and conflict that in reality produces deadly compliance. It is this trick of erasing destruction, which erases, too, the possibility for subjective engagement, that Loki points to and attempts to convey.

II Deprivation

Every morning during community meeting, patients offered a list of reasonable complaints – the plumbing in two bathrooms is not working, the food is terrible, there are not enough activities. Staff would agree, and most of the time have no solution. More broadly, patients often arrived homeless, without employment, and were discharged to whatever shelter among the boroughs had openings, with an appointment at a faraway psychiatric clinic in a month. In short, in the face of great need, we had close to nothing to offer.

The deprivation did not stop at patients. Staff were overworked, expected to do more than was possible, and without resources needed to perform basic tasks (such as printing paper). As an intern, I experienced the staff as having little capacity to help metabolize experience or think about our training needs. In a particularly challenging moment, immediately before my second rotation, the head psychologist and supervisor went on sudden medical leave, leaving me and another intern to carry the unit on our own, breaking APA internship requirements. Few times have I felt as greedy and as ungenerous as I did that year.

"I know what it is to be without milk that belongs to you" says ex-slave Sethe of Morrison's *Beloved* when she has given up on the social world, "to have to fight and holler for it, and to have so little left" (236). The novel depicts the violence of slavery as theft of the most basic human resources, largely figured through oral imagery. Sethe is pinned down and nursed by students of her plantation owner, robbed of both her daughter's food and her capacity to give. "They took my milk!" she repeats throughout the text. Another character is forced to wear an iron bit in his mouth, making both speech and taking in nourishment impossible. Sethe's husband, having witnessed Sethe's nursing, lives out his suffering by the dairy churn, representing the terrible scene with butter smeared all over his face. In short, the foundational elements of subjective life – giving, receiving, and speaking – are taken away. As the hospital's barren landscape illustrates, the deprivation so brutally and literally rendered in *Beloved* is no stranger to the present day, with a recent study reporting the median black family's wealth to be 2% that of the median white family's and projected to fall to zero by 2082.[4]

As if calling on Morrison's oral imagery, patients at the hospital often asked staff to bring them treats – a coffee, a donut, a juice. Something, anything. It would be tempting to respond, I think for selfish reasons; the deprivation we were witnessing and to a small degree experiencing was a daily reality for many on the unit, and to bring a coffee, a donut, a juice, would allow one to think it was, or could be, otherwise. The risk in such a response was covering over the deprivation, thereby refusing to confront and so too metabolize something of its experience.

One particularly insistent bargainer I'll call Sherwin made his demands less concrete – he did not want coffee, he wanted love. Brought in manic, after swinging a knife around at the train station and demanding a white woman marry him, Sherwin spent his days on the unit continuing his search. He would seek out light-skinned female staff, propose to them, and when they turned him down shout, "It's because I'm black!"

Over time, Sherwin's requests became less agitated and more fanciful – each encounter seemed to enact a ritual, although for whom and to what end remained unclear. One day, in a rare moment of privacy in the art room, Sherwin began to talk about his life. He told me of his father, a committed member of a Black nationalist organization, who had radicalized Sherwin as a child, expected much of him, and then was in and out of jail during Sherwin's adolescence. He spoke of his mother, who was light-skinned, also in and out of Sherwin's childhood, seemingly in response to conflict with his father. As Sherwin was speaking, another white staff member entered the space, and his open, wandering prose came to a sudden halt. He put on a large, flirtatious grin, told our visitor she was beautiful and asked her to marry him – she gave the shy smile most staff offered, and left.

"What just happened?" I asked

"What do you mean?"

"You completely transformed when Ms. Smith came into the room."

"You have to make white women think you want them. It's the only way to be safe," he replied

I was struck by this statement, as it seemed to flip the history it brought to mind, in which black men were lynched by mobs and then by courts under the accusation of having raped white women. Here it was not desire for white women but the absence of it that threatened safety. I wondered how Sherwin was right. In the following days I observed his interactions with light-skinned female staff and attended to my own response when Sherwin performed his marriage dance. I noticed a particularly disturbing aspect: while I think the mimicry of this historical and often deadly exchange made all white women on the unit uncomfortable, there was also a pleasure in it – in feeling one's desirability and so too one's purity (after all, the answer was no). Indeed, the female staff on the unit, for all their complaints, were drawn to Sherwin. It is this perverse underbelly of deprivation – the pleasure in withholding, in seeing the other want – to which Sherwin's proposals gave voice.

Near the end of his stay, following countless requests that I meet him at Starbucks after he left, after many refusals and much curiosity about his request, Sherwin broke down crying. He turned away from me and whispered, "I am your n** baby, and you are leaving me at the church steps." I was speechless. My mind went to Sherwin's light-skinned mother's departure, an articulation in his personal history of the social legacy of white female rejection of black masculinity. A rejection that Sherwin performed in his proposals, highlighting the use of black male desire in order to evacuate while also experiencing white female desire. But there seemed to be more in his words – why the church? Where and when was this scene? He left the next day, giving me a note with his address, in case I changed my mind about meeting again; I struggled to say good-bye amidst the questions his breakdown opened up.

III Broken mirrors

The last observation I'll share from the hospital is a frequent delusion I encountered among young black men of being a famous model. I was surprised by the recurrence of this particular delusion, perhaps especially in men. One patient, who reported himself "half white and half black," would spend sessions performing poses and asking which race I saw in each. Another patient spoke about his modeling in great detail – the clothes he wore, his fans. One session, about a week into our work together, he asked me if I had ever played a first-person shooter video game, where your hands are out in front of you. I had. He then said, "I feel like that all the time. My hands are in front of me, and I have no idea what is behind them, I have no idea what I look like."

Loss of one's image has been a trope in conceptualizing the psychic violence done to black Americans, and more specifically black men, since the early twentieth century, entering popular discourse through Ralph Ellison's *Invisible Man* (1947). This invisibility is also a structural reality, most clearly represented in the mass incarceration and subsequent political and financial disenfranchisement of young black men.

Davoine and Gaudilliere point to the devastating impact of a lost image on the body. Without representation, bodily experience cannot be inhabited as one's own. "Emotions and sensations" become "impossible to trust," often "anaesthetized" into what Davoine and Gaudilliere call "zones of petrification" (48–49). Ellison echoes the anesthetization at stake in the experience of invisibility throughout his novel, describing poignantly the resulting feeling of unreality. Along similar lines, Morrison articulates the path to freedom as re-imagining and so too reinvesting in the body:

> The only grace they could have was the grace they could imagine. . . . if they could not see it, they would not have it.
>   . . . [I]n this here place, we flesh; flesh that weeps, laughs; flesh that dances on bare feet in grass. Love it. Love it hard. Yonder they do not love your flesh. They despise it. . . . You got to love it.
> (102–104)

I am reminded of Ta-Nehisi Coates's plea to not forget the body, to understand that "racism is a visceral experience, that it dislodges brains, blocks airways, rips muscle, extracts organs, cracks bones, breaks teeth. You must never look away from this" (2015, 10).

One young man on the unit whom I'll call Joseph spoke exclusively of his body. It hurt. He experienced a series of odd and painful physical sensations, almost without pause. Following medical workups, his experience was marked as a somatic delusion; he was placed on multiple antipsychotic medications, all with little success. Hopeless for relief, Joseph mostly kept his pain a secret. Indeed, it was only during his second admission on the unit, following an attempt to cut into his body to stop the pain, that he finally revealed to me his physical suffering. Most days he sat home alone in his mother's apartment, attempting to think the pain away, wondering why on earth he had been saddled with it. "Pain behavior can point to a painful place," writes Wittgenstein, "but the subject of pain is the person who gives it expression" (in Davoine and Gaudilliere, 302). I, like Joseph, wonder after the contents of his pain – what was he working to express, that found its way into the most basic of signals? Pain. Pain in the body. What was he expressing on behalf of others, historic and present, who themselves were unable to feel?

One session Joseph and I sat together on the windowsill, and, for forty minutes, he communicated to me as best he could the bodily sensations that passed through him. It was devastating. I felt by the end drained of hope. Joseph then turned to me, lit up and said, "I feel like we just killed a deer!" I was both moved and confused by this image, which somehow felt right. In hindsight, I am struck by the resonance with Davoine and Gaudilliere's comparison of the psychoanalytic treatment of psychosis to hunting: "an arrow of language repeatedly shot at the Real Thing in order to force it to enter the realm of speech." Perhaps it was this traumatic real that Joseph was marking that we had, momentarily, shot into speech; this traumatic real that our psychotic patients keep alerting us to, that has yet to find its way into history, both individual and social.

Conclusion

> All survivors bear witness to the impossibility of surviving alone . . . without an other present, or, if necessary, hallucinated.
> (Davoine and Gaudilliere, 210)

At the opening of the first museum in the United States to memorialize victims of lynching, founder Bryan Stevenson articulated his vision as the confrontation of a shadow: "[C]ast across the American landscape. . . [, t]his shadow cannot be lifted until we shine the light of truth on the destructive violence that shaped our nation, traumatized people of color, and compromised our commitment to the rule of law and to equal justice."[5] Indeed, aspects of our history and present reality of racist violence that cannot be addressed do not disappear, but set up residence as shadows, gaps, or, in Davoine and Gaudilliere's term, "zones of petrification" – bits of catastrophic experience without representation. Their presence signals a threat to the foundational elements of social relations – the capacity to trust, to communicate, to be truthful. Ignored or denied by many, these gaps are left to those who cannot help but notice. As Davoine and Gaudilliere point out, it is often the children or grandchildren of the traumatized who take them up, unable to not register the shadows that cloud their caregivers' minds.

But how does one make sense of a shadow that no one else professes to see? Following Davoine and Gaudilliere, I contend that madness can be an effort at such sense-making – an attempt to represent what has been disavowed from the social world, in order to find one's way back into it. One way, then, to understand the elevated rates of psychosis in black Americans is as reflecting the kind of knowledge carried by this particular population, knowledge that has been denied or erased in the social inscription of American history.

Each in their own terms, Loki, Sherwin and Joseph grapple with shadows. Loki screams about coercion, Sherwin performs his marriage dance, Joseph bears inexplicable pain. All three invoke experiences that seem both of and beyond them, calling in more or less explicit ways on historical tropes. If we conceptualize these symptoms as purely individual, they become evidence of a faulty mind. But if we think of them as at once personal and historical, as a personal expression of contact with a historical shadow, they become "instruments of research" (78) to be respected, taken seriously, and eventually joined.

Such a shift has consequences for analytic work. First, it places history and social context more squarely at the center of how we listen. Paradoxically, symptoms that appear most detached from the social world are here thought of as most intimately connected to it. I have had fantasies since leaving of the hospital of setting up courses on the history of American slavery on the units or workshops to construct family maps, infusing the environment with the spirit of investigation and the importance of social and personal history. Second, the framework here espoused demands of clinicians for a particular kind of availability and assumption of responsibility. It requires us to tune in to the ways our patients live in and call on us – how we dream them, the parts of our own histories and experiences they evoke, and, perhaps most challenging, what they notice in us, which will inevitably become part of the investigative process. For it is in the meeting of two people who may each know something about catastrophe and so too one another, not in the sense of merger but in the sense of existing within the shared and intersecting paths of human history, that shadows can begin to be translated into a common language, freeing their explorers from the impossible task of surviving them alone. It is at this threshold of the representable that we face both risk and possibility; if we dismiss the mad, we further alienate those who dare to investigate historical catastrophe, but if we listen, we have the opportunity to join in the research, thereby fostering the development of a more just society.

Notes

1 As I am interested in the impact of the historical and social position of those defined as "black" in America (which cuts across ethnic origin), I will refer primarily to "black Americans." Some of the research has focused exclusively on African Americans, so I will use this term when appropriate.
2 While this research has been important in refuting an essentialist reading of the relation between black race and psychosis, it is important to note that it ends up relying on an essentialist conception of blackness, where people across different

societies and geographies are assumed to be part of an overarching category of "black" people, as if the term referred to an ontological reality and not a context-specific social construction.
3 It is worth noting that psychoanalysis in America was historically thought to be inappropriate for the treatment of psychosis as well as of those with significant socioeconomic stressors. To the contrary, I argue that working psychoanalytically can reveal links to historical trauma, often especially relevant to those cast out of the social order.
4 Institute for Policy Studies, *Dreams Deferred: How Enriching the 1% Widens the Racial Wealth Divide*, January 2019. Retrieved from: https://ips-dc.org/racial-wealth-divide-2019.
5 Why Build a Memorial to Victims of Racial Terror?, April 2018. Retrieved from: https://museumandmemorial.eji.org/memorial.

References

Anglin, D., Lee, R., Yang, L., Lo, G. & Opler, M. (2010). Ethnicity and Psychosis: Examining the Nature of the Relationship. In A. Fortier & S. Turcotte (eds.), *Health Education: Challenges, Issues and Impact*. Hauppage, New York: Nova Science Publishers, 119–144.

Arnold, L. M. et al. (2004). Ethnicity and First-Rank Symptoms in patients with Psychosis. *Schizophrenia Research*, 67:207–212.

Barnes, A. (2008). Race, Schizophrenia, and Admission to State Psychiatric *Administration and Policy in Mental Health*, 31:241–252.

Bresnahan, M. et al. (2007). Race and Risk of Schizophrenia in a US Birth Cohort: Another Example of Health Disparity? *International Journal of Epidemiology*, 36:751–758.

Coates, T. (2015). *Between the World and Me*. New York: Spiegal and Grau.

Davoine, F. & Gaudilliere, J. M. (2004). *History Beyond Trauma*, trans. S. Fairfield. New York: Other Press.

Eack, S. M., Bahorik, A. L., Newhill, C. E., Neighbors, H. W. & Davis, L. E. (2012). Interviewer-Perceived Honesty as a Mediator of Racial Disparities in the Diagnosis of Schizophrenia. *Psychiatric Services*, 63:875–880.

Ellison, R. (1947). *Invisible Man*. New York: Random House.

Hutchinson, S. (2017). *Black Women and the People's Temple in Jonestown*. Retrieved from: www.aaihs.org/black-women-and-the-peoples-temple-in-jonestown/.

Metzl, J. (2010). *The Protest Psychosis: How Schizophrenia Became a Black Disease*. Boston, MA: Beacon Press.

Morrison, T. (1987). *Beloved*. New York: Vintage Books.

Neighbors, H. W., Trierweiler, S. J., Ford, B. C. & Muroff, J. R. (2003). Racial Differences in DSM Diagnosis Using a Semi-Structured Instrument: The Importance of Clinical Judgment in the Diagnosis of African Americans. *Journal of Health and Social Behavior*, 44:237–256.

Olbert, C. M., Nagendra, A. & Buck, B. (2018). Meta-Analysis of Black vs. White Racial Disparity in Schizophrenia Diagnosis in the United States: Do Structured Assessments Attenuate Racial Disparities? *Journal of Abnormal Psychology*, 127(1):104–115.

Schwartz, R. C. & Blankenship, D. M. (2014). Racial Disparities in Psychotic Disorder Diagnoses: A Review of Empirical Literature. *World Journal of Psychiatry*, 4(4):133–140.

Winnicott, D. W. (1989). The Use of an Object in the Context of Moses and Monotheism. In C. Winnicott, R. Sheperd & M. Davis (eds.), *DW Winnicott: Psycho-Analytic Explorations*. Cambridge, MA: Harvard University Press, 240–246.

A psychoanalytic contribution to understanding anti-Latino discourse and violence

Ricardo C. Ainslie

> When Mexico sends its people, they're not sending their best. They're not sending you. They're not sending you. They're sending people that have lots of problems, and they're bringing those problems with us. They're bringing drugs. They're bringing crime. They're rapists. And some, I assume, are good people.
> – Presidential Candidate Donald Trump
> June 16, 2015e[1]

Racism is not new to American political discourse, but recent decades have seen a discernable rise in anti-Latino rhetoric and action. Like all political and social discourse, this rhetoric draws from a psychological space and from a cultural context. Political leaders do not invent their language or frame their views in a vacuum. On the contrary, whether consciously or unconsciously (or both), they draw from powerful currents; they articulate feelings held by the collective; more usually, a subset of the collective. That articulation, in turn, may attract more followers and may create a rhetorical space within which those views become amplified and those holding the same or related attitudes find common ground. In this manner, hate speech can ground collective identities; it invites a felt sense of coherence that draws from that shared prejudice. This turn is dangerous because once established, it is difficult to dismantle – attacking racist rhetoric becomes a threat to the individual and collective identities of those who have found coherence within such ideologies.

Donald Trump did not create anti-Latino[2] sentiment; he simply exploited and amplified it. In 2010, Arizona Governor Jan Brewer signed state law SB 1070, intended "to make attrition through enforcement the public policy of all state and local government entities in Arizona." The law set off a national furor and was widely reviled. The phrase "to make attrition" was commonly understood to be nativist code for ethnic cleansing because it invited racial profiling. Arizona law enforcement could now stop Latinos simply because they *appeared* to be individuals who were in the country illegally. It made all Latinos vulnerable to an unusual level of scrutiny by law enforcement. "Breathing-while-brown" could elicit a demand for documentation of legal status, and officers could apprehend anyone unable to produce the requisite papers.[3]

For many Americans, especially White Americans (who supported this bill/who found a community with the supporters of this bill), the feelings behind the Arizona measure resonated with their concerns and anxieties about immigration, especially that of undocumented immigrants. A contemporary poll (Rasmussen, 2010) found that 60% of Americans were in favor of similar legislation allowing local police to "stop and verify the immigration status of anyone they suspect of being an illegal immigrant." Reflecting this sentiment, similar laws were spawned in two dozen states, although few of those bills actually made it through the legislative process to become laws.

Just days after SB 1070 was signed into law in Arizona, Gary Kelley, a White man living in South Phoenix, accosted his neighbor, Juan Varela, while Varela stood in his own front yard. In a drunken rage, Kelley screamed "You fucking Mexican, go back to Mexico!" before shooting Varela to death in front of his family. Varela was, in fact, an American citizen; his family had been living in the United States for five generations, and he was an example of what SB 1070 opponents most feared: simply being brown-skinned was sufficient to question the legitimacy of one's legal status in the United States.

The rise in anti-Latino hate crimes and other forms of violence

Tracking hate crimes is notoriously difficult given that quite often it is not possible to know the intent of a perpetrator unless they explicitly invoke hate speech in relation to racial, ethnic, religious or sexual orientation in the course of committing an act of violence against another person or group. Further, states vary in regard to whether and how they collect this information, and not all law enforcement agencies track hate crimes with the same degree of enthusiasm or commitment. Finally, victims of hate crimes, especially those whose legal status in the United States is unauthorized, are often hesitant to report their victimization to law enforcement.

These caveats notwithstanding, there are consistent trends. The Southern Poverty Law Center, a nonpartisan center that tracks hate crime, reports that anti-Latino hate crimes rose every year between 2003 and 2007 (Potok, 2008). The same trend was reported by the U.S. Department of Justice, namely that between 2011 and 2012 attacks against the Hispanic community more than tripled, and during 2011–2015 Hispanics experienced a higher rate of violent hate crime victimization than non-Hispanic Whites and Blacks (Masucci & Langton, 2017). A 2016 FBI report comparing 2015 to 2016 statistics found that anti-Latino hate crimes rose by 15% (Criminal Justice Information Services Division, 2016).

In addition, a study by Stacey et al. (2011) found that the incidence level of anti-Hispanic crimes was associated with places with higher rates of Hispanic immigration, lending support to the thesis that Hispanic immigration was the leading cause of violence against Latinos. Specifically, they found support for their hypothesis that recent changes in Hispanic immigration were positively correlated to hate crimes targeting Hispanics.

The 2016 American presidential election placed immigration in the forefront of national debates in the United States. The anti-immigrant character of this discourse may have fueled an increase in anti-immigrant hate crimes, as some have contended (e.g., Los Angeles Commission of Human Relations, 2016). A 2018 study by Múller and Schwars, published in the online version of the Social Science Research Network, found a strong linkage between President Donald Trump's anti-immigrant rhetoric on Twitter during his first year in office and anti-Muslim and anti-Latino hate crimes as reported by the FBI.

Foreigners, strangers, and stranger anxiety

It is a truism of psychoanalytic developmental theory that, for infants, the anxious response to strangers is as universal as the need to attach oneself to caregivers (Bowlby, 1988; Spitz, 1965). In fact, in terms of the earliest, most primordial awareness of self and object, the infant's first year of life is marked by the two most fundamental organizers of social experience: the deepest love for the "we" of symbiotic immersion, and the deepest dread and fear in relation to the "not-me" Other. Fear of the

Other (along with curiosity and perplexity) is in clear evidence from the moment that the human infant begins to emerge into consciousness, as Margaret Mahler and her colleagues so beautifully documented in their now classic work, *The Psychological Birth of the Human Infant* (Mahler et al., 1975).

René Spitz's work helps us understand the underlying emotional structures involved in the formation of the construct of stranger as "enemy." Spitz theorizes that the presence of the stranger undermines the illusion of oneness-with-mother. It is the threat to that fantasy of symbiosis that is presumed to mobilize weariness and anxiety in relation to the stranger. Thus, from the beginnings of emotional life, the stranger, the Other, is configured as a threat that may engender destabilization and fragmentation of the self within the symbiotic space. Similarly, Winnicott's (1971) notion of the capacity to "hate" also begins here at this same developmental juncture. The formulations of these psychoanalytic developmental theorists help us understand the defensive character of the construction of the Other as enemy. This makes it useful to our efforts to understand the current climate of anti-Latino discourse and the accompanying manifestations of aggression against Latinos.

Psychoanalytic theorists such as Vamik Volkan (1988) have seized upon these developmental observations to underscore the link between stranger anxiety as a developmental circumstance and fear of the Other within a broader societal/social framework. Out of the polarities of love and the amalgam of fear and hate that govern the infant's early experience of the world of object(s), an affective framework of complex representational dimensions is established that later lends itself to shape the forms of self-other engagement. Every human being "knows," at a deep, phenomenological level, the experience of the Other as an object of ambivalence from the earliest moments of social awareness. However, Volkan adds an additional crucial element to this formulation, namely, the ways in which ethnic identity, religious belief, and language, among other cultural factors, create a framework within which we have both individualized enemies as well as created concepts of collective, shared enemies. In other words, our concept of "enemy" draws not only from individual, personal experiences but also from our participation in the concept of enemy as it is defined by the groups with which we identify. This also means that constructions of an enemy/Other are always intertwined with individual and collective identity processes.

The transformation of the American social space

In 2009, I wrote "Regression in the Construction of the Immigrant Other," drawing on the psychoanalytic concept of regression to understand the aftermath of a 2008 Immigration Customs and Enforcement (ICE) raid on the Iowa community of Postville and the social stressors that may have created the dehumanizing attitudes toward the immigrants who were apprehended. The raid on the Postville meatpacking plant resulted in the arrest of some 400 workers who were believed to be to be in the United States without legal authorization. Many of those who were detained had families, including children enrolled in Postville's public schools. The men were taken to detention centers and presumably most were eventually deported.

The raid sparked great outrage throughout the country, but in some quarters, also outcries of support for ICE and the policies that were "finally" beginning to rid the country of unwanted immigrants who lacked legal status to be here (Ainslie, 2009). I drew from Schafer's (1954/1967) use of the construct of "regression in the service of the ego" to discuss the ways in which, in the context of anxiety and stress, regression mobilizes a variety of defensive mechanisms. Some of these defenses, like splitting, projection, and the attendant dehumanization, could readily be seen at work in the responses within some sectors of the Postville community. They voiced their support for the ICE raids in terms that were striking for the intensity of their hostility and anger: "These are not immigrants; these are criminal invaders"; "It is about time that we start getting rid of the reason our economy is falling apart"; "Send all illegals back to their own countries after six months in jail. You will see crime go down, taxes go down, overcrowded schools get back to decent numbers and see real American citizens get back their jobs stolen by these illegal . . . criminals" "No illegal alien has the right to anything: he/she has no right to medical attention, hospital care, education, police protection, food shelter, utilities – for the illegal alien is no more than a common criminal. They should be herded onto trains and buses and deported to the borders and from there sent back to their countries after working for the US Government without being paid" (*Des Moines Register*, cited in Ainslie, ibid.). This later quote, calling for a group of people to be shipped off on trains to perform forced labor, seems eerily reminiscent of the attitudes that led to the Holocaust.

Social anxieties and the transformation of the American social landscape

Postville was a single incident, but the community itself was a reflection of what was taking place in many parts of America, setting off complex dynamics as people struggled to "digest" the radical transformation of the American social landscape. A 2009 *New York Times* interactive map (see "Remade in America: The Newest Immigrants and Their Impact") provides one of the clearest visual representations of the impact of immigration on American communities. The digital map goes back to 1880 and, in intervals of a decade, tracks the patterns of migration into the United States. An especially useful feature is the fact that one is able to click on filters that allow the viewer to focus on migratory patterns for particular countries of origin and see precisely where within the United States immigrants from that nation have settled over the ten-year increments.

Immigration patterns for some 20 nations are accessible at a keystroke, but none stands out more than immigration from Mexico. The brute numbers are telling – in the thirty years between 1980 and 2010 Mexican immigration into the United States went from approximately two million to nearly twelve million – creating an enormous impact on the American social landscape (see Stepler & Lopez, 2016). The interactive map provides a perspective that the numbers alone do not: the viewer can see how Mexican migration (by far the largest number of documented or undocumented immigrants) has transformed America radically and profoundly over a relatively short period of time. While America has witnessed prior migratory waves that have stirred ambivalence and xenophobia, the sheer number of immigrants from Latin America (primarily from Mexico, followed by representation from other countries, especially from Central America) is unprecedented.

This exercise provides a striking window into how much America has changed. During this thirty-year interval, the southeastern seaboard, from Louisiana to the Carolinas, went from having almost no Latinos to having a substantial presence throughout the region, Latinos assumed jobs working in slaughterhouses, cattle and poultry production, construction, agriculture, and the service industry. The same pattern is evident in the American agricultural heartland: in places like Iowa, Indiana, and Nebraska, significant numbers of Latino immigrants moved in to take similar jobs. Many communities that had never had a Latino presence suddenly found themselves with a significant number of Mexicans and

Central Americans (and the cultural currency that they brought with them), as well as Mexican restaurants, churches offering Spanish language services, and children showing up in their schools who spoke no English. Midwest communities that had been nearly entirely White for centuries (with the exception of scattered Native American communities pushed out of sight on remote reservations), suddenly found themselves "invaded" by Latino immigrants who looked different, who spoke little or no English, and who were culturally quite different from the local population. In the South, communities long used to the post–Civil War, post–Jim Crow White–Black racial divide suddenly had Latinos in their communities in significant numbers, creating new social tensions. Stepler and Lopez (2016) offer this telling detail: between 1990 and 2014, a record 1,579 counties (about half of all U.S. counties) had at least 1,000 Latinos, up from just 833 in 1990.

Relatedly, the number of new immigrants coupled with the higher birthrates within American communities of color, has translated into a new demographic reality in the United States: in many parts of the country, "majority minority" communities are increasingly common, and Whites are now clearly on a trajectory to become the minority population. The U.S. Census Bureau reported in 2014 that there were more than twenty million children under the age of 5 and that 50.2% of them were non-White, with the largest portion of these were Latino. By 2060 the United States is projected to be a "majority minority" country.

The impact of such enormous social change is palpable in every sphere of American life. The reins of political, economic, and cultural power are suddenly contested. It may be that Americans who reside in some of the country's urban centers have not fully grasped the great social transformation that has been taking place in recent decades. However, in broad swaths of the country, that change feels immediate and palpable. In urban zones, undocumented immigrants tend to inhabit the margins. They live in enclaves that are tucked out of sight; they work "invisible" jobs such as housekeepers, lawn workers, cooks, and manual laborers. For the historic residents of those metropolitan centers, it may be easy no not "see" the immigrant transformation (see Ainslie, 2017). But in much of the rest of America, this change is impossible to miss. Many American communities are small enough that these demographic changes exist in the open; they are inescapable and become foci of social tensions, much like what was evident in Postville.

Annihilation anxiety and the psychodynamics of collective regression

At an invited panel at the 2006 meetings of the American Psychoanalytic Association (Brenner, 2006), Vamik Volkan outlined key elements involved in within-group regression. Elsewhere, Volkan (1988) has theorized about the relationship between individual and collective identity. There is a sense of shared sameness in groups that share ethnic, religious, national, or ideological identity elements that serves to psychologically link members to one another. Individual identities exist within the "large tent" of the collective identity frameworks of which they are a part. These form a kind of backdrop, like a loosely fitting garment, until they come under duress, at which time they often become salient. What Volkan describes is a unique, collective mental representation of shared history that forms part of identity, an identity that is protected and maintained under the shared mental representation. In this way individual and collective identity processes are deeply entwined.

Volkan argues that when sufficient stressors impinge upon a group they may activate deep annihilation anxieties because the group feels threatened and endangered. The group's psychological moorings, as they relate to a sense of identity, are challenged and they become taxed. As a result, group identity processes are mobilized as a form of defense against those anxieties. The "us" versus "them" becomes accentuated. I would argue that the transformation of the American social landscape, both due to authorized and unauthorized immigration as well as to demographic trends, has destabilized the nation's collective identity, especially among segments of the White community, spawning a dangerous mix of anxiety and regressive group processes among those who feel threatened. This theoretical frame helps explain the surge in White Supremacist groups between 2015 and 2018. That tally has gone from 892 in 2015, to 917 in 2016, to 954 in 2018 (Southern Poverty Law Center, 2018). During this same interval, as well as the documented emergence of their ideology in the American mainstream, their efforts to psychically manage real and perceived threats, such groups simultaneously attack immigrants while arguing for the need to safeguard White identity.

In Volkan's 2006 observations (which are a synthesis of his prior work, e.g., 1988, 1997), he listed a number of behaviors and processes that are symptomatic of this kind of group regression, many of which might be readily applied to contemporary anti-immigrant discourse and anti-immigrant aggression. Among the collective symptoms or symptomatic processes that Volkan identifies can be found the following:

(1) Severe splitting, shared projections, and societal paranoia

Many of these indicators of regressive processes are readily evidenced in the climate of anti-immigrant discourse that has been evident for well over a decade but that has become more inflamed since the American presidential election of 2016. Splitting as well as projection and what Volkan has termed "societal paranoia" are reflected in entrenched "us"-versus-"them" positions in which immigrants are demonized while nativist positions are idealized. The vilification of immigrants, identifying them as murderers, rapists, and criminals, is not only demonstrably false, as crime statistics attest (Ewing et al., 2015), it turns immigrants into vessels for the collective fears and anxieties that are projected onto them. More generally, it creates a deeply polarized cleavage within the American polis.

(2) Dehumanization – first by identifying others as undesirable humans, followed by an active dehumanization

The dehumanization processes that are part of such collective regression are especially troubling and dangerous for they create an emotional context for acts of aggression against those now defined as Other. When candidate Trump first defines Mexicans as undesirables ("not the best" and as people who "have lots of problems") in the epigram to this chapter and then completes their dehumanization by saying that they are criminals to be feared (more recently he referred to immigrants as "animals" [see Valverde, 2018]), their dehumanization is complete and facilitates being targeted for aggression and violence.

(3) A shared narcissistic preoccupation

Volkan identifies the presence of shared narcissistic preoccupation as another characteristic of regressed groups. In the current anti-immigrant discourse, such narcissistic preoccupations are reflected in the refrain "Make American Great Again," which implies a narcissistic wounding based on the feeling that America has lost that position of greatness. Similarly, contemporary language describing American economic and foreign policy positions consistently underscores the belief that America has been taken advantage of by others, that America has been weak, and that foreign leaders are "laughing" at the United States. All of these are reflective of a collective sense of narcissistic wounding and preoccupation.

(4) Reactivation of "chosen glories"

The "Make America Great Again" refrain might also be thought of as the mobilization of Volkan's concept of "chosen glories" – the invocation of a group's prior greatness or victorious moments. Specifically, the phrase harkens to a time when America was unambiguously the world's foremost military, economic, and cultural power.

(5) Reactivation of "chosen trauma"

"Chosen glories" are often parallel to "chosen traumas" within the psychology of regressed group processes. As it relates to the immigration discourse, the September 11 attacks against the United States have figured prominently in the rise of anti-immigrant attitudes. While these have focused primarily on Muslims (for example, the Trump administration's attempt to ban Muslims from entering the country as part of a broader ant-immigrant posture), they form a seamless link with other xenophobic positions, including those that relate to the longer-standing concerns about Latino immigration.

(6) Inability to mourn or difficulty in mourning whereby a large group becomes a society of perennial mourners

Volkan notes that regressive shifts within groups often contain elements of an inability to mourn or difficulty in mourning. In some instances, members of a large group become a society of perennial mourners. Part of what is currently being mourned is the loss of the nation as it was once known by a particular group. The profound social changes secondary to the immigrant-driven transformation of the American social landscape has resulted, for some, in a conflictual and undigested sense of loss. America is no longer the same, and it will never be the same again, as demographic trends are unambiguous in this regard. White America is mourning a time when they were the majority, where they controlled the reins of power, where America mirrored them (on television, in movies, in the news, in its political leadership, etc.) and when they heard the content of what they wished to hear, affirming ideas that were present in every space.

(7) Border psychology

Volkan's Border Psychology phenomenon in regressed groups is perhaps best reflected in the obsession with border security in general and with the "wall" in particular. The latter is the most concise representation of xenophobic preoccupations in America's present-day body politic. Here, fear of the Other is concretized in the notion of terrorist threat and the need to keep the undesirable, dangerous Other contained and outside thea boundaries of an embattled and threatened group. This, too, is part of the nostalgia reflected in the "Make America Great Again" refrain.

(8) Ruining basic trust

The collection of regressive symptoms in the context of a distressed body politic also results in the erosion of basic trust. A healthy community (be it a city or a nation) requires social structures that foster a capacity to tolerate and absorb conflict and stress. When communities are taxed and regressed, those structures fail to "hold" (see Ainslie & Brabeck, 2003). The result is the fraying of basic trust within the community or group.

(9) Rallying around a leader and the importance of the leader's personality

Finally, Volkan underscores the enhanced power of a leader in the context of group regression. When groups are regressed, leaders may help contain the group's annihilation anxieties (for example, George W. Bush following the September 11 attacks attempted to articulate a distinction between Muslims in general and the Al Qaida operatives who wrapped themselves in religious justification). However, leaders may instead inflame collective anxieties and fears, furthering regressive shifts in the psychology of the group. The latter increases the likelihood of dangerous or even catastrophic consequences, as the group, having marginalized and dehumanized the Other, may now act aggressively against the "not-me" foreigners in their midst.

In sum, the rise in anti-Latino discourse and anti-Latino violence is theorized to be a function of the profound social change that the United States has undergone in the last three decades, coupled with political leadership that has further fueled the anxieties via anti-immigrant, dehumanizing rhetoric. This circumstance has mobilized collective processes that Volkan (2003) describes as characteristic of group regression.

Conclusion

On an individual level, psychoanalysis has long viewed the origins of prejudice as linked to threats to the self which are managed via projective processes in which unwanted or anxiety-producing elements are ascribed to others and then hated, devalued, and aggressed upon as a form of disavowal (Ainslie, 1995). Through this process, the self is momentarily protected via the extrusion of the emotional elements that threaten it from within. Thus threatening, ambiguous, or novel circumstances often mobilize regressive modes of thought and feeling as well as a variety of defensive postures because they threaten to disrupt our sense of ourselves or the world with which we identify.

Volkan's work helps us to theorize how individual psychology relates to broader group psychology. The murder of Juan Varela by Gary Kelley might be considered illustrative of this very linkage: whatever his individual psychodynamics or his long-standing, personal views about Mexicans, Kelley was living in a social-historical moment in which anti-immigrant sentiment was heightened and salient with the governor of Arizona having recently signed into law a very controversial anti-immigrant bill. Gary Kelley's actions are likely to have been an expression of his personal psychodynamics, but they took place within a resonant social context. The anti-immigrant posts to the *Des Moines Register* follow a very similar trajectory but at a collective level. They represent parallel tracks in which individual and collective psychodynamics employ similar mechanisms – regressive manifestations in which splitting, projection, and dehumanization pervade.

The sentiments reflected in the Postville incident, with varying degrees of intensity, capture the defensive expressions of collective anxiety for a subset of the American citizenry who believe their country has been fundamentally altered by the immigration phenomenon as well as by substantial demographic change, as the nation comes closer to being "majority minority." Though rife with falsehoods and dangerous dehumanization, candidate Trump could engage in anti-immigrant, anti-Mexican discourse precisely because he was tapping existent collective anxieties in a portion of the American electorate that found in his words a recognition and articulation of their deepest fears. These fears have activated regressive modes of thought and action, leading to a rise in anti-Latino hate crimes and violence against Latinos.

There are two potential outcomes to the present highly regressed and polarized condition of the American polis as it relates to the stressors created by the social transformation of the country. One is that regressive processes predominate, and immigrants continue to be scapegoated and attacked as the cause of perceived social ills. In the most extreme scenario, this circumstance could potentially parallel the processes governing the birth of Nazi Germany and the targeting of Jews that eventuated in the Holocaust. In the aftermath of the Japanese attacks on Pearl Harbor that brought the United States into the Second World War, over one hundred thousand Japanese Americans were dispossessed of their homes and their belongings and placed in detention centers. The anxiety-induced dehumanization of Americans of Japanese descent facilitated the processes that permitted acts of violence and injustice to be committed against them. Similarly, after the September 11 attacks in 2001, there were a surge of anti-Muslim, xenophobic responses that included wanton acts of violence and hate crimes against individuals and communities that were (or were perceived to be) Muslim.

However, the other potential outcome is that with time the United States will "digest" this wave of immigration and the resultant alteration of the American social landscape much as it has prior waves. Those prior immigrants (Irish, Italian, Polish, as well as Catholics and Jews, among others) were also met with considerable racism and opposition including hate crimes, scapegoating, and other acts of aggression. However, those immigrants were White, facilitating their assimilation into the mythic American Melting Pot. It remains to be seen whether America can similarly work its way through the "colorization" of the country or whether, instead, collective regression and polarization will deepen the social and cultural divide, bringing it to a breaking point. What psychoanalysis teaches us is that the best antidote to individual and collective regression is honest and direct engagement that offers the opportunity to reduce splitting and projection and enhances the potential for empathic understanding and acknowledgment of the subjectivity of the Other as different from the self.

Notes

1 Donald Trump Announces a Presidential Bid. *The Washington Post*, June 16, 2015. Retrieved from: www.washingtonpost.com/news/post-politics/wp/2015/06/16/full-text-donald-trump-announces-a-presidential-bid/.
2 The literature and media sources that I cite use the terms "Latino" or "Hispanic" to identify people who are Mexican or of Mexican ancestry or from Latin America. In this article I use them interchangeably, although I personally prefer the term "Latino."
3 In Havré, Montana, two Latinos who were acquaintances entered a convenience store one evening conversing in Spanish. A Border Patrol agent was also in the store and upon hearing them speak in Spanish, asked where they were born and demanded identification. After 20 minutes, during which he called in their IDs, they were allowed to leave. Both were United States citizens. *The New York Times*, May 22, 2018.

References

Ainslie, R. C. (1995). *No Dancin' in Anson: An American Story of Race and Social Change*. New York: Jason Aronson, Inc.

Ainslie, R. C. (2009). Regression in the Construction of the Immigrant Other. *Journal of Psychoanalysis, Culture & Society*, 14(1):49–57.

Ainslie, R. C. (2017). Immigration, Psychic Dislocation, and the Recreation of Community. *Psychoanalytic Review*, 104(6):695–706.

Ainslie, R. C. & Brabeck, K. (2003). Race Murder and Community Trauma: Psychoanalysis and Ethnography in Exploring the Impact of the Killing of James Byrd in Jasper, Texas. *Journal of Psychoanalysis, Culture & Society*, 8(1):42–51.

Bowlby, J. (1988). *A Secure Base: Parent-Child Attachment and Healthy Human Development*. Tavistock Professional Book. London: Routledge.

Brenner, I. (2006). Terror and Societal Regressions: Does Psychoanalysis Offer Insights for International Relations? *Journal of the American Psychoanalytic Association*, 54(3):977–988.

Criminal Justice Information Services Division. (2016). *Hate Crime Statistics*. Washington, DC: U.S. Department of Justice, Federal Bureau of Investigation.

Des Moines Register Blog. Retrieved from: www.desmoinesregister.com/apps/pbcs.dll/section?category=PluckForum&plckForumPage=ForumDiscussion&plckDiscussionId=Cat%3ad24d698a-c5dc-4ea1-8ae4-1a7b05fc9f5dForum%3ac68f2703-bb5e-4dda-a5cedec465d77bebDiscussion%3a17c75f99-73dd-4378-b2c6-870edcf0db3f&plckCategoryCurrentPage=0.

Ewing, W., Martinez, D. & Rumbaut, R. (2015). *The Criminalization of Immigration in the United States*. Washington, DC: American Immigration Council, Special Report, July 13.

Los Angeles Commission of Human Relations. (2016). *Hate Crime Report*, September 29. Retrieved from: https://hrc.lacounty.gov/wp-content/uploads/2019/08/2016-Annual-Report-of-Hate-Crime-in-Los-Angeles-County.pdf.

Mahler, M. S., Pine, F. & Bergman, A. (1975). *The Psychological Birth of the Human Infant: Symbiosis and Individuation.* New York: Basic Books.

Masucci, M. & Langton, L. (2017). *Hate Crime Victimization, 2004–2015.* Washington, DC: U.S. Department of Justice, Office of Justice Programs, Bureau of Justice Statistics.

Potok, M. (2008). *Anti-Latino Hate Crimes Rise for 4th Year in a Row.* Southern Poverty Law Center, October 29. Retrieved from: https://www.ojp.gov/pdffiles1/nij/grants/244755.pdf.

Rasmussen Reports. (2010). Retrieved from: https://en.wikipedia.org/wiki/Rasmussen_Reports.

Remade in America: The Newest Immigrants and Their Impact. (2009). *The New York Times*, interactive map, March 10. Retrieved from: https://archive.nytimes.com/www.nytimes.com/interactive/2009/03/10/us/20090310-immigration-explorer.html.

Schafer, R. (1954/1967). Regression in the Service of the Ego. In *Projective Testing and Psychoanalysis: Selected Papers*. New York: International Universities Press.

Spitz, R. A. (1965). *The First Year of Life: A Psychoanalytic Study of Normal and Deviant Development of Object Relations.* New York: International Universities Press.

Stacey, M., Carbone-Lopez, K. & Rosenfeld, R. (2011). Demographic Change and Ethnically Motivated Crime: The Impact of Immigration on Anti-Hispanic Hate Crime in the United States. *Journal of Contemporary Justice*, 27(3):378–398.

Stepler, R. & Lopez, M. (2016). *U.S. Latino Population Growth and Dispersion Has Slowed Since Onset of the Great Recession.* Washington, DC: Pew Hispanic Research Center.

Valverde, M. (2018). In Context: Donald Trump's Comments About Immigrants, "animals". *Politifact*, May 16. Retrieved from: www.politifact.com/truth-o-meter/article/2018/may/17/context-donald-trumps-comments-about-immigrants-an/.

Volkan, V. D. (1988). *The Need to Have Enemies & Allies: From Clinical Practice to International Relationships.* New York: Jason Aaronson.

Volkan, V. D. (1997). *Blood Lines: From Ethnic Pride to Ethnic Terrorism.* New York: Farrar, Straus & Giroux.

Volkan, V. D. (2003). Large-Group Identity: Border Psychology and Related Societal Processes. *Mind and Human Interaction*, 13:49–76.

Winnicott, D. (1971). *Playing and Reality.* London: Tavistock.

Part 3

This land

Whose is it, really?

Chapter 11

Trees and other psychoanalytic matters

Lindsay L. Clarkson

Introduction/context

As a single species we are transforming the planet in ways that we may not be able to put right. It seems we have allowed our destructive tendencies to prevail, resulting in not just climate change but environmental degradation, loss of natural habitats, desertification, and species extinction. Sequential global assessment reports from the Intergovernmental Panel on Climate Change describe the impact of human activities threatening ecosystems and causing a decline in biodiversity over the past fifty years (Diaz et al., 2019; Masson-Delmotte et al., 2018). The rate of global change is unprecedented in the course of human history on the planet. The situation we inhabit is captured by a quote from a recent essay in *Science* by Stephen T. Jackson (2009) on Alexander von Humboldt:

> Humans have been influencing the natural world at local, regional, and perhaps global scales for many millennia. The changing natural world has had reciprocal influences on human welfare and activities. Nature and humanity are now locked in lopsided coevolution – that is, nature would persist in the absence of humanity, but humanity cannot exist without nature.

We are not living in good contact with reality when we act as though we are self-sufficient and as though there are no limits to economic expansion or to exploitation of natural resources. Sanity founders if the sustaining aspects of the diverse biological world and larger life systems are disregarded and ignored. Fifty years ago, Harold Searles wrote about the ecological crisis and elucidated the primitive anxieties that might cause us to meet the massive changes in our environment with apparent apathy (Searles, 1972). He included psychoanalysts who have, for the most part, neglected explorations of our relationship to the natural world that might extend beyond "nature" as a mental construct and as a vehicle for projection of human object relatedness. As much as we humans can modify the natural environment or shape virtual worlds, the substrate for all of our efforts is provided by natural resources and processes. Andreas Malm, professor of human ecology, writes:

> Any toddler casting an eye towards her closest adults must grapple with the friction, the gravity, the light and the darkness, and the physicality of the objects surrounding her, and however perfectly she and her contemporaries subsequently learn to navigate, manipulate, refashion and seemingly subdue these and other aspects of nature, they cannot extricate themselves from the exterior materiality in which they once learned to walk and work. Some circumstances will never be of their making.
>
> (Malm, 2018, 158–159)

How is it that we psychoanalysts have left the emotional work that this reality demands of us so unformulated in our theories about our internal worlds? It is only recently that analysts, spurred by accumulating evidence of cascading changes in the environment, have begun to turn their attention to the psychological underpinnings of our attitude toward the earth. (see, e.g., Weintrobe, 2013; Clarkson, 2017a, 2017b; Orange, 2017). Just as psychoanalysts have been able to tune in to communications beyond words, it is feasible to bring to bear a psychoanalytic understanding to unfamiliar terrain: to the unconscious phantasies that structure our experiences with the natural world. Psychoanalytic inquiry can help us understand the reasons we disavow or cannot bring ourselves to face our own destructiveness as we alter the world and resist awareness of limits or mortality. On the other side, in the area of containment, a human potential for capaciousness exists that can allow us to acknowledge what is found in the nonhuman environment, instead of treating nature as foreign or a "green blur." Such awareness can enable us to cultivate our abilities to protect and preserve the web of life on which we depend and of which we are one strand.

Life in the consulting room

My consulting room window reveals a patch of forest with a brook. Each patient finds her own way to engage with or keep out the background experience of the natural world. On first encounter, G, a student in her twenties, described herself from a robot's vantage: an instrument to be tweaked and managed. G treated me as an automaton, a machine she sought out to provide adjustment to or riddance of faulty aspects of herself. She knew psychological terminology for feelings but had no personal experience of such things. When G mentioned "feelings," they bore no resemblance to intangible sensation or embodied experience but were instead metallic and heavy things to be moved around. I often felt purely practical myself in response. It took work to round myself to more usual human empathy.

G was uncomprehending or outright condescending when I tried to understand what she was saying to me rather than answer her direct queries in factual terms. Occasionally I noticed a glimmer of warmth in response to something I said that indicated that I could understand G's wariness to show me she had any life because of the great risk this entailed.

One day, after a number of years of treatment, G came in looking blue; she happened to notice an orchid in my consulting room and commented on the warmth of its color. Unexpectedly, she went on to survey her surroundings, newly aware of other plants. She said she expected that I thought carefully about what kind of environment would be good for my patients, how it might affect them. She implied this was a delicate situation. Glancing outside the window, G remarked on a goldfinch perched on the balcony railing, mentioning the vibrance of his yellow and the lightness of his movements. She told me she loved birds. Then G confided she had a hamster herself, but she was always worried she didn't pay enough attention to it – that it was neglected. The hamster had a rotating wheel in which to run, but G didn't provide much stimulation, nothing very interesting. Worse, she was afraid she would forget to feed the hamster, and it would die. The way she spoke made it clear that she felt this was an uninterruptable cycle and that her work with me followed a similar rotation without growth or life.

Prior to this session, it was my impression that she had not perceived, except momentarily, the life in me, in my office, or in herself. This day she not only was aware but could take in otherness, my attention to "patients," not yet specifically to her, but with the possibility of a mother who might not forget to feed or pay attention. G went on to say, speaking more formally, that she had heard "that walking in green spaces might alleviate depression." She did feel better when she was outside and was very worried about being forced to live in a small dark confined space, as she imagined an apartment in the future. I thought when she first spoke to me she was feeling more warmth, but then she found herself talking more formally, closing down, reentering the dark space.

G's original blindness to the natural world was a violent measure. I had the sense that as a young child to survive physically in a terrible situation, she ruptured her ability to be aware of a need for a living environment, turning to an autistic solution. A predictable mechanical world devoid of life was more reliable than a highly charged alternately intrusive and abandoning live relationship. What might appear to be a callous lack of attention to the natural world is a consequence of a desperate, vicious attack on any experience of meaningful kinship. The starvation of the caged and robotic hamster reflected an ongoing cruelty that created her internal poverty and despair. Her treatment of the hamster was both an identification with a murderous object and an identification with the helpless creature at the mercy of such a caretaker. G's dawning recognition of the life and otherness in the plants and birds was safer than extending herself to me as a trustworthy human presence but carried a tendency toward fuller contact and growth (modified from Clarkson, "The Window" in Moss, 2018).

This small clinical moment illustrates that the specifics of a person's internal situation matter in understanding what appears to be disinterest in the natural world and in gaining insight into tenacious resistance to life-affirming adaptation.

The internal and external worlds

I have had a longstanding concern for the natural world. It had always seemed a private matter, like a love of poetry, that I know enhanced my capacity for containment and enriched my ability to listen to words, metaphor, and harmonics. I have more recently begun to think that this affinity is not a separate concern from psychoanalysis but that, for me somehow, involves getting the right balance between appreciation of and attention to the inner and outer worlds. There are similarities: both studies involve privileging knowledge in depth. To know fully one mountain might be a lifetime's commitment: it is depth, not width that matters. Interdisciplinary discussions with evolutionary biologists, paleontologists, and ecologists concerned about the impact of humans on the natural world have impressed on me a perspective that humans exist as one species among many. The discussions highlighted the diminutive scope of the existence of *Homo sapiens* in the course of life on Earth. Such a view is radically different from the psychoanalytic preoccupation with humans at the center of attention (privileged and unique), disregarding our embeddedness in the natural world.

An increasing proportion of people live in a material world that appears to be created by human effort and expertise alone. Our daily urban environment has come to resemble the result of an omnipotent fantasy that we control the natural world. Nature is ours to be used, and it can endlessly absorb whatever waste we extrude. Technological miracles will result in limitless supplies of clean water, pure air, adequate food. However, the natural world is not solely a mental construct.

"Every creature is better alive than dead, men and moose and pine trees, and he who understands it aright will rather preserve life than destroy it," says Henry David Thoreau in *The Maine Woods* in 1864 (1988, 164). Thoreau refers to internal aliveness and vitality, not simply lifelike existence. The full range of being human includes our relationship to the natural world that exists without regard to our view of the centrality of human importance. The threesome, "men, moose and pine trees" broadens our community and speaks up for an awareness we have lost sight of. We evolved from, belong in, and are sustained by the nonhuman environment. But we often restrict what we observe, and the thinness of what we perceive is reinforced by the reality that an increasing proportion of people live in a material world that appears to be created solely by human effort and expertise out of manmade substances. Our glance remains at the surface and registers what is useful to us. Or we turn on a virtual reality that invites us to linger in a familiar setting under our dominion. Recently fires, floods, droughts, and storms burst through the marvels of human engineering. Nature, which we have treated as modular and reliable to provide what we need, is abruptly experienced as large, menacing, and uncontrollable.

"Strange that so few ever come to the woods to see how the pine tree lives and grows and spires, lifting its evergreen arms to the light, – to see its perfect success; but most are content to behold it in the shape of many broad boards brought to market, and deem *that* its true success!" writes

Thoreau (p. 163). It is our own loss. The natural world is inherent in the constitution of ourselves, and we are the poorer for our disconnection. If we take stock of ourselves as inhabitants of the Anthropocene, we know we are not living in a benign and creative relationship with respect to our planet. This may well reflect our relationship to ourselves. But mostly we seclude or distract ourselves from such knowledge.

There are subtle ways diminutions in awareness occur: in a passage from *Landmarks*, Robert Macfarlane (2015) describes the excision of certain words from the *Oxford Junior Dictionary* in 2007 during the course of a periodic update. Terms removed included "acorn," "buttercup," "dandelion," "fern," "heather," "heron," "kingfisher," "lark," "otter," "pasture." In their place, children now find definitions for "attachment," "blog," "bullet-point," "celebrity," "chatroom," "cut and paste." The poignancy of the loss of attention and location of childhood within the natural world is affecting at a deep level. Although the word "substitution" was probably not done by Oxford with a malevolent intent, one wonders whether there was a consideration about the emotional effect on children of the loss of language to designate the nonhuman inhabitants, fellow travelers really, in the woods and fields of the United Kingdom. Potential inquiries and research by children into their interdependence with other beings' lives, habitats, and approaches to the world are stunted, if not interrupted by such an absence. The loss of birds is not limited to their appearance in books; it is also apparent in the landscape. In a recent stark report in *Science*, three billion birds from North America were lost in the past fifty years, a decline of 29% of the avian population. (Rosenberg, 2019). The birds affected are only one component of an intricate web of life that human influence has affected amidst massive alterations of forests, rivers, oceans, and their inhabitants worldwide. There are similar findings recording the demise of insects, plants, and mammals.

A psychoanalytic query

Human relatedness to the natural world does not traditionally fall within the purview of psychoanalysis. In an effort to understand our lassitude with respect to the environmental crisis, as a psychoanalyst I have tried to use the tools I know. After describing the evolution of his premises regarding the source of mental illness and therefore of the mechanism of therapeutic action, Roger Money-Kyrle settles on the idea of unconscious "misconceptions" and "disorientations" about truth (Money-Kyrle, 1968). It is through persistent allegiance to distortions of reality that we become ill. Money-Kyrle formulates the aim of psychoanalysis "to help the patient understand and so overcome emotional impediments to his discovering *what he innately already knows*" (emphasis is mine). Money-Kyrle selects three central facts that we find difficult to face and with which we unconsciously delude ourselves to avoid an emotional reckoning: "the recognition of the breast as a supremely good object," "the recognition of the parents' intercourse as a supremely creative act," and the "recognition of the inevitability of time and ultimately death" (Money-Kyrle, 1971, 103–104). What he omits as a basic fact of life is the natural world's supporting the parental couple, an awareness that is present in the parents' minds. There is no possibility for triangular space or any other aspect of human existence without an encompassing, sustaining environment. Inherent in the aim of psychoanalysis is the search for truth, both internal and external, but it seems that our roots in the natural world have been excluded from our theorizing and clinical work.

How has this dependence on the natural world been neglected? The vital need to know in an ongoing way what is taking place in the natural world around us has deep roots in our survival as a species, roots that are now obscured by existence in modern human-dominant habitats. As primates, we are not only alert to our internal experience, to our group's state of mind, but if we are awake (in Thoreau's sense), we also tend to the details of what is happening now around us. As psychoanalysts, we are more likely to subsume this awareness of the environment into human object relatedness rather than to inquire about the separate importance of the natural world to our psychic balance. It is possible we are overwhelmed and intimidated by biodiversity and do not feel up to the task of contemplating the depth and richness of earth, the smallness of our stature in the universe, and the contrasting scope of the damage we have done to the natural environment. We react by evading the knowledge that would lead to pain or alarm.

Bion, in *Learning from Experience* (1962), goes a long way in helping us with our inquiry into the reluctance of humans to see themselves as dependent on and embedded in the natural world and the resultant penchant for lack of concern and exploitation. Bion describes the terrible consequences to an infant's growing personality of a disturbance in the relationship between a mother and infant. I think his insight is applicable to our relationship with the natural world. The mother's task from the infant's point of view is not only to provide physical safety and nurturance but to have the ability to gather the baby's early worries, frustrations, and sensitivities that are overwhelming. The infant projects such rudimentary and disorganized feelings into the mother who receives them, makes sense of them, and returns them to the infant in a form that is emotionally tolerable. The infant takes in not just the moderated and structured feelings from his mother but also a bit of his or her mother's capacity to tolerate frustration, pain, and anxiety. In certain situations, either from the infant's side of innate difficulties with aggression or from the mother's inability to engage with her infant, the baby is not helped to tolerate frustration or pain and instead goes down the path of evading reality. As the pain of frustration is unbearable, omnipotent thought substitutes a magically painless situation for the actual one. If one is in complete control, and there is no dependence on a living other, one does not have to deal with frustration. The problem is solved, but at the expense of living out of contact with reality.

Bion describes the:

> effect of splitting whose object and effect is to enable the infant to obtain what later in life would be called material comforts without acknowledging the existence of a live object on which these benefits depend. . . . Envy of the breast's capacity for love, understanding, wisdom, poses a problem solved by the destruction of alpha function. . . . The need for love, understanding and mental development is now deflected, since it cannot be satisfied, into the search for material comforts.
>
> (Bion, 1962, 10–11).

Board feet are the success, not the spire of the pine in its own habitat.

It appears that we find something in the undisturbed state of the natural world that is troubling and rouses our envy, instead of stirring a sane response of gratitude and concern. Our impulse is to interfere, to set ourselves above. We spoil the life that we feel excludes us from its riches and disdain the intricacy of our biologic home. Our solutions to environmental degradation that results from our material consumption involve omnipotent fantasies entailing further consumption and ingenious fixes created by technological finesse. Our thinking becomes simple and not based on science, reducing differentiation to sameness and asserting the world is created for humans and has no value in its own right. To protect ourselves from awareness of our losses and sensitivities, we have insulated ourselves from openness to actual experience with the natural world, our community. Harold Searles considered that our primitive fears of being nonhuman ourselves (ourselves as broad boards) interfere with our ability to embrace life in other beings.

In a contrasting mind-set, engagement with the natural world can enhance our sense of being meaningfully human. Although our internal object world affects our perception of nature, there are early and deep differences between our relationship to people and our relationship to the living, nonhuman world. We are all familiar with the solace found in the outdoors at times of loneliness or loss. The containment provided by the nonhuman environment provides a space and context to live within that is relieving in its sturdiness and indifference to our individual concerns. A good, not ideal environment is what the earth offers, as its persistence and unresponsiveness to human welfare are frustrating. The scale of our dependence on an environment that we cannot fully control is frightening. On balance, the earth's nonhuman inhabitants – animals, plants and microorganisms – provide a level of accompaniment in life: a quiet kinship paired with unlikeness, simply going on being. Our awareness of such a difference can provide a respite when we are weary of our relentless consciousness. Sensibility to the aesthetics and biologic complexity of nature can be sustaining when we are threatened by breakdown or terror of our transience. The resilience and interwoven complexity of the web of life in the face of our projected experiences of hate or despair can be strengthening and inspire us with courage to go on.

As we encounter aspects of ourselves that have been lost or split off, the company of the natural world can be steadying. The knowledge that the living external world persists provides an anchoring if we inhabit an internal world unmoored by reliable objects. Security, a sense of a home base, is founded on an orientation to a good internalized object, to a benign and generative parental couple, but this internalized object or couple does not exist in a vacuum. It is supported by good interactions with others, and, *if allowed*, with nourishment from the natural world. If we can tolerate knowledge in ourselves of the impact we have had on the earth, then we can experience ourselves as integral members of the ecological community. In this state of mind, we might care for the environment as we care for ourselves. There are qualities of the nonhuman world that deserve exploration in their own right, both to understand what might lead to a more preservative approach to the natural world but also what might have interfered with our knowledge of the place the natural world plays in our psychic equilibrium.

Nature: an understudied aspect of the psychoanalytic frame

Recently I have been trying to observe the impact the natural world has on me as I am working. I am accustomed to listening in the here and now, but simultaneously attending to another melody has been demanding. It reminded me of the strain of trying to discern a distant and unusual bird call amidst a chorus of familiar bird sounds. The influences that I was acquainted with to facilitate balanced listening were voices of my colleagues, my love of psychoanalytic understanding, the pleasures of inquiring more deeply or accurately. What I began to perceive was that my awareness of the natural world formed a near constant and balancing weight in my states of reverie, particularly relieving when I was subject to forceful and disturbing projections and pressures. The dependability of my affectionate regard for the trees around me provided an underpinning for my acceptance of my patient's disturbance and my ability to take in and understand and to find a way to talk about terrible anxieties and perceptions. Such experiences exist in mindless forms, both extremely urgent and uniquely configured. I think such work is more tolerable in me as a person in the internal company of other humans, moose, and pine trees.

In my situation, the window to the natural world is an essential and intrinsic aspect of the space I provide for my patients. I mean this both literally and as an awareness of a connection that I carry inside myself. Although I do not look out the window except peripherally while I am seeing patients, I know what is there. My consulting room overlooks a woodland area, with a small stream running through it. With the window open, the quiet murmur of the brook, the wind in the trees, the bird's songs, the dappled light are all part of the analytic setting. Sometimes torrential rains, thunderstorms, or heavy snowfalls impose themselves. The changing light throughout the year marks the passage of time. I know this is a small ark of richness, as roads I cannot see form boundaries to the west and south, and houses limit the northern edge. In the fall, leaf blowers intrude and require the windows to be closed. Nonetheless I am grateful for the life the trees contain and represent. The setting is infinitely variable, enriching and stabilizing for me as it can be for my patients. As patients become more comfortable in themselves and feel less alienated, they begin to notice the existence of life outside, often in fleeting moments, sometimes a whisper. Nonintrusive support of the natural world, uninterested in human-scale experience, allows me and my patient an ability to go toward primitive experience, as we can find grounding (as in feet on the ground or leaning up against a tree) despite internal emotional hurricane forces.

The world outside the window can also be put to other uses, as a distraction from the work at hand, or as a place to dissociate to, or as a site suitable for projection. The natural world can be so infiltrated by bizarre and aggressive fragments of a person's emotions and personality that it becomes useless for comfort or sane tethering. Whether insight gleaned from clinical work will be relevant to our larger societal disease, I do not know. In the two brief examples and the extended vignette that ensue, I will focus our inquiry on how an individual's state of mind affects his or her perception of the natural environment and the consequent engagement.

The window sash is slammed shut by Mr. Z to create a claustrophobic and stifling atmosphere that accords with his internal experience. He hates any comfort that he feels I derive from the ongoing world outside and feels triumphant that he has me captive. The shut window is also a communication about the hopelessness he feels of ever allowing a freer interchange with the reality of otherness; "taking in" is experienced as being taken over by.

Ms. N has often used the woods as a place to evacuate her experiencing self and emotions in small fragments, leaving her mindless in the room with me. It is so powerful and violent a projection that even her body in the room at such times is more a thing than a live entity. One day she observes "a large. . .," she pauses, "bird." She says it was bizarre, the bird was flying upside down with a wounded and misshapen wing. It appeared to be falling and its wings were flapping ineffectually. She wants to know did I see it? She feels it was odd and did not fit in in the midst of the ordinary woods. I think this "seeing" was more of a projection of a slightly cohering sense of herself; she is in partial contact with aspects of herself that feel malformed, disoriented, and inhuman. Such awareness (however partial) is devastating. She forcefully evacuates the splintered perception by means of her eyes into the misshapen, sinking bird, a different use of her eyes than seeing. Her inquiry to me explores whether or not I can "see it," i.e., bear to take in and know the disturbing quality of her internal world. For Ms. N, the small forest has no valence of comfort or belonging, and is not really seen. Rather, the woods are used as a site to receive the expelled aspects of her personality. Mindlessness induced by such mechanisms leaves no possibility for exploration of or consolation from the natural world.

A number of years ago, Mr. A, who had always been polite, said, frankly, he resented the fact that I was an analyst and a psychiatrist, as he was not. The weight of his statement was impersonal; I was divested of my particular self and became a professional title–comporting myself accordingly. For a long time, very little of what I thought or understood could be utilized by him for growth, as real exchange between separate and distinct beings was unendurable. Just as physically he was extremely sensitive to all manner of allergens or foreign substances, psychically we faced a similar dilemma.

Over time, Mr. A had spoken with some real affection for his garden and its resident birds. Frequently he dismissed the pleasure he avowed that he received from his encounters with nature, as an affectation of a desirable trait. At these times his engagement with the natural world devolved into a more acquisitive situation, in which he was in possession of a wonderful, precious observation that I was to admire while being hopelessly excluded from such a rare encounter. Mr. A would then speak down to me, "teaching" me about natural phenomena that he had researched. I was addressed as small and dim, made envious by his capacities. This treatment of me seemed to be a communication about his experience as a child and made me aware that for him to recognize that I had any understanding to offer him was a shaming and intolerable state of affairs. Mr. A's survival had depended on an ability to convincingly marvel at his fragile, easily injured parents and to protect himself from their forceful intrusion and disparagement. He kept the violence of what he actually thought to himself.

What I understood, from his perspective, was symmetrically filled with hate and designed to force a shameful awareness on him that he was imperfect and stupid. To depend on another was to risk a disastrous encounter with an archaic figure. Better to be the one "in the know" and to forswear familiarity with softer feelings.

When one day I made a comment about the disturbance Mr. A encountered when he felt he had learned something from me, Mr. A made it clear that I had misunderstood the situation. He said with a rueful smile, he was not interested in being given a good interpretation by me or being helped by me. He came to see me in order to *be* me. If he were me, he would not have to experience the pain or humiliation of being someone who was hungry or cold or needed something, nor would he have to experience envy of me. This was not total of course; a part of Mr. A *was* rueful and could be more receptive. Increasingly, Mr. A knew he missed a lot by severely restricting our relationship.

A few days later, as Mr. A entered, he commented on a palm frond that was hanging over the couch a bit. He has a complex way of taking the couch which gives a show of ease and settling. As he has become less wary, Mr. A allows that this artlessness is a pose. He feigns comfort to traverse the terrible danger of coming into contact with me, not me exactly. It is commonplace to encounter a "me" who in his mind might turn on him in a vicious attack, just at the moment he begins to feel he has a place. But if he finds a "me" in a comfortable and thoughtful mind-set, this too is agonizing when he is not in the same state. Today Mr. A signaled that he, good humoredly, would take the interfering leaf in stride but also more subtly that he was bothered that he had to accommodate the leaf to lie down. A smooth mechanical transition was interrupted by a muddle that was briefly visible. I was not perturbed by my part in the infringement of the errant leaf and actually felt a bit relieved to have some evidence of life.

Mr. A commented for the first time after many years of work, how well cared for the plants were in my consulting room, how much they had grown over his time here, how much they were a part of his experience coming every day to talk to me. He said fondly it was like being in a rain forest. His way of speaking was unusually personal and touching, somewhat wistful. The plants had grown and seemed to be thriving, whereas he had made do with thinner fare.

I thought it was not just the plants, well cared for, but some appreciation of a warmer, friendlier give-and-take that Mr. A could now tolerate. Momentarily, he seemed to take pleasure in a diverse and foreign environment, with potential for life, other creatures and ways of being, whether it be in the tropics, in my mind, or in his internal world in my company.

There was a recognition of me as other with a complexity of my own, with some ongoing capacity for attentiveness not just to the plants but to him. The way he was talking gave me to understand that he surmised I was not too envious of the plants' growth or too depleted by their demands and so could encourage them to develop.

Then a shift occurred. Mr. A became physically stiffer. He went on to tell me about a graduate school seminar that addressed setting up one's classroom. His professor made the point, if you are going to have plants in your classroom, then take good care of them. Their condition will give your students and their parents an impression of you and your abilities to take care of your class. Mr. A reported that then and there, he had decided never to have plants in his classroom, and this was still true. He said this with some firmness and evident relief that he had disposed of not just his risk of exposure as a person who might be neglectful and incapable of nurture but of any interest or longing for the potential richness and growth possible in the rain forest.

Briefly Mr. A had felt the beneficiary of my capacity to understand and care for him, that he himself was being tended to in a responsive, knowledgeable way, and that he felt appreciative. With a more benign experience of me, Mr. A felt more tolerant of an integrated understanding of himself. He was able to value the rain forest, and include the jungly aspects of himself. Here was the potential for development, based on internalization of a good, not ideal object. This awareness then became unbearable, and he dismantled his understanding. Mr. A reverted to a state of mind dominated by archaic figures who controlled all of the resources. In this state, the life was taken out of something he had recognized in me. Instead of a more organic connection with myself or the natural world, my cultivation of the plants now represented a false presentation, in which I was following a set of rules about how the "right kind of person" behaves. I was revealed to be making a show of nurture in order to influence people, to hold myself up as superior, and to display my beneficence in contrast to the depreciated others. On this day we were now in the realm of "broad boards." Valuing the pine as a separate and worthwhile entity, going its own way as part of a balancing ecosystem presented too painful a situation. In order to maintain his psychic equilibrium Mr. A dropped his concern for the natural world, valorizing a superior view of noncaring.

"Tree at my window"

Attention to both internal and external reality is important to sanity. We have complex fantasies about the motivations of the natural world toward ourselves. These fantasies may be an effort to make nature less other and more congruent with human inspiration. We also have the capacity to be aware that our community with the natural world entails recognition of the *absence* of motivation as understood along human lines in the other-than-human world. Such awareness can be a relief and strengthen our appreciation of our own way of being. Many poets have expressed the pulls and interdigitation of consciousness of one's own internal experience with consciousness of one's own place within and, in a felt way, apart from the natural world.

I would like to turn to a poem by Robert Frost entitled "Tree at my Window" from *West Running Brook* (1928). In four brief quatrains, the poet conveys an intricate dance of feeling with the tree adjacent to his house. When he falters psychically, he is strengthened by the tree's unwavering existence. What Frost addresses from his indoor vantage is not just a *view* of the tree, it is a relationship with another being who is embraced and tested for endurance. The bond is strained and ultimately found to hold. The poem illustrates the shifting states of mind that the poet encounters in his familiarity with the tree. Frost comes to find the tree as essential for his sanity.

As the poem commences, Frost welcomes the open dialogue with the tree implying an intimate companionship. The narrator remarks to the tree that although he may shut the window, he intends never to obscure their connection. The tree outside is created in the reader's mind as one with a substance of its own: roots, a trunk, a canopy of branches and leaves. In the second stanza, the scene alters, and we find ourselves in a nightmarish dream state. The tree has lost its grounding in the outside world. It has been lifted from its solid orientation to the earth. Now, the tree has become a figment of the poet's imagination with its leafy crown replaced by a menacing part-object human image. Leaves fluttering in the wind are replaced by uttered words. The reader is swirled and disoriented with the altered language of being. The poet has lost his bearings and projects his breakdown into the tree; it loses its separate rooted existence. In a state of madness, the poet folds in on himself, unsecured by the natural world.

In the subsequent stanza, the narrator recovers his wits. He remembers what he knows about the tree's otherness. The tree is recognized as not simply a mental construct of the poet. The poet's eye is unclouded, and he is shaken out of himself to see and witness the tree's separate existence and living place in nature. There is a relief in his observation (through the window) of the tree that is both affected by and able to withstand real winds and storms. The tree's resilient survival fortifies the poet's ability to contain his own anxieties, in an identification with the tree's capacity to endure and continue to grow. The narrator believes it is possible that in some way, unspecified, the tree has also beheld and survived Frost's own breakdown and recovery.

Frost concludes the poem with a light touch, as though he is moving away from the seriousness of the precarious experience of himself that he has just recounted. There is a playful invocation of the role of Fate in the creation of the link between himself and the tree. Noting the contrasts in their ways of being, he deftly depicts his preoccupation with the state of his inner world and the tree's involvement with the conditions of outer reality.

Awareness of both the state of one's internal environment and the condition of the external world leads to an appreciation of the complex live processes relating the two; this recognition is vital to the preservation of life in the current era, the Anthropocene. As psychoanalysts and as plain citizens of the earth, can we rouse ourselves to sensitivity, to perceive more fully our place in the natural world and to extend a hand to preserve the earth's richness?

References

Bion, W. R. (1962). *Learning from Experience*. London: Tavistock.

Clarkson, L. L. (2017a). Locating Ourselves in Relation to the Natural World. In J. Kress & J. Stine (eds.), *Living in the Anthropocene: Earth in the Age of Humans*. Washington, DC: Smithsonian Books, 48–52.

Clarkson, L. L. (2017b). Our Uneasy Relationship with the Natural World: Engaging with Climate Change. *Journal of the American Psychoanalytic Association*, 65:537–553.

Clarkson, L. L. (2018). The Window. In D. Moss et al. (eds.), *Violence to Our Planet/to Our Selves*. Retrieved from: www.psychoanalysis.today/CMSWebParts/CustomVAControls?ArticlePDF.ashx?NodeID-371&Culture=en-GB.

Diaz, S. et al. (2019). *Summary for Policy Makers of the Global Assessment Report of the Intergovernmental Science-Policy Platform on Biodiversity and*

Ecosystem Services (IPBES). Retrieved from: https://ipbes.net/sites/default/files/inline/files/ipbes_global_assessment_report_summary_for_policymakers.pdf.

Frost, R. (1928). Tree at My Window. In *West-Running Brook*. New York: Henry Holt.

Jackson, S. (2009, May 1). Alexander von Humboldt and the General Physics of the Earth. *Science*, 324(5927):596–597.

Macfarlane, R. (2015). *Landmarks*. London: Penguin.

Malm, A. (2018). *The Progress of This Storm, Nature and Society in a Warming World*. London: Verso.

Masson-Delmotte, V. et al. (eds.). (2018). *Global Warming of 1.5°C: An IPCC Special Report on the Impacts of Global Warming of 1.5°C Above Pre-Industrial Levels and Related Global Greenhouse Gas Emission Pathways, in the Context of Strengthening the Global Response to the Threat of Climate Change, Sustainable Development, and Efforts to Eradicate Poverty*. Geneva, Switzerland: IPCC.

Money-Kyrle, R. E. (1968). Cognitive Development. *International Journal of Psychoanalysis*, 49:691–698.

Money-Kyrle, R. E. (1971). The Aim of Psychoanalysis. *International Journal of Psychoanalysis*, 52:103–106.

Orange, D. M. (2017). *Climate Crisis, Psychoanalysis, and Radical Ethics*. New York: Routledge.

Rosenberg, K. V. et al. (2019). Decline of the North American Avifauna. *Science*. doi:10.1126/science.aaw1313.

Searles, H. F. (1972). Unconscious Processes in Relation to the Environmental Crisis. *Psychoanalysis Review*, 59(3):361–374.

Thoreau, H. D. (1988). *The Maine Woods*. New York: Penguin Books. Originally published 1864.

Weintrobe, S. (ed.). (2013). *Engaging with Climate Change*. New York: Routledge.

Chapter 12

Shame, envy, impasse, and hope

The psychopolitics of violence in South Africa

Wahbie Long

Introduction

In her celebrated collection of letters, the Madame de Sévigné would detail the hangings, quarterings, and wheelings of seventeenth-century France. On one occasion – the execution of a peasant – de Sévigné witnessed the condemned man's terror at his imminent death. He shivered and wailed, his body wriggling in the hangman's noose – a spectacle for the ladies and gentlemen gathered that morning. And yet de Sévigné was troubled: she could not fathom why a *commoner* should be so horrified at the prospect of his own death (Sennett & Cobb, 1972). She was not a particularly vicious woman – on the contrary, she was "a rich human creature of balance and sanity" (Bradford, 1915, 37), described as "delicious" (p. 41) by those who knew her. But in the words of Alexis de Tocqueville, "Madame de Sévigné had no clear notion of suffering in any one who was not a person of quality" (De Tocqueville, 1835/1889, 151).

One may interpret the madame's indifference as a historical artifact – the age of Enlightenment had not yet begun. In the mind of the aristocrat, it made perfect sense to treat the masses with a brutality that matched their supposedly brutish souls. It would fall to the humanists of the *eighteenth* century to formulate a belief in the dignity of "man" – albeit "man" of a certain hue. But in the intervening centuries, that belief has evolved into something we can all appreciate today: the idea that *all* human beings deserve to be treated with dignity. In his new book on identity, Francis Fukuyama goes as far as positing the universal existence of something the ancient Greeks called *thymos* – "the part of the soul that craves recognition of dignity" (Fukuyama, 2018). Human beings, that is, seek recognition from their peers, and when they do not receive it, one of two things happens. If they feel undervalued, they become resentful, and if they

DOI: 10.4324/9781003214342-16

reckon within themselves a failure to meet the standards of others, they feel ashamed. Human beings are not satisfied with only food and shelter: they also want *respect*.

In this chapter, I am concerned mainly with the question of dignity. My general position is that shame and envy – when framed at the societal level – are not only among the principal *drivers* of violence in South Africa, they are also *responses* to violence in the broadest sense of the term, that is, violence as "[a] manifestation of power that denies people their humanity" (Henry, 2000, 20). In support of this position, I offer three interlocking arguments. First, I contend that the poor and working classes respond to the shame inflicted on them by *structural violence* with a scarcely believable interpersonal violence of their own – directed against their own. Second, I suggest that the black aspiring middle class – the intellectual elite specifically – responds to *symbolic violence* by means of a reaction formation, an unconscious *ressentiment* according to Max Scheler's (1915/1961) rendition of that term. And third – following Alexandre Kojève's influential reading of Hegel – I maintain that many white South Africans are mired in an *existential impasse* that blocks reciprocal recognition and that they have settled for lives of alienated consumption instead. Finally, I consider the implications of widespread shame, envy, and impasse in this land of terrible beauty – as Yeats might have put it – for the cultivation of life-giving hope.

Shame

The history books tell us that much of twentieth-century politics was driven by economic issues: the left focused on workers, unions, and social democratic goals, while the right called for small government and free enterprise. In the twenty-first century, however, the political spectrum has constellated itself around markers of social difference: today, both the left *and* right advocate on behalf of groups they consider marginalized, be they women, black people, the white working class or nationalists. It is not that class politics has become irrelevant to cultural politics – what appears to have happened, rather, is that the politics of equality has been dissociated from the politics of difference in both public and intellectual life.

The Marxist feminist, Nancy Fraser (2003), identifies these two camps as the politics of *redistribution* and the politics of *recognition*, respectively. She describes how the concept of redistribution is rooted in liberal politics, whereas the notion of recognition draws heavily on Hegel's phenomenology of consciousness. In the public imagination, talk of redistribution is equated with *class politics* while recognition discourse is reduced usually to *identity politics*, which involves struggles over categories such as gender, "race," sexuality, and so on. What will interest us as psychologists is that the dominant political trend of our times – identity politics – is profoundly *psychological*, being organized around the injured dignity of oppressed groups. Each group, that is, claims an internal group identity that has been rejected by the outside world. For proponents of identity politics, therefore, the problem of dignity turns on a society that is pathologically unvalidating. Human beings are first and foremost social beings, and when social formations compromise the dignity of marginalized groups, the consequences can be devastating, involving either self-hating shame or envious resentment. For Hegel, therefore, the history of our species is a history of the struggle for recognition (Fukuyama, 2018). Human beings only become conscious of themselves when recognized by others, and the failure to attain this recognition must eventuate in conflict. History begins, therefore, with warriors who risk their lives in order to compel their adversaries to recognize them (Fukuyama, 2018). If they succeed, they become masters who are recognized without having to reciprocate, but if they fail, they become slaves who must recognize their vanquishers without themselves being recognized (Bulhan, 1985). Inside this matrix of unreciprocated recognition, Hegel's famous *master–slave dialectic* takes shape, the master affirmed in his dignity and the slave deprived of his humanity.

It goes without saying that the history of South Africa is a history of masters and slaves. Over the course of three centuries, European settlers subdued the native populations, confiscating their lands and exploiting their labor. It did not suffice, however, that the locals were defeated militarily and economically: the entire edifice of their cultural traditions had to be liquidated. Material domination, therefore, went hand in hand with ideological domination – and in the South African instance, that meant the denigration and shaming of all black people. Frantz Fanon explains how, in the colonial encounter, "[i]t is not possible to enslave men without logically making them inferior through and through" (Fanon, 1956/2006, 26). Henceforth, the native population looks on helplessly as the occupying powers set about obliterating its cultural forms, imposing "a pejorative judgment with respect to its original forms of existing" (p. 25). The natives are not recognized as human, being nothing more than an afterthought in virgin land. They live in "[a] world divided into compartments, a motionless, Manichaeanistic world, a world of statues: the statue of the general who carried out the conquest, the statue of the engineer who built the bridge; a world which is sure of itself, which crushes with its stones the backs flayed by whips: this is the colonial world" (Fanon, 1963/2001, 40). A catastrophe of such magnitude can mean only one thing – that "God is not on [their] side" (Fanon, 1956/2006, 25).

Fearing death, the black man is "[s]ealed into that crushing objecthood. . . . For not only *must* [he] be black; he must be black in relation to the white man. . . . [He] has no ontological resistance" (Fanon, 1952/2008, 82–83, emphasis added). He simply is what the white man says he must be. Feelings of inferiority and shame overwhelm him, but he never stops desiring the world of the master: "For the black man there is only one destiny. And it is white. Long ago the black man admitted the unarguable superiority of the white man, and all his efforts are aimed at achieving a white existence" (Fanon, 1952/2008, 178). This should not surprise us: the black man has no option but to *lactify* himself, having witnessed the wholesale destruction of his former mode of being. The problem, of course, is that the border between the black and white worlds is impregnable: "The native is a being hemmed in; apartheid is simply one form of the division into compartments of the colonial world. The first thing which the native learns is to stay in his place, and not to go beyond certain limits" (Fanon, 1963/2001, 40). The black man, accordingly, is released from his fetters only while he sleeps; he dreams constantly of physical prowess, Fanon claims, in a classic case of wish fulfilment. On returning to waking life, the wish is denied once more. Like Aesop's fox reaching for the grapes, the black man can never be white for that would mean being recognized as human.

Disrespect rains down on the black subject. Unable to resolve the existential dilemma, the shame becomes unbearable. The resentment toward the self is turned outward in an attempt to restore a sense of agency eroded by shame (Tangney et al., 1996). Soon enough, it erupts into senseless violence – but not against the oppressor. Instead, the victims of structural violence will vent their rage first against *themselves*, their violence so incomprehensible that – in the words of Fanon – "the police and magistrates do not know which way to turn" (1963/2001, 40). Poverty encourages "chaotic, arbitrary, and unpredictable behaviour" as it prevents people from "act[ing] rationally and exercis[ing] self-control" (Sennett & Cobb, 1972, 22). The shame of deprivation and the burning sense of injustice that goes with it undermine the legitimacy of the law in the eyes of the disenfranchised. Mindless violence breaks out as resentment toward the power establishment is displaced onto substitutes: women, children, refugees and – especially – other black men. What ethnographers call *everyday violence* starts to set in: the routinization of interpersonal aggression at the microlevel and the constitution during peacetime of a virtual "common-sense of violence" (Bourgois, 2001).

Displaced from its original object, the experience of bitterness explodes into the external world as spontaneous, sadistic, and often arbitrary violence (Wurmser, 2009) – a process borne out by statistics on violence in postapartheid South Africa (Coovadia et al., 2009; Seedat et al., 2009). For example, the national rate of violent deaths is five times the global average. The murder of women is six times the world average. The raw numbers confirm that most victims are black, while the highest rates are suffered by colored men and women. What we know about homicide hotspots is that Cape Town ranks fourteenth in the world and – by some distance – first in Africa (Long, 2017). Nationally, an estimated half a million rapes are perpetrated against women and girls every year. Outbreaks of xenophobic violence occur with regularity. Meanwhile, income inequality and male youth unemployment emerge as the strongest correlates of murder and major assault. In their widely praised book, *The Spirit Level*, epidemiologists Richard Wilkinson and Kate Pickett (2010) describe how inequality in modern, industrialized nations generates fear, envy and resentment, affecting the physical and mental well-being of both the poor and the well-to-do.

Feelings of shame, that is, are difficult to escape in class society. As Norbert Elias (2000) observes, the ubiquity of class contempt dictates that even young children intuit social stratification long before they acquire any understanding of it. In fact, the political conditions most conducive for the shaming of poor and working-class people are liberal bourgeois democracies, which are shot through with invidious cultures of social comparison. Democratic South Africa, that is, aggravates the psychological torture of its citizens: they live in a constitutional dispensation that guarantees the equality of all, yet they feel themselves barred from enjoying its material benefits. Social *ressentiment* – in the words of Scheler – "must therefore be strongest in a society like ours, where . . . formal social equality, publicly recognized, go[es] hand in hand with wide factual differences in power, property, and education" (Scheler, 1915/1961, 28). For ordinary people, such a divergence can only make sense by evaluating themselves negatively. By admitting that they lack all "badges of ability" (Sennett & Cobb, 1972, 62), the poor man and woman can lay to rest the question that has followed them all their lives: the question of why – despite their best efforts – they got nowhere in life. Assuming personal responsibility for a society that failed them, not only do they feel the pain of inadequacy – they resent themselves for feeling it.

But the injustice of it all does not end there. For those who believe they *do* possess a badge of ability, powerful sanctions will be levied against them should they ever resolve to wear it (Suskind, 1998). Consider, for example, the case of a school for working-class children (see Sennett & Cobb, 1972, 79–90). The teachers are anxious to enforce discipline; they imagine that their charges do not value order and routine, given their unruly backgrounds. The general mass is deemed unteachable while one or two are singled out as having potential. The few who are made to stand out must make an agonizing decision: excel and shame their peers – for which they will be bullied mercilessly – or accept the shaming of their teachers but enjoy the bonds of friendship. An identical scenario faces the worker who may harbor fantasies of excellence: get promoted to supervisor and earn the scorn of your colleagues or live with them as equals, sharing the common bond of indignity. It is no wonder that the few who rise above their class cannot live with the shame of having distinguished themselves. They can neither be who they are nor stay where they are: many will marry outside their circle, most will leave the neighborhood for good.

That is how class society operates: "In turning people against each other, the class system of authority and judgment-making goes itself into hiding; the system is left unchallenged as people enthralled by the enigmas of its power battle one another for respect" (Sennett & Cobb, p. 150). In an unequal society that professes equality for all, shame rears its head at every turn; for the poor and working classes in particular, substance use becomes a ready consolation. Indeed, South Africa – which has the second highest Gini coefficient for income inequality in the world (Burns, 2011) – also has one of the highest alcohol consumption rates in the world (Seedat et al., 2009, 1015). Alcohol misuse, in turn, is strongly related to the perpetration of acts of violence, and, according to the United Nations

Office on Drugs and Crime, South Africa has the fourth highest rate for drug-related offences in the world (Burns, 2011). Although the value of socioeconomic status as a predictor of substance use is contested (Galea et al., 2004), a growing body of research suggests that the relationship between addiction and *shame* – as distinct from guilt – is mutually reinforcing (Dearing et al., 2005; Wiechelt, 2007). The resort to substances, that is, can be conceptualized as a defense against chronic feelings of shame – as much as it can trigger the very same feelings.

Ressentiment

The Spanish philosopher, José Ortega y Gasset, once wrote of his German counterpart, Max Scheler, that he was "the first man [sic] of genius, the Adam of the new Paradise." Scheler was widely regarded as one of the most brilliant minds of the twentieth century, but, with his unexpected death in 1928 and the suppression of his work by the Nazis, his ideas faded rapidly (Frings, 1994). I want to resurrect one of Scheler's ideas today, namely, his reading of the concept *ressentiment* as laid out in his book, *The Role of Ressentiment in the Make-Up of Morals*. The concept was not originally his own: the first to elaborate *ressentiment* systematically was in fact Nietzsche who decried the Christian values of love, compassion, and humility as a form of slave morality. For Nietzsche, what lay at the heart of Christian ethics was, effectively, a reaction formation: the early Christians were motivated by impotence, hatred, and envy of their Roman masters – and they sought to reverse their lowliness by supplanting Roman morality with a value system of their own. Acknowledging his debt to his countryman, Scheler quotes as follows from Nietzsche's *Genealogy of Morals*:

> The inoffensiveness of the weak, even the cowardice in which he is rich, his unavoidable obligation to wait at the door acquires a good name, as "patience," it is also called virtue; the inability to avenge oneself is supposed to be a voluntary renunciation of revenge, sometimes it is even called forgiveness. . . . They also speak of "love for one's enemies" – and they sweat while doing so.
>
> (Scheler, 1915/1961, 45)

When approached through a social justice paradigm, Scheler's book is likely to offend: several commentators have suggested, even, that his work was a massive projection of his own *ressentiment* at the social leveling of the early twentieth century. His thinking was "deeply aristocratic," and his endorsement of social and value hierarchies meant that, for Scheler, inequality was a natural feature of human existence (Coser, 1915/1961). On the other hand, the rise of what Fukuyama calls "the politics of resentment" has transformed Scheler's *ressentiment* into a potentially valuable tool for analyzing the latest trend in local and global politics – identity politics – which threatens to shatter all possibilities for mutual recognition and reconciliation. It is towards Scheler's own treatment of *ressentiment* that I now turn.

In their efforts to preserve the specialized meaning of the term, Scheler's translators prefer the French *ressentiment* over the English "resentment." This is because Scheler himself has in mind something much deeper than "mere" resentment. In his view, *ressentiment* has several elements. First, a human being experiences some injury and an associated negative emotion. Second, he or she is unable to express this emotion directly, usually on account of occupying a lower position in a given status hierarchy. Third, the negative emotion is consequently repressed. And fourth, under the direction of a repressed desire for revenge that proceeds "via rancor, envy, and impulse to detract all the way to spite" (Scheler, 1915/1961, 47), the subject engages in value delusions and their corresponding judgments, demeaning values that are objectively superior while venerating those that are objectively inferior.

These are the essentials of Scheler's *ressentiment*, the practical meaning of which is best illustrated through examples – and Scheler himself provides several. The *priest*, for one, is a typical *ressentiment* subject: he is required to control his emotions and project himself as the embodiment of serenity. Then there is the *mother-in-law* who must not only relinquish her son to another woman but must "offer her congratulations, and receive the intruder with affection" (Scheler, 1915/1961, 64). Scheler reports a case of what he calls *class ressentiment* – specifically, an incident in 1912 near Berlin when someone tied a length of wire between two trees on either side of the road so that drivers passing through would be decapitated. What unites Scheler's collection of *ressentiment* characters is a "way of thinking which attributes creative power to mere *negation* and *criticism*" (1915/1961, 67, original emphasis).

Reaction formation

This preliminary account of *ressentiment* brings me to the second leg of my argument, which is an analysis of the black intellectual elite's response to the *symbolic violence* that pervades institutions of higher learning in South Africa. I do so partly in an attempt to understand a phenomenon in which my own working life is immersed but primarily to draw our attention to the pervasiveness of envious resentment in our public life. According to sociologist Pierre Bourdieu, symbolic violence designates the intimate encounter in which the oppressed cannot help but assess their predicament through the terms of reference provided by the oppressor and thereby participate unwittingly in their own subjugation. The protests that have shaken university campuses over the last four years, that is, signal a conscientization about the workings of symbolic violence. All the talk of *intellectual colonization, Eurocentrism, whiteness, privilege, epistemic violence*, and so on is university-speak for a perceived system of knowledge and an encompassing institutional culture that make it impossible for black students and academics to participate as their white counterparts' equals in intellectual life. Their argument is that the dice are loaded – that the rules of the game prevent them from challenging the ideological workings of the knowledge-making apparatus. Unable to challenge the system from the inside, they seek therefore to disrupt, their seemingly incoherent demands an example of Walter Benjamin's notion of "pure means" as a response to capitalist violence (Martel, 2017). Straightforward enough – except that, for anyone who believes in the existence of the unconscious, "the simple is never but the simplified," in the words of Gaston Bachelard (Bourdieu, 1989, 24).

Recall Fanon's reluctant admission in the opening pages of *Black Skin, White Masks* – that the only real destiny for black people is the color white. The psychological import of Fanon's verdict cannot be overestimated because it raises the crucial question of how – in the minds of student protesters – the pursuit of whiteness is transformed into its denigration. Freudian theory offers an elegant solution, namely, the *reaction formation*. As per Fanon, the black subject desires to be white. There is no fear of whiteness per se – but there is an overwhelming fear of the *desire* for whiteness. It is no longer the black subject but the white subject who becomes – in the words of Fanon – "a phobogenic object, a stimulus to anxiety" (Fanon, 1952/2008, 117). Whiteness is converted into a phobia: "We can't breathe!" the Fallists exclaim, expressing one of the classic symptoms of a panic attack. The deprecation of whiteness, in other words, attenuates the very desire for it (Hall, 1954, 92).

Political commentators suggest that Fallist fury has a touch of drama to it, that they doth protest too much. Adam Habib (2016), for example, has written about the "politics of spectacle," which he interprets as a strategy used by minority factions to seize control of the political narrative on campus. I would go further by suggesting that the *performative* aspect of Fallism is typical of reaction formations, which are habitually overelaborate and affected (Hall, 1954, 92). Moreover, the implacability of student anger has an almost *compulsive* feel to it – another characteristic of the reaction formation – for no matter how far backward university management bent, students could never feel satisfied. It was as if they *had* to be angry – regardless of the actual deal on the negotiating table.

Envy

Reaction formations aside, why does the wish for whiteness inspire such anxiety? It is here that the Kleinian theory of *envy* proves instructive. According to the standard version, envy is constitutional and enters the world with the neonate. The infant revels in gratification at the mother's nourishing breast but also has to contend with deprivation. It is this latter experience that generates the *persecutory anxiety* of the paranoid-schizoid position. The infant starts to hate the good breast and – as is also the case with gratification – spoils it with envy (Klein, 1975, 183–187). Sadistic attacks on the breast increase until it is entirely without value: in the words of Klein, "it has become bad by being bitten up and poisoned by urine and faeces" (p. 186). The stronger and more enduring the envy, the more difficult it becomes for the infant to reclaim the lost object; the ego becomes fragile, and the capacity for love and hope fades into obscurity.

Whereas Klein conceived of envy as an expression of the death drive, I want to approach it primarily as an intersubjective phenomenon (Orange, 1995), as a destructive mode of being resulting from persistently unequal social encounters. Viewed from this perspective, the relevance of Kleinian theory for a psychological analysis of Fallism becomes obvious upon recognizing the equivalence of elite institutions with the nourishing breast. The University of Cape Town, for example, dispenses precious knowledge, financial support, networking opportunities, and – above all – the promise of a life of dignity. But for Fallists, the internal logic of the institution is "white." They feel themselves deprived of the fruits they imagined a university education would confer, which triggers for many the familiar feeling of deprivation. They feel persecuted by an institution experienced as massively shaming, and as they begin to compare themselves to more privileged students, their shame turns to envy (Orange, 1995). In a literal display of anal sadism, they set about spoiling the university, unloading bins of human feces into lecture halls. Haunted by a relentless sense of grievance, they set fire to life-affirming artworks and shut down life-giving classes of knowledge. "If we cannot enjoy this place, then no one will," they may as well be saying. It does not matter that they may be damaging their own university – at least in the short run. As Freud observes, "[I]f one cannot be the favourite oneself, at all events nobody else shall be the favourite. . . . [S]ocial justice means that we deny ourselves many things so that others may have to do without them as well" (quoted in Hoggett, 2018, 400).

But this is a somewhat pragmatic assessment next to the *psychological* calculus that is now in play: the more the Fallists destroy the institution, the more impoverished the collective ego feels. Their envy grows stronger still, and the protests spiral out of control. The experience of deprivation and the destruction of the good object unleash a merciless persecutory anxiety; paranoia, aggression, and projection take over as the dominant psychological themes in university life. With the good object now spoiled, it becomes impossible to distinguish the good from the bad as the Fallists start agitating for the decolonization of the curriculum. The entire Enlightenment canon – they believe – must be dismantled because it stands for colonization by intellectual means. They insist that the Enlightenment values, ideals, and methods that came out of Western Europe are simply unworkable in the South African context. Reason itself becomes the object of their opprobrium – even science must fall – as *lived experience* emerges as the new basis for argumentation. The purported universals of the Enlightenment project are regarded as invalid in relation to the particulars found in the colonized world. A decolonial form of praxis is sought that will privilege the lived experiences of the oppressed here and around the world.

With the Fallists attempting to replace one set of academic values with another that must yet be determined, Scheler's *ressentiment* enters the frame – that special kind of envy concerned with value delusions. It may well be that their proposed reimagining of values stands on solid ground – but the ongoing confusion over what exactly decolonization entails suggests the presence of a "way of thinking which attributes creative power to mere negation." To be clear, talk of decolonizing consciousness has been a staple of the academic circuit for more than half a century – and it is the lack of resolution that turns Fallist politics into a legitimate object of *ressentiment* analysis.

It is my contention that several Fallist motifs bind the student movement to *ressentiment* politics. The first involves the *ressentiment* subject's adoption of what Léon Wurmser calls the position of *innocent victim* (2009, 387, 397). Regardless of their actual behavior – and this is a matter of public record – student activists considered themselves beyond reproach and therefore entirely free of guilt, there being (in Kleinian terms) no transition to depressive functioning. A second point of convergence – described again by Wurmser – is the *moral absolutism* of the *ressentiment* universe, which manifests itself at the individual level as an "anal-sadomasochistic superego operating in absolute polarities" (2009, 397). For those of us who followed the university protests, the twin tropes of *white privilege* and *black pain* were seared into our consciousness, leaving little room for the contemplation of moral and political ambiguities. The complexity of our political situation was whittled down to the simple moral binary of "with us or against us." And third, the classic sign of the *ressentiment* mood is the *displacement* of a suppressed impulse for revenge onto substitute objects (Wurmser, 2009, 396). Scheler describes how *ressentiment* – through repression – involves the disconnection of the person in question from "the original object of an emotion" with the result that the person "does not know 'of what' he [or she] is afraid or incapable" (Scheler, 1915/1961, 69). In this regard, as much as elite university culture can leave black students struggling with feelings of alienation, it is not the primary locus of the problem. My reading is that Fallist rage originates in prior humiliations – *misrecognitions* – that are raced, classed, and gendered in complex ways. Shame, after all, is hardwired into the chronicity of everyday and structural violence: unable to exact revenge, the original trauma that is structural violence is forgotten – but the sense of injury remains. It is picked at compulsively, eventually exploding without warning onto unwitting secondary targets. And as John Steiner points out in his work on grievance, the victim position is not easily relinquished: it is a source of satisfaction that is narcissistically invested (Hoggett, 2018), hence the seeming self-aggrandizement of Fallist supporters.

What remains to be examined, then, is the decisive matter of values. In my own writings, I have described the term "decolonization" as an *empty signifier* (Long, 2018): notice the oddity, for example, of intellectuals stressing the importance of "decolonizing" higher education *before* they commence discussions on what it actually means. Indeed – as the post-Marxist Ernesto Laclau (2005) points out – it is *because* it lacks any definite meaning that decolonization discourse can frame the political landscape – at least symbolically – in compelling ways. In a post-truth world that has presided over the relativization of all knowledge claims, decolonization discourse is not required to justify itself; its seat at the high table of epistemology is reserved. Yet it is a highly suspect form of politics because it often looks for problems in the wrong places. To begin with, proponents of decolonization almost never acknowledge one basic fact – that most poor and working-class students have suffered the indignity of being miseducated for twelve years of their lives. South Africa's schooling system ranks consistently among the worst in the world, and by the time these students enter elite universities, they are hopelessly underprepared for the academic life and struggle to cope with the unrelenting institutional demands. But instead of acknowledging these difficulties as areas for personal development, like Aesop's fox they conclude that the grapes must be sour *because* they are unreachable. The problem is not the collective injustice they suffered in our dysfunctional schools – rather, it becomes the university system and the Enlightenment values it espouses. It does not matter that no one knows what decolonization means – the university must be decolonized regardless – and so it comes to pass that what Vivek Chibber (2017a) calls "an orgy of bullshit" gets treated deferentially as bona fide scholarship.

It is no accident that – in the post-apartheid years – there has never been a Fallist movement in our township schools. Everyone receives the same inferior education and – because of Cape Town's enduring apartheid-style geography – there is scant awareness of the first-rate education learners in the leafy Southern Suburbs are receiving. But when these school-leavers enter elite universities, the inevitable social comparisons begin. A feeling of relative deprivation emerges as the political ideal of equality collides with the social reality of inequality. Poor and working-class students observe the ease with which their more privileged counterparts appear to negotiate university spaces. Envious resentment flares up among those students most alienated from the social order. What are they to do? Because they desire a middle-class existence – why else would anyone go to university? – they cannot draw on the traditional values of the working class (Coser, 1915/1961, 30; Scheler, 1915/1961, 66). Frustrated and without countervalues of their own, they can only attack the existing institutional order, despising it in public yet desiring it in secret (Coser, 1915/1961, 28–30). They have forgotten the original crime – their own miseducation – and vent their anger at the university authorities instead. At this point, the politics of decolonization becomes the politics of displacement. It does not stand on its own ground, being fundamentally a *reaction* against the Enlightenment tradition. It is a resounding "No!" to the affirmations of the academic establishment. Yet its proponents are also *tortured* by their own *ressentiment* – because the values they abhor consciously are the same values their educational aspirations demand that they embrace. On this point it is worth quoting Scheler once more:

> [A] man [sic] who "slanders" the unattainable values which oppress him is by no means completely unaware of their positive character ... the positive values are still felt as such, but they are *overcast* by the false values and can shine through only dimly. The *ressentiment* experience is always characterized by this "transparent" presence of the true and objective values behind the illusory ones – by that obscure awareness that one lives in a *sham world* which one is unable to penetrate.
>
> (1915/1961, 60)

One would be mistaken in assuming that the future of South Africa depends entirely on the condition of the poor and working classes. (I, for one, have made that assumption before.) To prove the point, one need only ask oneself why the country has not yet descended into civil war. The short answer is that the exploited classes do not have the wherewithal to organize themselves into a viable force – and that verdict has been reached on both the political left and right (Chibber, 2017b; Fukuyama, 2018). That is why the influence of *middle-class ressentiment* should not be underestimated. There is, of course, a substantial gap between the ivory tower and the street – but it is equally true that what happens on university campuses filters into public spaces. I mention this because research conducted in the middle of the twentieth century showed how followers of fascist movements were most likely to come from the lower strata of the middle classes who – because their strivings for self-improvement were continuously blocked – were most susceptible to developing feelings of *ressentiment* (Coser, 1915/1961). At present, colleagues around the country inform me of the increasingly fascist tenor of campus politics: they describe the suppression of dissent, rampant opportunism, and ideological dishonesty. We see the same in national politics as quasi-fascist movements swim ever closer to the political mainstream. With the degree of cooperation between the two spheres increasing all the time – and with social inequality showing few signs of abating – it is only a matter of time before impotent rage – *ressentiment* – gets channeled into the creation of antidemocratic political movements.

Impasse

In the mid-1950s, the French psychoanalyst, Octave Mannoni, published what would become his most famous work, *Prospero and Caliban*. In his attempt to understand the psychological workings of colonialism, Mannoni assigned a dependency complex to the colonized, which he believed expressed itself via a reaction formation in the shape of a pathological desire for freedom. It is a highly contentious argument that I cannot take up now. Instead, I want to focus on two of Mannoni's observations on the psychology of the *colonizer*. First, Mannoni reasoned that the cultural and technological achievements of Europe – powered by enterprise, ingenuity, and an urge to dominate – were in fact the products of a defensive maneuver against an underlying inferiority complex. Second, he suggested that the need to rule in faraway lands stemmed from a paradoxical hatred of humankind. Pouring out of Europe – spurred on by their own misanthropy – the colonizers set out in search of worlds they fantasized would bear no trace of a human presence. High on "the lure of a world without men" (Mannoni, 1956, 101), it was easy to convince themselves that they had "discovered" America and Australia and southern Africa – in spite of the presence of the local populations – because the locals did not qualify as fully human. Rather, the colonizers would project their own forbidden impulses onto the subhuman creatures they encountered. Obsessed especially with the sexual rapacity of the natives and the clear and present danger to their own delicate women, the savages had to be infantilized, paternalized, or subdued by force – and any attempt by the colonized to declare their own humanity was to be suppressed by all means necessary. This was no simple matter of economic or strategic interest – the *psychological* equilibrium of the colonial project was at stake – in Mannoni's words,

> we are perfectly happy if we can project the fantasies of our own unconscious on to the outside world, but if we suddenly find that these creatures are not pure projections but real beings with claims to liberty, we consider it outrageous.
>
> (1956, 117)

As the Fanonian scholar Hussein Bulhan explains, colonizers are tragic figures. On the one hand, they need the colonized to remain in their place, to serve as the repository of their projections, a fate that no human being will tolerate indefinitely. On the other – since the colonial relationship is a recapitulation of the master–slave dialectic (Bulhan, 1985, 116) – the colonizer never feels recognized as human because the act of recognition is made by a slave and is therefore worthless. It is this hapless situation that constitutes what Kojève calls the *existential impasse* of the master (1947/1980, 19) – a situation that I believe may apply to many white South Africans today.

Progressive white psychoanalysts including Gillian Straker (2004) and Melanie Suchet (2012) have written courageously about their racial melancholia as "the *unwilling* beneficiaries of Whiteness" (Suchet, 2012, 211). But we neglect at our peril those whites whose racial melancholia is all about a "*refusal* to relinquish what has been lost" (Suchet, 2012, 217). As Suchet admits in the postscript to her chapter, "Unraveling Whiteness," this refusal involves *most* white South Africans. Indeed, the end of apartheid has not led to significant changes in the distribution of material resources – but the passage of time does appear to have exposed the fragility of whiteness. Uncertain of their place in South African life, many whites have withdrawn from public spaces into fortified enclaves (Lemanski, 2004) – "their gated communities with high walls, electrified fences, closed-circuit television and private [armies]" (Long, 2017, 308). The steady erosion of whiteness has produced a sense of loss and confusion: as per Suchet's analysis, what was once a narcissistic veneer has been replaced by a melancholic structure. No longer do black people submit to the white subject's fantasy: they are exiting the dialectic en masse, leaving the master without a raison d'être. Disoriented, it is as though white South Africans were asking their black counterparts – and I quote Suchet again – "If you are no longer that to me, then who am I to myself?" (2012, 217). But rather than step into the void between whiteness and blackness, many white people have simply battened down the hatches, retreating still further into their whiteness: they live (barely) in an *existential impasse*, refusing to recognize black people, and, being unable to resolve their grief, they cling stubbornly to their lost object – just as Freud's melancholics once did. In an evident case of *disavowal*, they *know* what is happening yet *still* they believe (Straker, 2004), or, as Slavoj Žižek puts it, "I know, but I don't want to know that I know, so I don't know" (2008, 53).

Disavowal is made possible through its connection with *fetishism*. Marx described the commodity fetish as the expropriation of workers' labor power, which then reappears magically in the products of their labor (Woodfin & Zarate, 2004). The commodity comes to represent what has been lost: the target of powerful identifications, it is converted readily into a fetish. Following Straker's line of argument, one may reason that white South Africans manage their experience of lack and loss through fetishism, their castrated whiteness affirmed and negated simultaneously. Locked away in their gated communities – a symbol of what Stephen Mitchell has called an "internal protection racket" (2000, 731) – commodities overcome them in splendid isolation (Altman, 2004), this their defense against the brittleness of whiteness (Suchet, 2012). *Perversion* has entered the scene, the anxiety generated by lack papered over by the fetish (Straker, 2004).

Deborah Posel notes how "[r]ace is always a relational construct" (2010, 167) – the meaning of whiteness both implies and depends on the meaning of blackness – but with black people refusing to endorse the historical terms of reference, white people find themselves in psychic freefall, cut loose from what was once subjective *and* objective truth. Too many deny their moral culpability, their defensiveness typical of paranoid-schizoid *guiltiness* rather than depressive guilt (Harris, 2012; Mitchell, 2000). Reflecting on this inability to mourn, Adrienne Harris describes a gap in the white psyche that functions as "an imploding star, refusing signification" (2012, 207), where not only trauma but also destructiveness have been bleached out. All the while, the loss of the white ideal is disavowed through the commodity fetish with its stockpiling of economic power, no matter the attendant psychosocial damage.

Strictly speaking, Kojève's *existential impasse* refers to the *master's* realization that he has not been intersubjectively confirmed: he turns the Other into his slave in order to be recognized, yet the slave by definition is not worthy of recognizing him. The situation I am describing, however, is one in which it is *black* people who see through the rules of engagement – although the outcome for white people as putative masters is still the same. Kojève explains how the master realizes that he is on the "wrong track [yet he] has no desire to 'overcome' . . . himself as master . . . he cannot be transformed, educated. . . . Mastery is the supreme given value for him, beyond which he cannot go" (1947/1980, 19, 21–22). Without the prospect of redemption, the master can only continue as before. Kojève again: "The Master . . . does not work, [he] produces nothing stable outside of himself. He merely destroys the products of the Slave's work [by consuming them]. Thus his enjoyment and his satisfaction remain purely subjective: they are of interest only to him and therefore can be recognized only by him; they have no 'truth,' no objective reality revealed to all. Accordingly, this 'consumption,' this idle enjoyment of the Master's, which results from the 'immediate' satisfaction of desire, can at the most procure some pleasure for man; it can never give him complete and definitive satisfaction" (1947/1980, 24).

Whereas the style of the black middle class is to consume their goods in plain sight (Burger et al., 2015), white consumers do so seemingly in private. As far as I can tell, this is not because white people do not need to signal their status; it is rather the case that white consumption is an exercise submerged in guiltiness. The difference in consumption habits may explain why we still know rather little about the goings-on in the homes of the white elite; indeed, it is only by "studying up" (Connell, 2007, 216) that the workings of the master–slave dialectic can be articulated in full. On the basis of this analysis, however, it would appear that, in the drawing rooms of private urban enclaves, it is impasse, inwardness, and joylessness that prevail, the hallmarks of whiteness in post-apartheid South Africa.

Hope

In tracing the trajectories of shame, envy, and impasse in our national life, I have attempted to place Hegel's master–slave dialectic front and center. But one also needs to situate the question of equality in historical context: never mind South Africa, it is a sobering fact that the history of our *species* is a history of masters and slaves. In his account of social organization from the Stone Age to the present, Walter Scheidel (2017) contends that a combination of domesticated food production, sedentism, state formation, and hereditary property rights ensured that material inequality became a central feature of human coexistence. A fundamental part of the civilizing process, in other words, is inequality itself. But history is not without surprises. What Scheidel calls the *Four Horsemen of Leveling* is proof that unequal societies can be leveled – in exchange for a monumental loss of life. *Mass mobilization warfare* is one of those horsemen involving the kind of killing contract that more or less seeps into every segment of society. The two world wars are fitting examples where industrial-scale warfare, aggressive taxation, rising costs of living, state involvement in the economy, and trade disruptions ravaged the wealth of the rich, leading to unionization and the creation of welfare states that would level inequality on a scale almost unparalleled in human history. *Transformative revolution* is another notable leveler. Communist takeovers – exemplified by expropriation, redistribution, and collectivization – succeeded in challenging inequality in extraordinary ways, rivaling even the world wars for number of fatalities and human suffering in general. *State failure* is the third horseman: when states fall apart, the rich simply have more to lose so the playing fields get evened out. And finally, there are *lethal pandemics*: when sufficient numbers of people die, the balance between capital and labor can shift so dramatically that one can be left with Black Death–type situations where the workers make merry on meat and beer while the nobles run around trying to maintain appearances.

Acts of God aside, Scheidel is clear that *exemplary violence alone* has been shown to address inequality in genuine ways – not democracy, not macroeconomic crises, not modern economic development, not even radical policy reforms. Fanon may well have intuited this when he declared that "decolonization is always a violent phenomenon" (1963/2001, 27). Naturally, the irony of seeking to end structural and symbolic violence with *revolutionary* violence is not lost on anyone; indeed, the wellsprings of life-giving hope may have to be sought elsewhere. But the basic point is this: the cultivation of hope in the absence of actual material prospects amounts to little more than another cheap opiate for the masses. Real hope cannot exist within a matrix of shame, envy, and impasse when the material base of our disfigured national psyche remains locked in place. As for the observable correlates of everyday violence, *ressentiment*-driven value delusions, and alienated consumptiveness, these should remind us that nothing less than our shared humanity is at stake.

The only way to dissolve the master–slave dialectic is to resolve the problem of unreciprocated recognition in which the master insists on remaining the master. Fanon envisioned a particular outcome to the deadlock, but it is not a solution that builds nations. As psychologists, we tend to treat misrecognition as a "psychical deformation"; philosophers regard it as a matter of "ethical self-realization" (Fraser, 2003, 29). Neither of these positions will suffice. Following Nancy Fraser, I want to reframe the question of misrecognition as a question of *justice* – because misrecognition involves "an institutionalized relation of *subordination*" (2003, 29, original emphasis), a relation that prevents South Africans from participating as peers in a dignified social life.

But what makes for a life of dignity? What makes a life incontrovertibly human? One can hardly do better than Martha Nussbaum's (1999) catalogue of ten central human capabilities. This is not the occasion to repeat the entire list, so allow me to quote only those of her reflections that are of immediate relevance. For Nussbaum, being human means:

> Being able to move freely from place to place. . . . Being able to use the senses; being able to imagine, to think, and to reason and to do these things in a "truly human" way, a way informed and cultivated by an adequate education. . . . Being able to form a conception of the good and to engage in critical reflection about the planning of one's own life. . . . Being able to live for and in relation to others, to recognize and show concern for other human beings, to engage in various forms of social interaction; being able to imagine the situation of another and to have compassion for that situation; having the capability for both justice and friendship. . . . Having the social bases of self-respect and nonhumiliation; being able to be treated as a dignified being whose worth is equal to that of others. . . . [B]eing able to participate effectively in political choices that govern one's life. . . . [B]eing able to

> hold property. . . . [B]eing able to work as a human being, exercising practical reason and entering into meaningful relationships of mutual recognition with other workers.
>
> (1999, 41–42)

Anything less than the life under consideration is no longer a human life.

Notice Nussbaum's emphasis on *material* space: the freedom to move from one place to another, the reality of owning property. These are among the attributes that make us human. For the millions of disenfranchised South Africans, therefore, the question of landlessness is not only of practical importance: it is an existential question. To own land is to own oneself, to live with confidence in the world, to build communities of feeling, to pursue questions of meaning rather than survival, to have the sense that one is ontologically real (Long, 2017). To deny a people their land, therefore, is to deny them their humanity. Ominously, Scheidel makes the point that land reform – when accompanied by violence or the threat of violence – is an effective strategy for levelling inequality. Why is violence or the threat of it effective? Because no one gives up anything worthwhile without a struggle. One can only hope that it does not come to that, that the power elite in this country will recognize that the interests of the dispossessed are the interests of us all.

But Nussbaum also discusses *psychological* capacities in her account of what it is to be human. We should not make the error, therefore, of imagining that the psychological is trivial in contexts of massive material deprivation. The land question is critical – and its resolution will go some way towards restoring dignity to the lives of South Africans – but we must not underestimate the *political* relevance of our ability for recognizing and validating the mental states of others. Treat others as you wish to be treated, and do not treat others in a manner that you do not wish to be treated: this is the so-called Golden Rule that underpins almost every religious, cultural, and ethical system known to humankind. Yet one cannot realize this principle without a capacity for empathy – and that is what marks us out as psychotherapists. We are experts at holding minds in mind – at perspective-taking – a prerequisite for ethical living. But it is just as true that empathic sensitivity becomes damaging when it is oblivious to the political struggles of ordinary people. That is why critical theory matters, why sociology matters, why philosophy matters, why history matters, why economics matters. The parent discipline we call psychology is a discipline of the status quo (Prilleltensky, 1989): progressive practice requires of us a preparedness to venture outside our home discipline. The splitting of the psychological from the social domain has made it difficult for psychologists to have any kind of moral voice in the struggles of the everyday. On the other hand, the tendency among many activists to dismiss psychology as false consciousness is premature to say the least. The bottom line is that personal change and social transformation are inseparable: as much as we need programs for social improvement, we also need to remember that the small things still matter. That is just one of the things we as psychotherapists do: we nurture hope – that most fragile of cargoes – with the realization that what each of us does in our lives on a moment-to-moment basis will ripple through the ages.

References

Altman, N. (2004). Whiteness Uncovered: Commentary on Papers by Melanie Suchet and Gillian Straker. *Psychoanalytic Dialogues*, 14(4):439–446.

Bourdieu, P. (1989). Social Space and Symbolic Power. *Sociological Theory*, 7(1):14–25.

Bourgois, P. (2001). The Power of Violence in War and Peace: Post-Cold War Lessons from El Salvador. *Ethnography*, 2(1):5–34.

Bradford, G. (1915). Portrait of a Lady: Madame de Sévigné. *Sewanee Review*, 23(1):36–48.

Bulhan, H. A. (1985). *Frantz Fanon and the Psychology of Oppression*. New York: Plenum Press.

Burger, R., Louw, M., Pegado, B. B. I. O. & van der Berg, S. (2015). Understanding Consumption Patterns of the Established and Emerging South African Black Middle Class. *Development Southern Africa*, 32(1):41–56.

Burns, J. K. (2011). The Mental Health Gap in South Africa – a Human Rights Issue. *Equal Rights Review*, 6:99–113.

Chibber, V. (2017a). *Social Determinants of Psychological Suffering (with Reference to Marx's Theory of Alienation)*. Seminar delivered at Child Guidance Clinic, University of Cape Town, Cape Town, August 8.

Chibber, V. (2017b). Rescuing Class from the Cultural Turn. *Catalyst*, 1(1):27–56.

Connell, R. (2007). *Southern Theory: The Global Dynamics of Knowledge in Social Science*. Cambridge: Polity Press.

Coovadia, H., Jewkes, R., Barron, P., Sanders, D. & McIntyre, D. (2009). The Health and Health System of South Africa: Historical Roots of Current Public Health Challenges. *Lancet*, 374:817–834.

Coser, L. A. (1915/1961). Max Scheler: An Introduction. In M. Scheler (ed.), *Ressentiment*. New York: Free Press, 5–36.

Dearing, R. L., Stuewig, J. & Tangney, J. P. (2005). On the Importance of Distinguishing Shame from Guilt: Relations to Problematic Alcohol and Drug Use. *Addictive Behaviors*, 30(7):1392–1404.

De Tocqueville, A. (1835/1889). *Democracy in America*, trans. H. Reeve. London: Longmans, vol. 2.

Elias, N. (2000). *The Civilizing Process: Sociogenetic and Psychogenetic Investigations*. Malden: Blackwell.

Fanon, F. (1963/2001). *The Wretched of the Earth*. London: Penguin.

Fanon, F. (1956/2006). Racism and Culture. In A. Haddour (ed.), *The Fanon Reader*. London: Pluto Press, 19–29.

Fanon, F. (1952/2008). *Black Skin, White Masks*. London: Pluto Press.

Fraser, N. (2003). *Redistribution or Recognition? A Political-Philosophical Exchange*. London: Verso.

Frings, M. S. (1994). Introduction. In M. Scheler (ed.), *Ressentiment*. Milwaukee: Marquette University Press, 1–18.

Fukuyama, F. (2018). *Identity: Contemporary Identity Politics and the Struggle for Recognition*. London: Profile Books.

Galea, S., Nandi, A. & Vlahov, D. (2004). The Social Epidemiology of Substance Use. *Epidemiologic Reviews*, 26(1):36–52.

Habib, A. (2016). *The Politics of Spectacle – Reflections on the 2016 Student Protests*, December 5. Retrieved from: www.dailymaverick.co.za/article/2016-12-05-op-ed-the-politics-of-spectacle-reflections-on-the-2016-student-protests/.

Hall, C. S. (1954). *A Primer of Freudian Psychology*. New York: World Publishing Company.

Harris, A. (2012). The House of Difference, or White Silence. *Studies in Gender and Sexuality*, 13(3):197–216.

Henry, S. (2000). What Is School Violence? An Integrated Definition. *Annals of the American Academy of Political and Social Science*, 567:16–29.

Hoggett, P. (2018). Ressentiment and Grievance. *British Journal of Psychotherapy*, 34(3):393–407.

Klein, M. (1975). *Envy and Gratitude and Other Works 1946–1963*. New York: Free Press.

Kojève, A. (1947/1980). *Introduction to the Reading of Hegel: Lectures on the Phenomenology of Spirit*, trans. J. H. Nichols, Jr. Ithaca: Cornell University Press.

Laclau, E. (2005). *On Populist Reason*. London: Verso.

Lemanski, C. (2004). A New Apartheid? The Spatial Implications of Fear of Crime in Cape Town, South Africa. *Environment and Urbanization*, 16(2):101–111.

Long, W. (2017). Essence or Experience? A New Direction for African Psychology. *Theory & Psychology*, 27(3):293–312.

Long, W. (2018). Decolonizing Higher Education: Postcolonial Theory and the Invisible Hand of Student Politics. *New Agenda*, 69:20–25.

Mannoni, O. (1956). *Prospero and Caliban: The Psychology of Colonization*, trans. P. Powesland. London: Methuen.

Martel, J. (2017). Walter Benjamin. In B. Evans & T. Carver (eds.), *Histories of Violence: Post-War Critical Thought*. London: Zed Books, 14–30.

Mitchell, S. (2000). You've Got to Suffer if You Want to Sing the Blues: Psychoanalytic Reflections on Guilt and Self-Pity. *Psychoanalytic Dialogues*, 10(5):713–733.

Nussbaum, M. (1999). *Sex and Social Justice*. New York: Oxford University Press.

Orange, D. M. (1995). *Emotional Understanding: Studies in Psychoanalytic Epistemology*. New York: Guilford Press.

Posel, D. (2010). Races to Consume: Revisiting South Africa's History of Race, Consumption and the Struggle for Freedom. *Ethnic and Racial Studies*, 33(2):157–175.

Prilleltensky, I. (1989). Psychology and the Status Quo. *American Psychologist*, 44(5):795–802.

Scheidel, W. (2017). *The Great Leveler: Violence and the History of Inequality from the Stone Age to the Twenty-First Century*. Princeton: Princeton University Press.

Scheler, M. (1915/1961). *Ressentiment*, trans. W. W. Holdheim. New York: Free Press.

Seedat, M., van Niekerk, A., Jewkes, R., Suffla, S. & Ratele, K. (2009). Violence and Injuries in South Africa: Prioritising an Agenda for Prevention. *Lancet*, 374:1011–1022.

Sennett, R. & Cobb, J. (1972). *The Hidden Injuries of Class*. London: Faber & Faber.

Straker, G. (2004). Race for Cover: Castrated Whiteness, Perverse Consequences. *Psychoanalytic Dialogues*, 14(4):405–422.

Suchet, M. (2012). Unraveling Whiteness. In L. Aron & A. Harris (eds.), *Relational Psychoanalysis: Expansion of Theory*. New York: Routledge, vol. 4, 199–220.

Suskind, R. (1998). *A Hope in the Unseen*. New York: Broadway Books.

Tangney, J. P., Wagner, P. E., Hill-Barlow, D., Marschall, D. E. & Gramzow, R. (1996). Relation of Shame and Guilt to Constructive Versus Destructive Responses to Anger Across the Lifespan. *Journal of Personality & Social Psychology*, 70 (4):797–809.

Wiechelt, S. A. (2007). The Specter of Shame in Substance Misuse. *Substance Use & Misuse*, 42(2–3):399–409.

Wilkinson, R. & Pickett, K. (2010). *The Spirit Level: Why Equality Is Better for Everyone*. London: Penguin.

Woodfin, R. & Zarate, O. (2004). *Introducing Marxism*. Royston: Icon Books.

Wurmser, L. (2009). The Superego as Herald of Resentment. *Psychoanalytic Inquiry*, 29(5):386–410.

Žižek, S. (2008). *Violence: Six Sideways Reflections*. New York: Picador.

Index

Note: Page numbers followed by an 'n' indicate a note on the corresponding page.

abjection 103–104
accusing eyes 143
Adorno, Theodor W. 98–99, 100–101, 102–105, 107, 111, 112n6, 116n71
affairs 91–92
agitators 104–105
anger, uses of 35, 45–46
annihilation anxiety 206–211
antiracism 137
appetitive regulations 6
authoritarianism 97–98, 106
authoritarian personality 102
autonomy 101, 116n75

Ballenger, James 171
Bell, Derrick 43
Biden, Joe 37
Bion, Wilfred 21, 223–224
biopolitics of the population 33–34
Biss, Eula 139
Black Lives Matter 34, 188; *see also* race and racism
Blackness and black people 137, 237; and psychosis 182–196, 196n2, 197n3; *see also* race and racism; South Africa
Bleger, Jose 64
body, the 4
border psychology 209
borders 66–72
boundaries 65–66
Breivik, Anders 111
Brewer, Jan 200
Brexit Party 116n71
Bruck, David 169
Bulhan, Hussein 249
Butler, Daniel 69

Cambridge Analytica 110
capitalism 97–98, 105–107
Cartwright, Samuel 183
Charny, Israel 178–179
chosen glories 208
chosen trauma 208
civilization 99
Civil Rights Movement 40–41
class politics 236, 238–239
climate change 217
clinical work 128–133, 219–220; and natural world 219–220
Clinton, Hillary 108
Coates, Ta-Nehisi 144, 194
Cohen, Roger 89
collective regression 206–211
colonization 248–249
color blindness 41–42, 148–149, 185; *see also* structural racism
commons 8–9
consciousness 3–4
COVID-19 32–33, 38, 51–52, 68, 89; and Trump, Donald 94–95
crime 135, 147, 149, 151; *see also* violence
Critical Race Theory 37–38, 42, 44, 49n25; *see also* race and racism
Cuba 56
culture industry 105, 109–110
Cummings, Elijah 109

Davoine, Francoise 185–186, 195
death penalty 169, 173–180
debt 139–140
dehumanization 207
Deleuze, Gilles 76n7
delusion 166–167

demarcation 67–69, 72, 74
democracy 97, 111, 123
depressive guilt 140
deprivation 190–193
Derrida, Jacques 173–179
destruction 186–190
dictionaries 222
disidentification 14–15
diversity training 37, 44
dreaming 62–63, 75
dreams 43

ego 83–84
Ellison, Ralph 193
emotional attachment 30
entitlement 122
envy 243–248
epistemology of identificatory obligation 131–133
ethics 72–75
eugenics 183; see also Nazis; race and racism
Evarts, Arrah 183
everyday violence 237–238
"excess deaths" 32–34
excitement 85–88, 91–92; and Whiteness 121
"Executive Order on Combatting Race and Sex Stereotyping" 37–42, 44
external world 3–7

Fallism 243–245
Fanon, Franz 64, 236–237, 242
fantasy 19
Farage, Nigel 116n71
fascism 97, 100–103, 107
fathers 79–84, 86–95
feminization 113n21
fetishism 250
fight/flight 14, 21
fires 51–54
first person plural 8–9, 145
first world problems 53, 57
Floyd, George 33, 75n4
Foucault, Michel 98, 99, 177; on power 43; on racism 33–35
fragility 147–150
framing 64–67
Fraser, Nancy 235–236
freedom 101, 106–107
Freud, Sigmund 3–5, 30, 99, 100, 104–105, 113n19, 244; and death

drive 165; and dreaming 75; and hate 160–161, 163; and narcissism 164; and topographical regression 26; and vertical planes 122–123
Frieden, Thomas R. 79
Frost, Robert 231–232

gated communities 54–55
Gaudilliere, Jean-Max 185–186, 195
genocide 158–159, 162, 176–180; see also hate crimes; murderous racism; Nazis; race and racism
globalization 61–62
Glover, Calvin 27
grievance 46
groping 79–83
group mentality 21–22
Guiliani, Rudy 37
guilt 138–144, 153n3

hate crimes 201; see also genocide; murderous racism
hatred and hating 8–9, 160–164; and I (first-person singular) 13–14
Hegel, Georg Wilhelm Friedrich 236
Hispanics 201, 212n2
Hitler, Adolf 99–100, 102
HIV 129
Holocaust 111
homeless people 58–60
homophobia 13; and disidentification 15; and psychoanalysis 19–20
homosexuality 23–25
hope 252–255
Horkenheimer, Max 103
Horney, Karen 116n71

I 10
identification 93, 133n1; with the aggressor 107; and authoritarian personality 102; and clinical work 16; ethics of 17–18; and misogyny 86–87, 90; and privilege 71; and structured hatreds 27–30; through idealization 101, 108
identity politics 236
I (first-person singular) 13–14
illiberal democracy 97
immigrants 200–211
Immigration Customs and Enforcement (ICE) 203
impasse 248–251
inequality 108, 238

innocent victim 245
insidious excitement 87–92
internal racism 143
internal world 220–222
invisibles 58–59

Jews 16–19, 103, 106, 211; and psychology 158, 168, 171; *see also* Nazis; race and racism
Jones, Jim 189–190
justice 18, 253

Kavanaugh, Brett 85–86, 88–89
Kelley, Gary 200, 210
King Jr., Martin Luther 40–41, 42–43
Klein, Melanie 136, 141–144, 151, 167–168
knowledge 72
Kojève, Alexandre 251
Kristeva, Julia 103–104
Kuper, Leo 158–159

land 10–11
Latinos 199–211, 212n2, 212n3
Lawrence, Charles 39
Layton, Lynn 154n8
leaders 209
Levinsian ethics 72–73
liberals 135–137, 141–144, 148–150
liquid modernity 60
lone shooter 158–160
Lorde, Audre 35, 45, 138
lynching 195

Mahler, Margaret 202
manic society 60
Mannoni, Octave 248
maps 127–128, 129
Martin, Trayvon 159
memes 53
#MeToo 88–89
Metzl, Jonathan 182–183
Mexico 204, 207
Milner, Marion 64
mischief makers 165
misogyny 13; and disidentification 15; and hermeneutics of transparency 27–29; and psychoanalysis 19–20; and transmission 83; and Trump, Donald 109; *see also* sex and sexism
Money-Kyrle, Roger 222–223
moral instruction 16–17
Morrison, Toni 191, 194

mourning 208–209
murderous racism 162, 173–180; *see also* genocide; hate crimes
Muslims 208, 209, 211

narcissism 164–165, 207–208
natural world 217–218; and clinical work 219–220; and internal world 220–222; and psychoanalytic frame 222–231; and tree at the window 231–232
Nazis 16–19, 99–100, 176–177, 211; *see also* genocide
neo-Nazis 160; *see also* white supremacy
Nussbaum, Martha 253–254

objects 3–5, 7; of hatred 13–14, 20–21, 22–23; sexual 23–24
Occupy movement 55
Oedipal complex 113n19
opinions 63–64
oral type 108
ordinary 152–153
O'Shaughnessy, E. 22

pandemic 51–54
patriarchy 80
perception 26–27, 29
persecutory anxiety 243
persecutory guilt 136, 141–144
place 55–56; and demarcation 67–69
plants 229–230
Plessy v Ferguson 36
politics of spectacle 243
populism 105, 107
power 43, 57–58; *see also* privilege
privilege 57
property 146
psychoanalysis: and framing 64–66; and hatred 19–20; and Levinasian ethics 72–73; and natural world 220–231; and opinions 63–64; and power 57–58; and the social 60–62, 73–75
psychosis: and deprivation 190–193; and destruction 186–190; and racism 182–186, 197n3; and self-image 193–196
Puget, Janine 58–59, 61, 63

race and racism 9–10, 13, 50n35; and COVID-19 32–33, 95; and disidentification 14–15; and "Executive Order on Combatting Race and Sex

Stereotyping" 37–42; and guilt 135–136; murderous racism 162, 173–180; and psychoanalysis 19–20; and psychosis 182–196; as relational construct 250–251; and reparations 46; and self-preservation 160–166; and Trump, Donald 35–37, 48n4, 48n5, 50n27, 108–109; and white defensiveness 46–47; *see also* Black Lives Matter; Critical Race Theory; genocide; Jews; privilege; slavery; South Africa; Whiteness
Rankine, Claudia 151
Raspail, Jean 109
Ray, Victor 44
reason 160–164; and murder 179
refugees 73, 109
regressive egalitarianism 103
reparations 46, 135–136, 150–153, 154n5, 154n6, 154n8; *see also* race and racism; slavery
reparative guilt 140, 141–144
respect 234–235, 237
ressentiment 235, 238, 240–243
Roberts, John Glover 42–43
Roof, Dylann 158–160, 165, 167–177, 180

sadism 87
safety 57–58
San Francisco 51–52, 53–54
Scheidel, Walter 252
Scheler, Max 240–241, 245–247
schizophrenia 183–184
self-destruction 164–166
self-esteem 27–30
self-image 193–196
self-preservation 160–166
Sévigné, Madame de (Marie de Rabutin-Chantal) 234
sex and sexism 41–42; *see also* misogyny
sexuality 23–25, 93, 121, 130–132; and racism 170
shame 154n4, 235–240
shared projections 207
slavery 121; and psychosis 182–183; *see also* race and racism; reparations
Smith, Gerald 98
social anxieties 204–205
social bond 99–100
social landscapes 203–204
social media 110–111, 116n71
social nausea 57–61
social positioning 64

social subjectivity 61
social unconscious 66–72
societal paranoia 207
Sodre, Ignes 93, 143–144
South Africa 235–236; and envy 243–248; and existential impasse 248–251; and hope 252–255; and *ressentiment* 240–243; and shame 235–240; *see also* race and racism
Southern Baptist Convention (SBC) 49n25
splitting 207
Stevenson, Bryan 195
Straker, Gillian 249
strangers 120, 201–203
structural hatreds 23, 30–31; *see also* homophobia; misogyny; race and racism
structural racism 38–40; *see also* Critical Race Theory; race and racism
subjectivity 76n6
subjects 5
Suchet, Melanie 249–250
suffering 72
Sullivan, Shannon 151
Summers, Lawrence 127
Szymborska, Wisława 65

Tarrant, Brenton 111
Taylor, Breonna 33
Thoreau, Henry David 221
topographical regression 26
topology 66–72
transmission 83–84
transparency 24–26; hermeneutics of 27
Trump, Donald 85, 94; and anti-Latino sentiment 199–200, 201, 207; and authoritarianism 112n6; identification with 108; and misogyny 89–90; and racism 32–33, 36–37, 38–40, 48n4, 48n5, 50n27, 108–109
trust 209

unconscious bias 38–39, 47
universities 44–45

Varela, Juan 200, 210
vertical planes 122–125, 129
violence 84–85, 135; epistemic 242; everyday 237–238; exemplary 253; and persecutory guilt 143–144; symbolic 241–242; *see also* crime
virtuality 76n7
Volkan, Vamik 202, 206–211

wealth 59–60; *see also* class politics; inequality
welfare 106
white fragility 140, 147–150
white guilt 135
Whiteness and white people 9–10, 71, 119–120; centering of 137–138; in clinical work 128–133; and defensiveness 46–47; and fragility 147–150; and geography 127–128; and grievance 35–36; and guilt 138–144, 153n3; inside and out 122–124; and the irreparable 144–147; personal reflections on 124–127; and privilege 245; and reparations 150–153; and schizophrenia 183; and shame 154n4; as a way of being and knowing 120–122; *see also* race and racism; reparations
white supremacy 94, 145
WikiLeaks 110
wishing 4, 6
woke 63
women: as daughters 79–84, 86–96; and Trump, Donald 85–86

Zimmerman, George 160

Printed in the United States
by Baker & Taylor Publisher Services